The Monster Hunter in Modern Popular Culture

The Monster Hunter in Modern Popular Culture

Heather L. Duda

McFarland & Company, Inc., Publishers
Jefferson, North Carolina, and London

LIBRARY OF CONGRESS CATALOGUING-IN-PUBLICATION DATA

Duda, Heather L. 1976–
　　The monster hunter in modern popular culture : Heather L. Duda.
　　　　p.　　cm.
　　Includes bibliographical references and index.

　　ISBN 978-0-7864-3406-0
　　softcover : 50# alkaline paper ∞

　　1. Heroes in mass media.　2. Monsters in mass media.
I. Title.
P96.H46D83　　2008
302.2308 — dc22　　　　　　　　　　　　　　　　　　2008027621

British Library cataloguing data are available

©2008 Heather L. Duda. All rights reserved

No part of this book may be reproduced or transmitted in any form or by any means, electronic or mechanical, including photocopying or recording, or by any information storage and retrieval system, without permission in writing from the publisher.

On the cover: Wesley Snipes in a publicity shot from the 2004 film *Blade: Trinity* (New Line Cinema/Photofest)

Manufactured in the United States of America

McFarland & Company, Inc., Publishers
　Box 611, Jefferson, North Carolina 28640
　　www.mcfarlandpub.com

Table of Contents

Preface   1

1. A History of the Monster Hunter   7
2. Humanity and the Contemporary Vampire   37
3. Vigilantism and the Graphic Novel's Monster Hunters   67
4. The Advent of the Female Monster Hunter   101
5. Monster Hunters for the New Millennium   142

Conclusion   166
Chapter Notes   171
Works Cited   175
Index   181

For Mom and Dad.
Because you're wonderful.

Preface

Although I have only been working on this text for the last four years, I have been preparing for it most of my life. When people ask me why I love horror, I smile and tell them about my mother. My mother loves horror films—the sillier and the gorier the better. She will watch whatever slasher film is playing on late-night television and laugh her way through it. Thanks to her, my genetic makeup naturally drew me to the genre. Before discovering the joys of Freddy Krueger, Michael Myers, and Jason Voorhees, I read such books as *Scary Stories to Tell in the Dark* and sat in rapt attention as people told me their own stories about spooky events. To me, a good scare was better than anything else. At an early age I discovered a collection of cartoons by Charles Addams in my local library; even if I could not always understand them, they fascinated me. I also liked watching reruns of *The Addams Family* and *The Munsters* on television. While other girls my age were reading *Sweet Valley High* and *The Baby-sitters Club* books, I was drawn to the odd and supernatural. When Lydia from *Beetlejuice* said, "I myself am strange and unusual," she could have been talking about me, a girl interested in popular culture slightly off the beaten path.

To this day I remember my first scary movie: Stephen King's *It*. My mother had borrowed it from a friend at work, who had taped it only weeks before from television. One night I was home alone and decided to watch it. Foolishly I turned off the lights—making the house very dark since we lived out in the country—and proceeded to watch. Halfway through my parents arrived home to find a frightened yet fascinated daughter curled up in the recliner, unable to move for fear of clowns and the risk of missing an important moment. I was definitely afraid in all the right moments, but I also remember enjoying that fear. The shiver that went up my back while watching *It* was the same shiver I felt when I read ghost stories. In a way, it was like a drug. None of my friends were horror fans so they could not understand, but my mother could at least relate. From that night on, we watched scary film after scary film, some classic (like *The Shining*) and some not (like *Dr. Giggles*). Together we held our breath and laughed as the film dictated.

Over the years some works have stood out more than others: Stephen King's *The Stand*, Stanley Kubrick's *The Shining*, Joss Whedon's *Buffy the Vampire Slayer* and *Angel*, just to name a few off the top of the list. The genre excited me but I never found an outlet for my love, just odd looks from classmates who did not understand why I could not read romances like a "proper" teenage girl. Then I went to college and met many fellow horror fans. We watched movies together and critiqued the effectiveness of the special effects. I will never forget debating *The Exorcist* one evening with a few friends. We could not come to a conclusion about whether or not you needed to be Catholic to truly appreciate the film. (I still do not have an answer to that question.) In college I also discovered where contemporary horror came from as I discussed the gothic elements of *Jane Eyre* and *Frankenstein* with my classmates and professor. Finally, I could put a name to my reaction to horror. I understood how Romantic and Victorian sensibilities paved the way for American fears about infiltration and motherhood. After graduate school, I could tell people why they needed horror and the principles of transference. I could also explain what cinematic techniques were most effective when trying to scare audiences. My appreciation of the genre suddenly took on a more academic tone. Instead of defending my interest in what my early peers had thought a silly genre, I was now a part of an ongoing academic discussion about the genre. Who knew?

Yet, even though I understand how the genre works and what it tries to accomplish, I still get excited over a good, scary movie. A while back my mother and I watched *The Descent*. We turned off all the lights and enjoyed watching a group of spelunking women slowly descend into madness. Afterwards, I did not lecture my mother about the technical aspects of the film; instead, we both agreed it was a good watch and I left wondering when the next good, scary movie would come out.

* * *

This book is, like any book, a work of love. While studying for my comprehensive exams, I went to see a movie and came face-to-face with a poster for *Van Helsing*. The poster got me thinking about monster hunters. With the help of my dissertation committee, I came up with the idea to write about the Van Helsing character in literature, film, and television and how that character has evolved over the last century from a "good" guy to a monstrously "good" guy. Once I had my idea, I realized, much to my surprise and excitement, that very few gothic and horror critics write about Van Helsing. While I cannot say for sure why the monster hunter has been largely ignored by critics, I can say that the character deserves much more attention. Hopefully, I have given the character his due. If nothing else, hopefully I have at least opened the door for a wider discussion of the character.

After careful consideration of several texts, I have found that the trauma of the Vietnam War and the rise of feminism have, among other things, contributed to a new type of monster hunter. Whether male or female, this character is much more monstrous than his/her Victorian counterpart. But this is where the gender similarities end. The male monster hunter, because he is almost always a monster as well as a monster hunter, is often driven by redemption; he has a need to atone for his monstrous deeds. Until he learns that monster hunting is about saving those around him rather than saving himself, the male monster hunter can never truly be effective. The female monster hunter, however, is not driven by redemption. Because of her long connection with the monster, the female monster hunter understands that it is her very monstrosity that makes her powerful. In coming to this realization, the female monster hunter is able to transcend traditional gender roles and become a powerful force who time and again saves the world.

Throughout my discussion of monster hunters, I rely on three theoretical frameworks: horror criticism by such scholars as Nina Auerbach, Paul Wells, and Jonathan Lake Crane to better understand the monster and the history of the horror film; posthumanism to understand the ruptures in humanistic ideology; and feminist criticism to understand why there is a difference in goals between the male and female monster hunters.

This book is a greatly revised version of my dissertation. I say "greatly revised" because one chapter has been discarded and two new ones have been added. I have also discussed new texts that deserve a place within the history of the monster hunter but were left out of the original work. For one, I did not read Alan Moore's *Watchmen* until after getting my Ph. D., and only then realized that graphic novels gave me a new set of monster hunters. After reading *Watchmen*, I moved on to *V for Vendetta*, *The League of Extraordinary Gentlemen*, and Frank Miller's *The Dark Knight Returns*. I was hooked on graphic novels. In the free time I had after graduation, I also finally got around to watching *Deadwood*, *Pitch Black*, and *Dexter*. The men in these works all needed a place in my manuscript. I began forming a fifth chapter, one which would discuss post–9/11 developments in the monster hunter. As I waited with bated breath to read the final *Harry Potter* novel, I even wondered if Severus Snape would find a place in the chapter. (He did.) Suddenly monster hunters were turning up all over the place and I was spending hours watching movies and television. Another big change occurred with Chapter 4, the chapter I always lovingly refer to as "The Chick Chapter." I wanted more from this chapter because it had never come together like I wanted it to, even though its main character — Buffy — was one of my dissertation's inspirations. I happened upon an article on the *Alien* films and could not believe I had made such an omission in my dissertation. Where was Ellen Ripley? She ended up being the glue for Chapter 4. Once I included her evolution as a monster hunter, the rest fell into place. I am pleased with how this book came together and am happy to have another shot to enhance my dissertation and to smooth out its rough edges.

That said, at some point, I had to draw the line, and it was a difficult one to draw. To keep my sanity, I had to let the western fall by the wayside (the one exception is HBO's *Deadwood*). Perhaps my next project will be to write about films like *High Plains Drifter*, *Unforgiven*, and *3:10 to Yuma*. These films all feature a type of monster hunter but their characters just did not gel with my fantasy literature monstrous monster hunters. Likewise, the rape-revenge film, although mentioned briefly in Chapter 5, did not get the attention it probably should have. After the westerns, maybe I'll work on a project to include *The Accused*, *The Brave One*, and *Descent*. Finally, much to the chagrin of one of my friends, I had to let anime go — although it, too, does get a brief mention in Chapter 1. Alas, there are only so many texts one can work with before saying no. I have done my best to stick with my beloved fantasy literature and no more. For the most part, I think I have succeeded; however, I am sure someone, somewhere will come up with a text I innocently omitted. In addition, some of my texts — like *Dexter* and *Terminator: The Sarah Connor Chronicles* — are ongoing. By the time this book is published, they may have been cancelled or something may have occurred on the show to contradict my reading of those texts. Please keep that in mind when reading my analysis.

In organizing this book I have tried to be as clear as possible when dealing with overlapping events. Chapter 1 includes a thorough look at Bram Stoker's Van Helsing and a definition of the monster hunter as I see the character. I then construct a timeline of the character's evolution. In this first chapter I set up the vital change in the character from saint to sinner; a change that has led to a renewed interest in the character from writers and both television and filmmakers. In Chapter 2 I focus on this change and flesh out the necessary components needed to make a monster a monster hunter. I use Nick from the television show *Forever Knight*, Blade from the *Blade* trilogy, and Angel and Spike from *Buffy the Vampire Slayer* and *Angel* as my case studies. Parallel to these vampires' change in the horror genre are the contributions of both Frank Miller and Alan Moore to the graphic novel monster hunter. In Chapter 3 I discuss the ways in which these men also deal with the traditional monster hunter's necessary shift in light of a post–Vietnam, post–Watergate, and Cold War world. Up to this point in the book all the monster hunters discussed are men, but in the 1990s female monster hunters arrive with a vengeance, most notably Anita Blake in literature and Buffy Summers on television. Chapter 4 deals with these women and their evolution not from Van Helsing but from Stoker's Mina Harker, the slasher's Final Girl, and Ellen Ripley. Finally, in Chapter 5 I take a look at the new millennium's monster hunters and consider how they both follow their predecessors in some areas and branch off in new directions in other areas.

* * *

In the end, there are so many people who need to be thanked; I hope I can do their contributions justice. My parents, Charles and Linda, have been with me every step of the way. Not only do I thank them for never over-censoring my popular culture intake as a child, but I also thank them for their enduring support of my academic endeavors. My siblings Ben and Alison basically put up with me during all my stress and pretended to care when I endlessly went on and on about my findings. Thanks, guys! My dissertation committee at Indiana University of Pennsylvania—Dr. Thomas Slater (my chair), Dr. Wendy Carse, and Dr. Lingyan Yang—took on a project that must have seemed unorthodox at best. Yet, despite my crazy ideas about popular culture, they helped me throughout with their support and criticism. They asked excellent questions in all the necessary places and really made me think about my ideas. Without them, I would never have made it past Chapter 1. My dissertation copyeditor and dear friend Erin Gyomber is not a horror fan in general, although I did persuade her over to the dark side of *Buffy* fandom. Despite not loving the genre, she still agreed to tackle the tough job of editing my dissertation. Along the way, she asked great questions in places where I thought the argument was obvious. Without her this project would not be the same. I also thank Photofest for their patience with my photo requests. Although I ultimately chose not to use any photos in the book, they did a fantastic job finding relevant pictures. Finally, to all my friends and family who have had to hear about this project for four years, I thank all of you for your patience, generosity, laughter, and lunch breaks. I have learned that support is the most important thing when taking on a book project and I luckily have that in spades. Thank you one and all for everything; you know who you are.

Heather L. Duda
Fall 2008

Chapter 1

A History of the Monster Hunter

"Some say you're a murderer, Mr. Van Helsing. Others say you're a holy man. Which is it?"
— *Van Helsing*

What does it mean to be human? This question has been asked in some way or another throughout the history of mankind. At first, the answer seems simple enough: every person is human. While this may be biologically true, humanity is a tenuous term at best with multiple interpretations differing from society to society. For example, to cannibals, it is humanly acceptable to eat other humans; for much of the western world, cannibalism is the opposite of what humans are: monstrous. Humanity, then, is "a name not merely for a species but for a quality" (Williams 22). It is ultimately a homogenizing term that separates people into two categories: those who are human — who follow a society's rules and regulations and demonstrate that society's "humane" qualities — and those who are inhuman, or monstrous — who go against the grain and act in ways that are opposite to society's homogenizing apparatuses like law, education, and religion. For the most part, to define someone as human would not necessarily be a bad thing. Many would agree that, despite the risk of homogeneity, some apparatuses — like laws — need to be in place. It is when the desire for homogeneity gets out of control that dangers appear. While it may be acceptable to set laws concerning murder, theft, and assault, among other things, it is not acceptable to claim that everyone must work a certain way or practice a certain religion. While these examples are certainly extremes, they illustrate a large gray area between human and inhuman and this is the area that garners the most discussion in places like art, literature, and film. There is one genre in particular that enjoys questioning humanizing apparatuses and practically resides in the gray area: horror.

From its very inception, gothic and horror have been a playground for the human and monstrous alike. (Although I do understand that the gothic and horror genres do have their own characteristics, for my purposes I am going to use them simultaneously because they have the monster hunter character in common.) Both enjoy employing supernatural elements and somewhat monstrous characters to make a point about culture and society. The genres' writers and filmmakers love to question what it means to be both human and monstrous. Even the "gothic" name derives from a description of a monstrous society. When the Goths invaded Rome, their actions were inhuman by Roman standards. According to Richard Davenport-Hines, in his *Gothic: Four Hundred Years of Excess, Horror, Evil and Ruin*, "The tribes originally from Scandinavia and eastern Europe which broke Roman power and sacked the capital in AD 410 were called Goths by Greek and Roman writers. [...] Their love of plunder and revenge ushered in a dark age, and the word 'goth' is still associated with dark powers, the lust for domination and inveterate cruelty" (1). Yet, horror and gothic are not simply about human and monstrous locked in a bloodthirsty battle of good-versus-evil. In fact, the very popularity of the genre, with its obsession with the monstrous, demonstrates that society is not entirely sure that the boundaries between human and inhuman are solid and unyielding. If we were so sure about ourselves and our civility, why would we need to keep dredging up our repression in the form of such popular monsters as vampires, werewolves, and the ever popular slasher villain? Why do these genres continue to make so much money?

Of all the gothic and horror texts that deal with humanity and inhumanity, there is one type of story that focuses on the eternal struggle between traditional good and evil: the monster/monster hunter battle. Bram Stoker's *Dracula* is the epitome of the monster-hunting narrative. Published in 1897, *Dracula* is, at its basic level, about the need for humanity to prevail over monstrosity. The two characters locked in battle for the sanctity of Victorian England's ideals are Dr. Abraham Van Helsing — the ultimate monster hunter — and Count Dracula — the ultimate monster. As the prototype of all that is good and right in Victorian society, Van Helsing is described thusly by John Seward:

> He is a philosopher and a metaphysician, and one of the most advanced scientists of his day; and he has, I believe, an absolutely open mind. This, with an iron nerve, a temper of the ice-brook, an indomitable resolution, self-command and toleration exalted from virtues to blessings, and the kindliest and truest heart that

beats [...] work both in theory and practice, for his views are as wide as his all-embracing sympathy [Stoker 129].

Van Helsing is an educated man, a mentor, a father figure, and a friend. Encompassing the best that Victorian masculinity has to offer, he is the ideal monster hunter — a man within whom intellect and nerve combine but never overpower his compassion. In comparison, Jonathan Harker's description of the Count is not so noble:

> Hitherto I had noticed the backs of his hands as they lay on his knees in the firelight, and they had seemed rather white and fine; but seeing them now close to me, I could not but notice that they were rather coarse — broad, with squat fingers. Strange to say, there were hairs in the centre of the palm. The nails were long and fine, and cut to a sharp point. As the Count leaned over me and his hands touched me, I could not repress a shudder [43].

If Van Helsing represents all that is good, the Count must be all that is bad. Van Helsing would never invoke such a disturbing reaction from another character. Readers understand that Van Helsing is the novel's humanizing agent while Dracula is clearly the monster.

Yet, for all his importance as the humanizing agent, an odd thing happens to the monster hunter in horror criticism: he is virtually ignored. Andrew Tudor, one of the few horror critics to write about the horror expert, claims that this character is akin to a hero, but is among the least developed of the genre: "Although in strict story terms they may be their movies' protagonists, and although their capacity for autonomous action is an essential constituent of the genre's narrative progress through disorder to order, they are rarely afforded the same kind of attention routinely paid to heroic figures in other narrative forms" (113). Even though Van Helsing and his students share virtually all of the action in Stoker's novel, it is the monster who receives the most attention in horror scholarship. Perhaps this is because Van Helsing's job is to uphold the status quo, which means that the monster must represent all that is villainous, chaotic, and repressed in society. A creature so laden with symbolism and cultural baggage would inevitably receive far more interest and attention than a human character who is virtuous, kindly, and near perfection. Heroic though he may be, Van Helsing and his monster-hunting successors are not the reason people read, watch, or critique horror. Then why do we need such characters?

The answer can be found in the purpose of horror. The elegant Eastern European outsider, the sexually promiscuous woman, the mad scientist — all of these characters exemplify the fears lurking within the horror genre. Horror is about dredging up that which is repressed by society, allowing the reader or viewer to experience his repressed desires within the controlled environment of the movie theater or his own home. According to Stephen King, "Horror appeals to us because it says, in a symbolic way, things we would be afraid to say right out straight, with the bark still on; it offers us a chance to exercise [...] emotions which society demands we keep closely at hand" (31). Audiences project their repression onto the monster — enjoying for a brief time the monster's villainy — so that when the film is over, they can return the book to the shelf or leave the theater and return to socially-dictated normality.[1] Horror critic Robin Wood provides readers with a list of repressions the monster can symbolize: sexual energy, bisexuality, female sexuality and creativity, children's sexuality, and the "Other" (specifically women, the proletariat, other cultures, ethnic groups, alternative ideologies, sexual deviants, and children) (166–170). In other words, the monster symbolizes everyone who is not a white, educated, upper-class male. No society is truly homogenous. No matter how good the humanizing apparatuses of a culture, there are always those attributes that do not fit in. To remain one of society's members, a person will repress those qualities. That is why horror is so enticing. For a short period of time, repression can run free via transference, thus purging audience members of any guilt or frustration they may experience by keeping their repressions to themselves. Because the monster hunter is there to make sure that the status quo remains, the monster hunter becomes less of a hero and more of an annoyance. Readers and viewers do not want to dwell on the character who will force them back into reality. They know the character is present and they know his function. For a brief moment, they want to focus their attention on what it is like to be monstrous. The monster hunter has a clear reason for being and needs little analysis by either the audience or the critics.

Because horror critics often fail to speculate on the role of the monster hunter, there is no consensual definition of the character. Therefore, to understand the hunter, we must first understand what it is he seeks to do. Since we know that the monster can stand in for everything from repressed sexuality to a fear of the Other, by destroying the monster the monster hunter seeks to reinstate the status quo of his time by destroying that repression. In simpler horror times, such as the Victorian Era, it was entirely possible to completely destroy the monster. Van Helsing and his small band of monster hunters successfully defeat the vampire. Yes, Quincey Morris — one of Van Helsing's monster hunters — dies in battle, but it is a heroic death and his memory lives on in the naming of Jonathan and Mina's son: "His [Jonathan and Mina's son] mother holds, I [Van Helsing] know, the secret belief that some of our brave friend's spirit has passed into him. His bundle of names links all our little band of men together; but we call him Quincey" (Stoker 368). At the end of the novel everything is as it should be: Dracula and his wives are destroyed and the family unit has been upheld. For Stoker and other Victorian writers, it was acceptable to question their society's humanity just as long as the text contained a happy ending by that society's standards.

Not only must these early monster hunters be pure and good, they must also make the choice to be monster hunters. This is not to say that they always come willingly to the vocation. In fact, the only reason Harker, Seward, Morris, and Holmwood fight is to save their women. (That said, based on Harker's reaction when he sees Dracula in England, he might have come willingly to the battle even without Mina, for he has seen what the vampire is capable of.) Seward, Morris, and Holmwood have lost the woman they love to Dracula and they band together to prevent the same fate happening to Jonathan. While they are driven by revenge in some ways, it is still their choice to join Van Helsing; they could certainly choose to walk away. This choice also marks the early monster hunter as being a "good" character. In Western society, the Golden Rule is upheld as a significant aspect of what it means to be human. From an early age, most members of western civilization are taught some version of "Do unto others as you would have them do unto you." While there is certainly criticism about the underlying humanizing agenda of this statement, it still forms the basis of Western society. To be considered good, a person must do good things to and for others and, in turn, he will be rewarded with goodness from others. By agreeing to risk their own lives to protect the life of a woman, these men are demonstrating great humanity by their society's standards; their choice to fight is what makes them "good" men. Unfortunately, this choice also makes them boring men by the standards of the typical horror consumer. On the other side of the spectrum, there is no sense of choice on the part of Dracula. Readers get the sense he was always monstrous. There is no chance, then, that he would abide by, or even care about, the Golden Rule. Therefore, he is more exciting and enticing than Van Helsing's band of monster hunters.

Of all the three primary horror archetypes — the vampire, Frankenstein's Monster, and the werewolf — only the vampire has traditionally been plagued with an untiring monster hunter. This is most likely due in part to the fact that Stoker's novel inspired the majority of other vampire texts. But there is also the necessity of a monster hunter in the vampire texts because vampires are possibly the most interesting of all horror archetypes, thus making them the most dangerous. Why is the vampire so popular and fascinating? According to Veronica Hollinger, "The deconstruction of boundaries helps to explain why the vampire is a monster-of-choice these days, since it is itself an inherently deconstructive figure; it is the monster that used to be human; it is the undead that used to be alive; it is the monster that *looks like us*" (201). Nina Auerbach's seminal study, *Our Vampires, Ourselves*, continues this line of thought: "Vampires are neither inhuman nor nonhuman nor all-too-human; they are simply more alive than they should be" (6). Vampires do not morph into howling, hairy wolves at the full moon, nor are they pieced together with rotting parts from dead men like Frankenstein's Monster. Vampires can assimilate themselves into mortal society and, in doing so, they cannot be easily differentiated from us. It is both fascinating and frightening to think that a monster can be hiding in plain sight. The whole point of humanizing apparatuses is to prevent the monstrous from walking around with the human. A great fear of any society is the inability to differentiate between "good" and "evil." Vampires understand, better than any other monster, mortals' need to easily recognize monsters. Assimilation, after all, was always the goal of Stoker's Dracula: "Here I am noble; I am *boyer*; the common people know me, and I am master. But a stranger in a strange land, he is no one; men know him not— and to know not is to care not for. I am content if I am like the rest, so that no man stops if he see me, or pause in his speaking if he hear my words, to say, 'Ha, ha! A stranger!'" (Stoker 45). Herein lies the fear of Dracula. If he is given the opportunity to assimilate himself, he will be virtually impossible to detect. Once he gets a foothold in a foreign country—and a Western one at that—he will be unstoppable. He could, potentially, bring down the entire British Empire, which is very similar to what happens in Brian Stableford's 1988 novel, *The Empire of Fear*, a vision of an alternate history in which vampires are the world's elite and mortals are nothing more than playthings. Kim Newman's *Anno Dracula* (1992) offers a similar fate when Van Helsing fails to kill the Count and the vampire goes on to wed the Queen and rule England. These alternate realities are exactly what Stoker's Van Helsing cannot allow to happen.

If Stoker's Dracula represents a fear of the outside infiltrating the homeland, then Van Helsing seeks to maintain the cultural purity of Victorian England. If Dracula threatens to rip apart the Victorian family, then Van Helsing must help Jonathan Harker reclaim his wife, Mina, from the villainous "home wrecker," thus allowing Victorian family values to persevere. If Dracula dares to practice sexually taboo unions like polygamy, then Van

Helsing must kill the vampire's wives. No matter what his task, the most important thing to remember is that Van Helsing chooses to take these actions, and this choice — the one element every true monster hunter has in common — sets him apart from his contemporaries. The original monster hunter is a brave man with noble intentions who is admired and respected for his choice to face the dangerous monster. Whatever name he goes by, we will see in the following pages that whatever else may be, the monster hunter's chosen job is to restore some semblance of order to the lives of those around him.

Because the monster hunter's role is to defeat the monster, there is a strong bond between the two adversaries. This bond could include a mutual respect of one another's intellect or a similar age or even the fact that both are equally powerful in his own way. Their strongest connection may well be the fact that the monster hunter often comes from outside the culture he is trying to protect, just like the vampire. Because he is an outsider, the monster hunter has the necessary understanding to fight the vampire, distancing himself from the culture around him just enough to notice the inconsistencies that inevitably show the vampire's true colors. According to Auerbach, "Van Helsing is not a vampire, but he is the sole possible vampire-killer; only another ponderous foreigner can fulfill Dracula's need to die" (116). While she is referring specifically to the 1931 Universal film version, *Dracula*, her sentiments can easily be applied to the role of every Van Helsing character. From Stoker's novel to the present day, the monster hunter is an outsider of some type. Stoker's Van Helsing is from Amsterdam, so he is literally an outsider to England. But even when he is from the same culture or society, the Van Helsing character type is different in some way. He may be much more educated than those around him, he may be single, or he may speak with a slight accent or irregularity. Van Helsing's difference sets him apart from the other characters and allows him some measure of awe and reverence from those around him, lending credence to his ideas and knowledge. Not only that, his status as Other gives him power. As will be examined throughout this study, former monsters make for powerful monster hunters because they understand the culture of monsters. It is only by embracing, rather than fighting, his outsider status that the contemporary monster hunter can prove victorious time and again.

Although they may be victorious in some ways, this is not to say that monster hunters have remained the same for the last century. While early texts wrap everything up in a nice, happy ending, horror changes drastically in the second half of the twentieth century and the monster hunter changes with it. It is at this time that humanity no longer prevails in horror texts and the monster hunter begins to fade out of the genre. When Alfred Hitchcock's *Psycho* was released in 1960, it helped to usher in a new era of horror films. In this new era, the monster becomes even more complex yet also surprisingly single-minded. Although the sub-genre would not hit the mainstream until the middle of the 1970s, *Psycho* was the first of the slasher films: films which feature a somewhat mortal monster on a killing spree of mostly teenagers. These monsters do not have a plan of attack like Dracula's desire to infiltrate England. Instead, they mindlessly kill all those in their path with neither rhyme nor reason. In addition, these monsters are seemingly immortal in that no matter how many times they are shot, stabbed, or fall several stories, they just keep on coming. With their single-mindedness and refusal to play by traditional horror rules, the slasher monsters represent chaos. Chaos is the ultimate fear of the humanizing apparatus. When there is chaos all rules and order are thrown by the wayside and the feeling is one of "every man for himself." When the humanizing apparatuses are thrown into disarray, those people who championed them have nothing left to cling to.

Writing about slasher films of the late 1970s and early 1980s, Andrew Tudor claims, "In the typical narratives of paranoid horror, the defenses protecting this world from the other have long since disappeared. Van Helsing is in his grave, the old remedies do not work and the lurker has crossed the threshold for good" (184). He is right. Monster hunters from Stoker's Van Helsing up through the first half of the twentieth century worked because the monsters played by the rules. Van Helsing knew Dracula's weaknesses and, with the help of his friends, he could track and destroy the vampire. In the slasher films, there are no apparent weaknesses and no rules. Monsters kill for the joy of killing and cannot seemingly be killed. How can the traditional monster hunter work within these new parameters where it is no longer about upholding the status quo but simply about staying alive? It is no wonder that Van Helsing goes to his grave during this time period. In his place arrives the character of the Final Girl—the one character in the slasher film other than the monster who manages to survive. But, as we will see in Chapter 4, the Final Girl is not really a monster hunter. Instead, she is the one character lucky—and I use the term loosely—enough to stay alive. But the monster hunter also has the ability to change with the times, and change he does. To better understand this progression in the history of the monster hunter, it is important to see how the Van Helsing prototype has evolved over its first century and how that evolution relates to the study of humanity.

Browning's Dracula and Fisher's Dracula: Two Test Cases

Tod Browning's 1931 adaptation of Stoker's novel is one of the most well-known of all vampire films and really emphasizes society's need for a happy ending. By the time Van Helsing (Edward Van Sloan) appears in the film, Dracula (Bela Lugosi) has already assimilated himself into British culture — he is even able to walk down the street to the theater without being noticed. The camera follows Dracula through the street while people pass him on either side without even giving the Count a second glance, thus making him especially dangerous. When Dracula introduces himself to Dr. Seward (Herbert Bunston), Lucy (Frances Dade), Mina (Helen Chandler), and Jonathan Harker (David Manners), they take him for an unusual foreign dignitary. The only comment made about his manner is when Mina tells Lucy she prefers someone "more normal." Like Jonathan Harker in Stoker's text, Mina recognizes an odd quality in the Count, but she brushes it off without fear. Yet the viewer recognizes Dracula's inability to completely assimilate to England's "human" traits as a mark of his monstrosity. He is different, even if only slightly, and that marks him as both dangerous and enticing.

When Van Helsing finally appears, the shot is a medium close-up of him examining a sample of Renfield's (Dwight Frye) blood. He is speaking with Dr. Seward and another gentleman in Latin. With his chemistry set and knowledge of Latin, Professor Van Helsing is clearly marked as an educated man, a mark further demonstrated when he becomes the first to realize the connection between Renfield's actions — his appetite for flies and spiders — and vampirism. When Seward claims that vampirism is just folklore, Van Helsing responds, "I may be able to bring you proof that the superstition of yesterday can become the scientific reality of today." While Seward may not believe everything that Van Helsing is saying, it is clear to the viewer that Seward has faith in the professor. As a matter of fact, Seward turns the care of Renfield over to Van Helsing. In this Van Helsing we have a classic monster hunter: one who is educated and respected. It also should be noted that he is white and, by the looks of his clothing, financially well-off. As with most early monster hunters, the character needs to represent the ruling — and humanizing — class. Only then can he successfully restore the cultural norm.

While Van Helsing is the vampire expert and Dracula his nemesis, the two men share many traits, a requirement that helps the two understand one another. First, Edward Van Sloan speaks slowly and with a slight accent.

While his accent is not quite as pronounced as Lugosi's—suggesting that his Van Helsing is less of an outsider than Lugosi's Dracula—the pace of his words almost matches Lugosi's lengthened speech pattern. Likewise, both men exude an air of power and strength. When Renfield (in Browning's adaptation, Jonathan Harker never visits Transylvania) first enters Dracula's castle, Dracula descends on him from the top of a long staircase. Lugosi himself is a tall man often hovering over the other characters in the film, thus linking height and power. While Van Sloan may be shorter than Lugosi, Van Sloan's character still manages to hold sway over Seward, Mina, and Jonathan. When Van Helsing is in Seward's office, Seward is sitting and Van Helsing is standing, allowing him to bend over to talk to Seward. In addition, when Mina is explaining a dream to Jonathan, Seward and Van Helsing are descending the staircase in Seward's home. Rather than continuing into the room, Van Helsing remains on the stairs, allowing him to listen from afar and above. This constant emphasis on height is a mark of power for Browning, and both Van Helsing and Dracula possess that power.

Perhaps no scene in the film better demonstrates the equality of Dracula and Van Helsing than when the two men face one another in Seward's living room. Dracula enters from the right while Van Helsing enters from the left. Dracula tells Van Helsing that he should return to his own country, thus reminding the audience that Van Helsing is also an outsider. Van Helsing responds, "I prefer to remain and protect those whom you would destroy." What follows is a battle of the wills edited as shot/reverse shot. Dracula, with his hypnotic eyes, tries to summon Van Helsing to him. Van Helsing resists. As the shot/reverse shot continues, the viewer sees Van Helsing take one step and then another step towards Dracula. Then, suddenly, Van Helsing stops. He takes one step backward and then another. Dracula responds, "Your will is strong, Van Helsing," and attacks the Professor. Dracula is only driven back when Van Helsing produces a crucifix. Dracula's supernatural abilities are the key to his power; Van Helsing's power lies in his knowledge. He understands what Dracula wants to do and is able to resist.

Ultimately, Van Helsing's knowledge saves the day. After Dracula has rushed to Carfax Abbey with Mina, Van Helsing and Jonathan pursue. The two men split up to search for the Count. It is Van Helsing who finds him, and it is Van Helsing who drives the stake into Dracula's heart. After being rescued by Jonathan, Mina asks if Van Helsing is coming. He tells her to go ahead as he stays behind. The viewer does not know what Van Helsing is going to do and is left with the image of Mina and Jonathan ascending the stairs of the Abbey into the daylight. According to Nina Auerbach, "With his ceremonial line readings and foreign accent, Van Sloan is a pale parody of Lugosi, even, like him, shunning daylight; at the end, he stays in the crypt with the dead Dracula, directing the young lovers as they walk somnambulistically up a huge staircase toward the light" (116). Yet Van Sloan's Van Helsing is less a "pale parody" than a type of doppelganger. As will be shown, to be an effective monster hunter one must understand the monster without becoming the monster. For viewers to believe that Van Helsing can actually defeat the mysterious and mesmerizing Dracula, they must believe that Van Helsing is intimately connected to the vampire. Van Sloan may not be quite as dramatic a Van Helsing as Peter Cushing will be in the Hammer vampire films, but he does make a visual connection between his character and Lugosi's. And that visual connection helps to alert the audience that he is the film's expert who will save the day.

Once the vampire is dead, does this always make for a happy ending for the good doctor? Yes and no. He has done his job by helping the younger generation destroy the vampire; he has upheld the status quo and for that he should be relieved. But what does he receive in return? Just the knowledge that there will be other vampires and other battles. In many ways, Van Helsing does not bask in the warmth of the new day shining over Dracula's empty coffin. Perhaps this is because the monster hunter secretly knows that there will be other monsters to battle. Perhaps filmmakers like Browning knew that true humanity cannot even be achieved.[2] Perhaps Van Helsing and his successors are just too much like the monsters they fight to ever truly be accepted by society. No matter what the reason, monster hunters usually remain on the fringes of the society they protect. They are there when needed, but offer a reminder that there are certainly things that go bump in the night. In fact, as the years roll on, it becomes clear that monster hunters can only truly be accepted into a society of other monster hunters, something which Stoker hints at when he has Van Helsing maintain contact with the Harkers even after Dracula's death.

As the classic vampire film, Tod Browning's *Dracula* gives us a template to which future monster hunters can be compared. Because the film is adapted from the quintessential vampire narrative, the film becomes the quintessential vampire film. Bela Lugosi remains to this day the man many picture when thinking of Count Dracula. However, when asked about Van Helsing, few could probably pull up Edward Van Sloan's name or face. Despite being the film's hero, he is not the most remembered actor in the ensemble. Still, the portrayals of Lugosi and Van Sloan must have been accurate enough for future filmmakers because the things that Browning did with his adaptation in terms of monster and monster hunter remain within subsequent significant vampire films.

By the end of the 1940s, the Universal monsters had run their course. The monsters themselves, once respected and feared, had become caricatures in a madhouse run by Abbott and Costello. Luckily, 1958 brought a resurrection for the undead. Terence Fisher and Hammer Studios in England decided to return a little respectability to the horror archetypes, especially to the vampire. Fisher based his vampire film —*Horror of Dracula*— on Stoker's text, albeit very loosely. In the Hammer adaptation, the names are the same, but the characters are very different. Jonathan Harker (John Van Eyssen) is a vampire hunter from the very beginning. When he ventures to Castle Dracula in search of the Count, he kills a female vampire, a murder that enrages Dracula (Christopher Lee), who then makes Jonathan a vampire. To seek vengeance for his "wife's" death at Harker's hands, Dracula travels to England to kill Harker's fiancée, Lucy Holmwood (Carol Marsh). When Lucy's brother, Arthur (Michael Gough), interferes, Dracula pursues Arthur's wife, Mina (Melissa Stribling). The only names that remain the same in the Hammer film are, of course, the vital ones: Dracula and Van Helsing (Peter Cushing). In this film, Dracula is dangerous not for his assimilation potential, but for his sexuality. He seduces Lucy and does the same to Mina, so much so that she actually brings his coffin into her basement so Dracula can have easy access to her bedroom. Heightened sexuality has long been a favorite repression of both gothic and horror and here it is obviously linked to monstrosity.

Unlike Universal's 1931 *Dracula*— where the first confrontation between Dracula and Van Helsing occurs in the middle of the film–Dracula and Van Helsing do not meet until the very end of Fisher's film. In *Horror of Dracula* there is only one scene before the final confrontation that expresses the equality of hunter and vampire. After Van Helsing tells Arthur and Mina of Jonathan's death, he returns to his home to read Jonathan's diary, listening to his own phonographic recording as he reads. When the recording comes to an end, he picks up the microphone to record more and the viewer sees Van Helsing in a medium close-up speaking into the phonograph. The shot cuts to Dracula, standing in the same space within the camera's frame, as he enters Lucy's bedroom. This cut suggests that the two men are linked to one another, perhaps even equals.

Although the doubling between Dracula and Van Helsing may not be as blatant in the Hammer film as it is in the Universal release, Cushing's Van Helsing is still every bit as attentive and knowledgeable as Van Sloan's. It is Van Helsing who follows Jonathan to Castle Dracula and learns that he has been turned into a vampire; it is also Van Helsing who drives the stake into Jonathan's heart, as well as into Lucy's. In addition, Arthur turns to and allies himself with Van Helsing in order to defeat Dracula. While it is Dracula who acknowledges Van Helsing's intellect in the Universal film, here it is Van Helsing himself who explains his credentials to Arthur: "Holmwood, the study of these creatures has been my life's work. I've carried out research for some of the greatest authorities in Europe and yet we've only just scratched the surface." Even though Van Helsing may not know everything about vampires, he knows more than the average man, and is thus able to answer Arthur's questions and dispel his misconceptions. Once again, the monster hunter is an educated, white male. However, something interesting happens to Van Helsing through Cushing's portrayal. Whether it is because Fisher wanted a strong link between vampire and hunter or because Hammer films were synonymous with sexuality, Cushing's Van Helsing is both charismatic and sensual. As Nina Auerbach comments, "He [Dracula] is pursued by Peter Cushing's athletic Van Helsing, who is less an occultist or sonorous patriarch than a shrewd fighter who, like his double Dracula, exists above all as a body" (121). This film marks the first time Van Helsing is associated with sexuality and a power that comes from physicality as opposed to only knowledge. Cushing's Van Helsing does not need young, virile men to fight his fight; he can hunt down and kill Dracula on his own. This is certainly not the grandfatherly monster hunter of Stoker's novel.

In the final sequence, Van Helsing and Arthur pursue Dracula to his castle. Once there, Arthur rescues Mina while Van Helsing chases after the vampire. This confrontation scene is much more exciting than that in either the Universal film — where there is no final confrontation between the men as Dracula is already in his casket when Van Helsing arrives to stake him — or the novel — where Jonathan quickly cuts Dracula's throat. Here Van Helsing and Dracula race through the rooms of the castle. When the monster and monster hunter finally find themselves in the same room, Dracula seems to immediately have the upper hand. He knocks Van Helsing to the floor and begins choking him.

The two are predominantly shot from a low angle so that Dracula looms above Van Helsing. At the last moment, as Dracula is moving in to bite Van Helsing, the doctor pushes the vampire aside. The two men face one another with Dracula moving towards Van Helsing and Van Helsing moving away. Suddenly, Van Helsing leaps onto the table and runs to the window to throw open the curtains. Dracula is caught in the sunlight and begins to turn to ash. Grabbing a candlestick, Van Helsing makes his way to the other end of the table and the matching candlestick. He holds the two together in the form of a cross, which he uses to push Dracula back into the light.

As Dracula turns to ash, the shot is from a high camera angle and shows Van Helsing looming over the vampire. In the end, it is Van Helsing who has the power. Just before the credits roll, Van Helsing puts on his gloves and watches the ash blow away; his work is done. Mina is cured — we see the burn mark from a crucifix disappear — and reunited with Arthur; their happy home is restored. Hammer's Van Helsing — just like Stoker's — has destroyed the sexual predator and the family morals of Victorian England are as they should be. In addition, the audience believes that Dracula is truly dead when the film ends. While there are other films in the Hammer Dracula series, Fisher offers his viewers closure; the status quo has successfully been maintained.

Although Fisher's adaptation prompted numerous sequels that only began to die out when the slashers took over, Dracula's and Van Helsing's roles remain much the same through the 1960s and into the early 1970s. It was then that, as Andrew Tudor argues, Van Helsing begins to go to his grave. There are, however, two movies from that time period that deserve mention here: *The Fearless Vampire Killers* (1967) and *Captain Kronos — Vampire Hunter* (1974). These films deserve some attention not because they are especially good, but because they are among the first to focus specifically on the role of the monster hunter, thus predicting a trend that will take almost twenty-five years to fully materialize. *The Fearless Vampire Killers* is a spoof on the vampire genre. Two inept vampire hunters — Professor Abronsius (Jack MacGowran) and his assistant Alfie (Roman Polanski, who also directs) — try to destroy Count von Krolock (Ferdy Mayne) and his vampire horde. Mostly the two run around the Count's castle avoiding near-misses with the vampires in an attempt to save Alfie's love, Sarah (Sharon Tate). While the three do escape the Count's domain, it is too late. Sarah has already been turned into a vampire and proceeds to bite Alfie. The Professor, who is driving their sleigh and is oblivious to the whole affair, ends up releasing the very nightmare on society that he hoped to prevent (at least that is what the voice-over informs the audience). If the 1970s signaled the downfall of the monster hunter, *The Fearless Vampire Killers*, with its inept Abronsius and Alfie, is certainly an early nail in his coffin.

In contrast, *Captain Kronos* (released by Hammer Studios) is not a spoof. This film follows Kronos (Horst Janson) and his sidekick, Professor Grust (John Gater), as they seek out and destroy vampires. For Kronos, the battle is personal since both his mother and sister were turned into vampires. However, the film itself spends less time on the role of the monster hunter than on the lust-filled romance of Kronos and Carla (Caroline Munro). That said, *Captain Kronos* is a precursor to films such as *Blade* (1998) and *Van Helsing* (2004). With the creation of the character Kronos, the vampire expert moves from the realm of the learned, distinguished gentleman to the realm of the young, sexy fighter. If *The Fearless Vampire Killers* helps to send the traditional expert to his grave, *Captain Kronos— Vampire Hunter* branches off in another direction and paves the way for the younger, sexier monster hunter. In addition, the film gives the young fighter a sidekick who is knowledgeable in monster folklore. As the century moves to a close, Professor Grust will morph into such characters as Whistler (Kris Kristofferson) from *Blade* and Carl (David Wenham) from *Van Helsing*.

While the monster hunter does, indeed, go to his grave in the 1970s, two important political events occur which help bring him back: the Vietnam War and Watergate. Vietnam was the first major defeat of America's powerful military. This defeat would have been difficult enough to take, but the media's presence during the War allowed all of America to witness the events first hand, and some of those events were monstrous by American standards. The military personnel arrived home from World War II as heroes, but the public was not so quick to bestow such an honor on men who had raped and killed innocent Vietnamese citizens. The stories of military units who acted like monsters had been beamed into homes across the country. How could American military personnel act this way? The Watergate scandal came on the heels of Vietnam and once again flooded American news outlets with tales of corruption and villainy. Yet again the people who were supposed to know right from wrong and protect the American public were reduced to scoundrels, liars, and monsters. Suddenly, the American boundaries between human and monster were not quite as solid as they used to be. Americans were quickly realizing that monstrous intentions were not so easily contained and suppressed. For perhaps the first time, consumers of gothic and horror texts saw their fictional characters' attributes manifested in their heroes and leaders. The questions gothic and horror texts had always asked were being asked on a much larger scale. However, this real-life monstrosity actually set the stage for a significant transformation in the gothic and horror genres. According to Auerbach, "The corporate corruption revealed by the Watergate investigations seems to have been decisive in the transformation of vampires into potential saviors" (152). When reality is as frightening as horror, horror characters may not seem quite so abhorrent.

Around the same time that Vietnam and Watergate were on the minds of the public, a new school of theoretical thought was rising: posthumanism. Prompted by Edward Steichen's photography exhibit entitled "The Family of Man," the posthumanists questioned whether or not there could really be a "family of man." To the posthumanists, "family of man" implied that all biological humans are the same. However, this new group of theorists doubted that such a sweeping generalization could do justice to the diverse cultures existing on Earth. Posthumanism borrows concepts from a wide variety of other theories. Like the deconstructionists, the posthumanists refuse to accept hierarchical binaries like human and inhuman or good and evil. These theorists also pull from postmodernists like Jean Baudrillard and Michel Foucault who understand that order and homogeneity are fraught with problems. Posthumanists recognize that we are always already living within a society that has a certain humanist ideology from which we cannot ever successfully escape, something horror texts—at least the early ones—imply in their monster hunters who successfully defeat the inhuman creatures. Neil Badmington, one of the leading posthumanists, facetiously argues, "'We' need to be kept in check, kept human. The inhuman is never too far away. Through its institutions, its apparatuses—education, law, religion, morality, ethics, common sense—culture ceaselessly (re)makes humans (why else would 'we' need such entities in our adult lives?)" (*Alien Chic* 126). Our humanizing apparatuses are everywhere. However, buried within these very apparatuses is the contemporary monster hunter who, like the posthumanists, picks away at the ideologies he appears to be defending.

Not only does posthumanism seek to deconstruct how humanism is formed, it also seeks to exploit the homogenizing qualities of humanism, those qualities which immediately mark a gap between "us" and "them." In her famous essay, "A Cyborg Manifesto," Donna J. Haraway argues, "The dichotomies between mind and body, animal and human, organism and machine, public and private, nature and culture, men and women, primitive and civilized are all in question ideologically" (163). Haraway does an excellent job of demonstrating how boundaries are constantly in flux and constantly being transgressed. The dichotomies to which she refers—and many others—are not stable but are tenuous at best; order is never permanently defined or upheld. In his introduction to a collection of essays entitled *Posthumanism*, Neil Badmington claims, "What the contributors seem to recognise as they map posthumanism is that the crisis in humanism is happening *everywhere*. Although it continues to be debated by critical theorists, the reign of Man is simultaneously being called into question by literature, politics, cinema, anthropology, feminism, and technology" (9).

Again, as with Haraway's argument, Badmington recognizes that on every front order is failing. An "us-versus-them" mentality is no longer a good enough way to define human and monster in a postmodern world.

When we analyze a horror text from the 1970s, it becomes less about the need to maintain the status quo and more about the need to understand the monster, or at least understand that the monster (read: society's repressed desires) is not going away. The slasher villain returns again and again because contemporary society realizes it can never really get rid of its inhumanity. In *Terror in Everyday Life*, Jonathan Lake Crane argues, "The underlying problem here [in slasher films] is one which suggests that the essence of humanity *is* to be violent, anti-social and auto-satisfied, and that socialising structures merely attempt to prevent, hide, or police these tendencies" (87). Crane also sees these slasher films as representing a very negative image of society when he discusses the immortality of the slasher villain as it applies to Jason Voorhees of the *Friday the 13th* franchise: "Any large human who can don a goalie mask and wield something sharp can play Jason. Jason is a cipher; a stumbling mute who lurches through his appearances without benefit of voice or personalized gestures. He is a murderous blank, well-known and well-regarded for killing in great numbers, and being in turn unkillable. That is all" (142). Monster hunters are useless because, thanks to the Vietnam War and Watergate, there are no pure, unselfish heroes left to the save the world. Chaos rules. Or does it? Yes, the slasher films were the focus of the horror genre in the 1970s. But while Michael Meyers was running rampant through the streets of Haddonfield, Illinois in *Halloween* (1978) and Jason Voorhees was terrorizing the counselors of Camp Crystal Lake in *Friday the 13th, Part 2* (1981), the vampire was making a comeback and the monster hunter was about to be resurrected as a member of the undead.

Murderers and Men of God

By the end of the 1970s, the vampire becomes less a figure to fear than one to admire. Horror readers and viewers of this time wanted to discover and emulate the sexy and eternal undead. According to Margaret L. Carter, "In novels and stories published in the United States since 1970 [...] the vampire often appears as an attractive figure precisely *because* he or she is a vampire" (27). One reason for this attraction is that the 1970s allowed the vampire to reinvent itself. Through this reinvention, vampires began to take on new roles, including actually becoming the monster experts, a knowledge which will lead some of them to become monster hunters:

"Vampires in the 1970s *became* authorities. Hovering between animal and angel, they are paragons of emotional complexity and discernment, stealing from Van Helsing the role of knower but adding a tenderness and ineffable sorrow human beings have become too monstrous to comprehend" (Auerbach 131). While Auerbach recognizes that vampires have become the experts, she does not take this implication further: in the process these new vampires suddenly take on a duality of sorts. On the one hand, they are still monstrous and represent the repressed; on the other hand, they usually impart their expertise and experience to a younger character through some type of confession. In becoming a sage like Van Helsing, the vampire regains a measure of humanity and, in the process, sympathy. The beginning of this trend occurs with the creation of two vampires: Louis and Lestat.

In 1976, Anne Rice published Book 1 of her Vampire Chronicles: *Interview with the Vampire*, the first vampire text to deal extensively with the implications of immortality and inhumanity. Gone is the lone vampire cooped up in his run-down castle in the middle of nowhere with his brides and minions. In his place is an entire culture and society of the undead who have successfully infiltrated mortal society. *Interview* is an important step in the vampire genre: not only does it create a new breed of vampire, one which demonstrates the ideas of humanity and expertise just mentioned, but it also suggests a new breed of vampire hunter that will, in turn, influence an entire generation of horror writers and filmmakers.

Louis, the novel's main character, chooses to become a vampire. As he tells his interviewer, "But the other light was my wish for self-destruction. My desire to be thoroughly damned. [...] But this was what I wanted, you see. It didn't matter. This was what I thought I wanted" (17). In the prominent vampire texts up to this point, the vampire's choice is neither discussed nor even imagined. Yet Rice wants her readers to immediately connect with Louis, so she explains his motivations for becoming a monster: Louis is so bitter about life that he ceases to live. He wants an escape, and that escape is gleefully provided by Lestat, the vampire who sires, or changes, him. However, from the very beginning of his immortality, Louis has difficulty killing humans and behaving as a "proper" vampire should. After his first kill, Louis makes an astonishing discovery: "And what I felt, most profoundly, for everything, even the sound of the playing cards being laid down one by one upon the shining rows of solitaire, was respect. Lestat felt the opposite" (31). Louis is a new breed of vampire. He is not the selfish, sexual being of Lugosi's Dracula or even Lee's Count. That role is given over to Lestat. Louis shows himself as a breed apart, filled with respect—both for his own vampirism and the world around him. At this point, Louis is considered an outsider in two different worlds. As a vampire, he is certainly not human by mortal standards. However, in questioning his necessity to kill, he is also not considered normal by vampire standards. Louis is accepted into neither society and this causes his continual wavering, a trait which many future vampires-turned-monster hunters will share.

From this moment on, Louis understands that he is, as he says, completely superior to Lestat, a superiority that allows him to distance himself from Lestat and what he holds dear. Louis kills but the kill always arouses a personal battle in which his humanity and inhumanity fight one another for control of his conscience. As he says before first meeting Claudia (the young girl he and Lestat turn into a vampire),

> And all the while, as the death wish caused me to neglect my thirst, my thirst grew hotter; my veins were veritable threads of pain in my flesh; my temples throbbed; and finally I could stand it no longer. Torn apart by the wish to take no action — to starve, to wither in thought on the one hand; and driven to kill on the other — I stood in an empty, desolate street and heard the sound of a child crying [73].

Louis does give in to his hunger, just as other vampires have before him. However, with Louis, this need is never without its guilt. Because he respects life and all that is in it, he does not kill for the sake of killing. Instead, Louis constantly tries to reconcile his vampiric needs with his remaining shreds of humanity. This attempt at reconciliation is Anne Rice's most significant contribution to the vampire narrative.

Claudia, in contrast to Louis, is very comfortable as a vampire. She may look like a child but she is certainly not innocent: "for little child she was, but also fierce killer now capable of the ruthless pursuit of blood with all a child's demanding" (97). Wise beyond her years, it is Claudia who eventually opens Louis's eyes to his servitude to Lestat. And it is Claudia who decides that she will kill Lestat: "And why not kill him! [...] I have no use for him! I can get nothing from him! And he causes me pain, which I will not abide!" (123). Lestat is of no use to Louis and Claudia, but he will also not let them go on without him. Therefore, Claudia's only course of action is to become both vampire and vampire slayer, perhaps the first of her kind. And because he is so in love with her, Louis sheds his indentured servitude to Lestat only to give it to Claudia.

Lestat's murder is very much like a ritual. Claudia drugs two young boys with absinthe and laudanum. When Lestat drinks from the boys, he is both drugged and poisoned. Once he realizes what is happening, Lestat calls for Louis, but Louis does nothing. Claudia then pulls a knife from the couch cushions and slits Lestat's throat. She follows that by drinking the remainder of his blood. Once they believe Lestat to be dead, Claudia and

Louis take him to the swamp and dump him. It is not until much later that the two learn the one sin for vampires: "It is the crime that means death to any vampire anywhere who commits it. It is to kill your own kind!" (247). While it is not explained why to kill one's own kind is so villainous, it is clear that the vampire community takes the rule very seriously. For Van Helsing, murdering vampires is a duty to society; for Claudia and Louis, murdering Lestat becomes a crime punishable by death. Before *Interview*, monsters did not actively plan one another's death. They may kill one another as a primal urge (for example, to be the alpha monster), but they do not pass judgment on one another. Louis and Claudia's action is the transition between monsters who do not bother one another to monsters who become judge and jury for their own kind.

While Claudia is the first vampire-turned-vampire-hunter, Louis soon follows in her footsteps. Lestat survives the attempted murder and the swamp and follows Claudia and Louis to France. Once there, he seeks his vengeance on Claudia by telling his story to the vampires at the Theatre des Vampires (the same vampires who explain the aforementioned cardinal sin). The vampires imprison Louis in a wall vault and kill Claudia. When Armand (the leader of the Theatre des Vampires) frees Louis, he explains that he could not have saved the vampire child, but Louis does not want to hear his excuses and blames Armand for allowing the vampires their vengeance. With Claudia's murder, something changes in Louis: "That passivity in me has been the core of it all, the real evil. That weakness, that refusal to compromise a fractured and stupid mortality, that awful pride!" (307). In other words, Louis believes his humanity has made him weak and passive. It is time for him to give in to his vampire nature and kill. But instead of killing just any mortal, Louis chooses first to kill those he believes wronged him. He returns to the Theatre, taking with him kerosene with which to ignite the entire building: "They would be destroyed. I ran for the stairs, a distant cry rising over the crackling and roaring of flames, my torch scraping the kerosene-soaked rafters above me, the flames enveloping the old wood, curling against the damp ceiling" (311). Although Louis sheds his final shreds of humanity, he still can never be a true member of the vampire community because he has killed many of his own. Like the monster hunters before him, Louis is an outsider; he can only truly belong to a community of monster hunters. Since Claudia is gone, he must now go through immortality as a loner.

While Louis helps to usher in a new type of monster hunter, the fact that he must lose his humanity to do it presents a rather bleak picture. Luckily, Louis is one of the only monster hunters who must make this sacrifice. As will be discussed throughout this study, it is only when the reformed monster seeks humanity that he becomes a monster hunter. However, the humanity Louis struggles with in *Interview* is not entirely new to the horror genre, although he is one of the first vampires to focus a great deal of time and thought on its implications. Mary Shelley imbues her Monster with a certain level of humanity, at least until he learns he can never really be a part of society. Other monsters have also shown glimmers of humanity, and it is this glimmer which leads to an audience's sympathy. For example, when Bela Lugosi's Dracula wishes to be "truly dead," we do feel a bit of sympathy for him. However, this sympathy is short-lived when the glimmer dies away and leaves the inhuman monster in its place. The vampires of the 1970s and their followers may not necessarily become less evil, but they certainly become more sympathetic. Often in these texts, a love story is added to enhance the vampire's humanity, and thus our sympathy. Or, as in *Interview*, the reader is forced to realize that immortality is, in fact, extremely boring. Yet something singular occurs when vampires become sympathetic: when vampires begin to feel emotion, they can begin to feel pain and guilt and regret. With these feelings can also come a sense of duty. And with that sense of duty, the vampire may choose to move from the role of the monster into the role of the monster hunter, a choice not evident before the 1970s.

Three vampire films in particular demonstrate the move to a more sympathetic vampire: William Crain's *Blacula* (1972), John Badham's *Dracula* (1979), and Francis Ford Coppola's *Bram Stoker's Dracula* (1992), all three of which will be discussed in much greater detail in Chapter 2. What I want to point out here is the focus on the love story in all three films. Each film's vampire falls in love with a woman and that love — rather than primal instinct — controls the monster's actions. Instead of trying to infiltrate western culture, each of these vampires wants only to be left alone with his love. As a result, the films' monster hunters actually become the bad guys as they try to keep the lovers apart. These three vampires demonstrate that love can bring about a type of humanity and with that humanity comes viewer sympathy, and, in some cases, the discrediting of the traditional monster hunter.

What this shift to a sympathetic monster shows is that the ideas behind posthumanism are seeping into horror. As I have said, questioning humanity has long been a pastime of gothic and horror creators. However, this questioning is usually in the form of two separate characters like Dr. Frankenstein and his Monster or Van Helsing and Dracula. In the 1970s, the characters merge into one. Beginning with Louis, the monster can shift between human and inhuman, actually making a conscious effort to do so. The focus becomes less on maintaining the status quo—after all, Louis is only one of many vampires worldwide and he cannot, nor does he want to, kill them all—and more on the characters themselves. What makes a vampire inhuman? Why does he choose the path to immortality? What does he do with his power? Who is that power benefiting? Why are these creatures deemed monstrous? These are the questions asked by the posthumanists and these are the questions now asked by horror audiences.

As the twentieth century drew to an end, the monster hunter was slowly getting ready to make a reappearance. Although that reappearance happens ever so slightly in *Interview with the Vampire*, the monster hunter truly reemerges in the 1990s. When he does, this monster hunter drastically differs from Stoker's Van Helsing. While the iron nerve may remain, that is, at first, one of Van Helsing's only traits to readily reappear. This new breed of monster hunter are in many cases past monsters or they are humans who use monstrous means. This movement between worlds gives them the knowledge they need to fight others like them, but it also causes great conflict as they are constantly being pulled between two selves: their monstrous nature and their desire to either regain or hold on to their humanity. It is this constant battle for redemption that allows them to be both human and monster and yet neither: the perfect poster children for posthumanism.

In 1992, a Canadian television show entitled *Forever Knight* (1992–1996) premiered, presenting one of the first true monster-turned-monster-hunters. The show follows the life of an eight-hundred-year-old vampire, Nick Knight (Geraint Wyn Davies). Knight, an angst-ridden detective, has decided that killing is no longer for him—yet, he cannot forgive himself for his past wrongs against society. To atone, he becomes a homicide detective in Toronto. His mentor Lacroix (Nigel Bennett) and old flame Janette (Deborah Duchene)—both vampires—think he is foolish. But Knight perseveres and tries to protect the unsuspecting citizens of Toronto and his unknowing partner, Schanke (John Kapelos), from the horrors of the night. Knight's search for redemption propels him to protect the very people he used to hunt. Although there will be more on Knight in Chapter 2, it is important to point out here that he protects mortals from other mortals. The other monster hunters discussed below mostly protect mortals from immortals. Knight is first and foremost a detective and his ultimate goal is to regain his mortality; this desire to reenter humanity will be the hallmark of many contemporary monster hunters.

Through the end of the twentieth century and the beginning of the twenty-first, the monster hunter continued to flourish on television with

Buffy the Vampire Slayer (1997–2003) and its spin-off *Angel* (1999–2004). In May 1997, Joss Whedon brought Buffy Summers (Sarah Michelle Gellar), the Chosen One, into America's living rooms. Buffy is, as the show's title indicates, a vampire slayer. But she is not alone in her quest to destroy demons and vampires. She is backed by an entire group of monster hunters: the Scoobies.[3] Of her group, five people fit the role of monster/monster hunter: Angel (David Boreanaz), Spike (James Marsters), Oz (Seth Green), Willow (Alyson Hannigan), and Faith (Eliza Dushku). Because it is a television show that spanned from 1997 (the premier) to 2004 (the season finale of *Angel*), *Buffy the Vampire Slayer* had plenty of time to develop its characters. The television show explores the complex posthuman relationship of monster and monster hunter in a way that is unattainable in a two-hour film. While most of these characters will get a more in-depth examination in chapters to come, it is important to highlight the five here because they further demonstrate the change begun by Anne Rice.

Angel and Spike are both vampires. But unlike "normal" vampires in the "Buffyverse"—what fans call the fictional world created by Whedon—these two possess their souls. In the Buffyverse, a human who is bitten and becomes a vampire loses his soul. This allows the vampire to pillage and plunder, devouring and/or killing anyone in his path without remorse. Because both Angel and Spike have their souls, they also have consciences. For the first time in their vampiric lives, these two vampires feel extreme guilt about the men and women they have destroyed. To repent for their actions, both vampires fight with Buffy against their own kind.

Oz, Willow, and Faith have a different story. They begin their time on the show as monster hunters, become monsters, and return to monster hunting. In the second season episode "Phases," Oz is turned into a werewolf. He begins to lock himself in a cage during the full moon to avoid killing anyone. And while he occasionally manages to break free, the viewer never sees him murder humans, nor is there any indication that he ever does after discovering his alter ego. When his wolfishness gets out of hand, he leaves Sunnydale looking for a way to control his inner demon. At the show's beginning, Willow is a wallflower with a natural affinity for magic. Over the course of several seasons, she develops her power to assist Buffy. But when her girlfriend, Tara (Amber Benson), is murdered in the sixth season episode "Seeing Red," Willow goes over the edge. She transforms from wallflower to powerful witch and nearly brings about the destruction of the entire world. After spending a summer learning to control her power, Willow returns to her friends as an even more powerful ally. Faith, another slayer, finds herself on a similar path. Unfortunately, Faith lets her jealousy of Buffy lead her to work for Season Three's monster, Mayor Richard Wilkins III (Harry Groener). Once joined with him, she tries to make Angel evil and battles Buffy. She is in a coma when the season ends. When she wakes, she does not repent her actions. Instead, after wreaking havoc in Sunnydale, she moves on to L.A. to torture her old Watcher, Wesley (Alexis Denisof). With Angel's help, Faith learns to live with and control her dark side and her jealousy and returns to Sunnydale to help Buffy defeat the First, the great evil of Season Seven.

In addition to "softer" vampires and complex character development, the end of the twentieth century also brought with it a whole new vampire: the half-breed. These vampires usually have a male vampire sire and a human mother. In many cases, the half-breed, like other vampires of the late twentieth century, takes on the role of both monster and monster hunter. Possibly the most popular half-breed to date is the Daywalker, Blade (Wesley Snipes) from the trilogy *Blade*, *Blade II* (2002), and *Blade: Trinity* (2004). Again, while there will be more on Blade in Chapter 2, it is important to see how he fits in with the monster hunter timeline. Blade's mother was bitten the day she gave birth to him, and this bite causes some sort of genetic mutation. As Whistler — Blade's partner and father figure — explains, he can go out in the day and is immune to garlic but has a vampire's strength, regenerative powers, and, unfortunately, a thirst for blood. As the vampire Deacon Frost (Stephen Dorff) puts it, "You have all of our strengths and none of our weaknesses." Blade sees it differently and uses a serum to quench his thirst for blood. He abhors what he is and puts that anger toward and hatred of his own kind into his work. When he goes out hunting, Blade takes out hordes of vampires at once, using all of the latest technologies and weapons. In a way, Blade is a "postvampire" in that he is neither human nor vampire but a mixture of both.

An interesting thing happens to the Van Helsing stereotype in the first Blade movie: he is split into three separate characters. First is Blade himself. He is the strength, the fighter, the "iron nerve." He has an intimate knowledge of vampires because he is one of them. Then there is Whistler who understands and knows the vampire folklore. He is the technician of the group who builds and fixes Blade's weaponry. It can even be said that his is the "temper of the ice-brook" (Stoker 125) with a cool resolve. But Whistler, unlike Van Helsing, is no doctor or scientist. Instead, that role is given to Blade's romantic interest: Karen (N'Bushe Wright). She is a doctor, a hematologist to be exact. It is she who creates a vaccine for vampirism, at least one that can be used on vampires who are bitten, not ones like Blade or those who are born vampires. Although she offers to find Blade a cure for his vampirism, he tells her that the war is not yet over and he is not yet ready to become human (a sentiment that Angel echoes in his spin-off series); if she wants to help, she needs to make him a better serum. Together, the three make up one super Van Helsing. They have the knowledge, the skills, and the background needed to fight the vampires. Even though their job is not as easy as Van Helsing's—they have many vampires to fight while he has only one—as a group they have the strength needed to keep the monsters from passing too far beyond the threshold.

Unfortunately, not all changes in the monster hunter have met with positive reviews. In 2004, Universal finally released a film that focuses on Stoker's monster hunter: *Van Helsing*. The film's Van Helsing (Hugh Jackman) is not a great, educated man. In fact, he is nothing more than a henchman, a hired thug, for a group of priests calling themselves the Knights of the Holy Order. Unlike his Victorian predecessor, he does not seek knowledge about the things he goes after. When Anna (Kate Beckinsale), the gypsy princess who helps him fight Dracula (Richard Roxburgh) and his wives, accuses him of asking a lot of questions, Van Helsing responds, "Usually I ask only two: what are we dealing with and how do I kill it." For good or bad, this is not the Van Helsing of Stoker's creation. As with *Blade*, the original Van Helsing character seems to be split, this time into two characters: Van Helsing, the fighter, and Carl, the learned man who makes Van Helsing's James Bond-like weaponry. When Van Helsing comes to him for weapons to fight Dracula, Carl is the one to educate him about vampires, for Van Helsing says, "Vampires, gargoyles, warlocks, they're all the same." The original Van Helsing would certainly know better. Even Blade has a certain level of understanding and respect for his adversaries. This contemporary Van Helsing knows little more than fighting techniques and needs both Carl and Anna to rescue him from his own ignorance.

In addition to losing his credibility as a man of intellect, *Van Helsing*'s protagonist has lost the respect of others. Stoker's Van Helsing is an important doctor, specifically sent for by his colleague and student, Dr. Seward. The 2004 Van Helsing is a wanted man, an outlaw, and, to many, a murderer. Even though people know of him, they acknowledge his presence with a sneer. When Van Helsing goes after Mr. Hyde (Robbie Coltrane), the monster says, "So you're the great Van Helsing," not with respect but with contempt. After Van Helsing kills Hyde, a French policeman yells to him that he is a murderer. And even Anna questions his motives when she asks, "Some say you're a murderer, Mr. Van Helsing. Others say you're a holy man. Which is it?" Van Helsing responds, "It's a bit of both, I think." This Van Helsing is a product of the twenty-first century. Gone is the public's respect for scientific knowledge and intellect. In their place is a respect for muscle and weaponry. Van Helsing is really only as good as his best gadget. Without his machine-gun crossbow and fancy handsaws, he is really nothing more than any other hired gun.

Yet, despite his weakened reputation, one aspect of Van Helsing remains consistent with his predecessors: he is still linked directly to Dracula. Jackman's Van Helsing does not remember who or what he is, only that he was found in Rome four hundred years before the film's action date of 1888. When Carl asks him what he remembers, Van Helsing responds that he remembers fighting the Romans, a battle which occurred in 73 A.D. Clearly this Van Helsing is as much a supernatural being as those he seeks to destroy. When he first appears before Dracula, Dracula greets him by using his first name, thus suggesting a certain level of intimacy between the two. Dracula knows Van Helsing, yet Van Helsing does not know Dracula. While their bond is not emphasized by the cinematography like that used in other films, their histories are deeply connected. Dracula explains Van Helsing's role in acting as the Left Hand of God, the man who took the vampire's mortal life. Being called the Left Hand of God makes Van Helsing the Wrath of God, a significant change from Stoker's Van Helsing, who seems more a Christ-figure than a destroyer of men.[4] Dracula offers to tell Van Helsing more about his past, but Van Helsing responds, "Some things are better left forgotten," and proceeds to kill the vampire. Despite facing box office disappointment, this film still plays an important role in the continuing evolution of the monster hunter. Although Jackman's monster hunter may be less complex than the other contemporary monster hunters, he still represents the posthumanist trend that there can be no true human and no true monster; both are intertwined.

There are two significant distinctions that need to take place at this point. First, these contemporary monster hunters are not necessarily heroes in the traditional sense. As consumers of these texts, we do not look up to characters like Blade or Spike. We must remember that when it comes to male monster hunters—women deserve their own analysis, which comes in Chapter 4—the characters are not what is traditionally thought of as "good." These are past monsters who have committed horrendous acts. They have killed and destroyed innocent people. In most cases they are only fighting monsters for selfish means, at least at first. These characters—while heroic during the texts—should not be compared with traditional heroic characters like Beowulf, Saint George, or even Frodo Baggins. The contemporary male monster hunter will almost always have an ulterior motive for his actions and this puts him in a category of his own.

Second, the contemporary monster hunter is not a case of a "good" person going "bad" for a short time. For example, there are works in which the protagonist must lower himself to the level of the villain in order to save the day. Some examples of this would be Leonardo DiCaprio in the 2006 film *The Departed* or Jodi Foster in the 2007 film *The Brave One*. In these films it can be argued that the hero's monstrosity is excusable because it brings down a bigger monster. While it is not my goal to argue such a presumption, I do want to point out that the contemporary monster hunter should not be forgiven for his evil deeds. It is just such a background that makes the monster hunter effective. He must understand what it is like to freely terrorize so that he knows how to stop that terrorization. These characters can get in the heads of the contemporary villain because they once were the villains. Pessimistic as it may sound — and despite the fact that they are their works' protagonists — the contemporary monster hunter should not immediately be pardoned for his past actions.

The World Beyond

The focus on human and monster within the same person is not confined specifically to gothic and horror texts. Since the 1970s, the trend has also seeped into other genres, most notably the graphic novel and anime. There will be more on graphic novels in Chapter 3, but Alan Moore's *The League of Extraordinary Gentlemen, Volume 1* (1999) deserves mention here within the timeline as it is an excellent demonstration of other traditional monsters becoming monster hunters. In this novel, Mina Murray gathers together Allan Quatermain, Captain Nemo, Dr. Jekyll (and of course Mr. Hyde), and Hawley Griffin (the Invisible Man) to form the League: a group united to seek out a special anti-gravity material known as cavorite.

While the group members do not always see eye-to-eye, they do manage to come together for the good of the British populace. Mina, the group's leader, even manages to calm the beast Hyde. At one point, when he grips her arm and will not let go, Mina states very firmly, "Mr. Hyde, you are hurting my hand, sir, and I will not allow that. I should be grateful if you would release me" (134). The next panel shows the two staring at each other. The third panel has Hyde releasing Mina. In Stevenson's novel, Mr. Hyde is abusive to women; having him respect Mina here is certainly in line with the changes to the late-twentieth-century monster who tends to harbor a glimmer of humanity. At the novel's end, the Head of Intelligence tells the League that they should not disband as he is keeping them on retainer. Quatermain comments that, "He's paying us an awful lot of money to sit around doing nothing," to which Mina responds, "We'll see. These are tumultuous times, Mr. Quatermain....I'm sure something will turn up" (145–146). Not only does Moore create a group of monster hunters who work together for the good of humanity, he also gives the reader an open ending, another characteristic of the contemporary horror text. Today's horror audiences are not nearly as naïve as their Victorian or early twentieth-century counterparts. Contemporary audiences understand that monstrosity never really goes away. Emphasizing that these are tumultuous times reminds the reader — and the monster hunter — that things are only safe for the time being and there is no telling when and where the next inhuman act will occur.

Anime is another genre where the human and the monstrous collide. An excellent example is the movie *Vampire Hunter D* (1985) where D is half human and half vampire but beset with a sense of duty. As the film opens, a young woman is fighting monsters. She fails in her quest and is bitten by an ancient vampire lord who hopes to take her as his new wife. Doris, the young woman, enlists D, a vampire hunter, to help her kill the vampire lord and release her from her fate. Yet, unbeknownst to her and her brother Dan, D is actually a vampeal, the name for one who is half vampire and half human.

As a half-breed, D is the epitome of vampire as Byronic Hero. According to Carrol L. Fry, "The Byronic hero, then, is an intimidating man with a glittering eye: a man alone, alienated from his fellows by his passionate nature and aristocratic background and a character whose genesis clearly derives from the Gothic villain as created by [Ann] Radcliffe and her imitators" (273). D certainly fits this definition. He is a man traveling alone, both in the beginning of the film and at the end. His very nature as a half-breed immediately sets him apart from his fellow beings. The full-blood vampires in the film abhor vampeals, as do the mortals. This makes for a double-strike against D. D is also Dracula's son; a more aristocratic father in the vampire world would be difficult to find. Fry goes on to claim, "Some of Byron's heroes are noble outlaws from the romantic tradition, but redeemed by the depth of their passion: a passion — expressed in undying love for a woman — that excuses all other faults" (273). Doris must convince D that he should help her kill the vampire lord because, at the beginning, he is resistant. However, he begins to fall in love with Doris and therefore risks his life for her and Dan. In his wish for humanity and love, D is very much like Rice's Louis and other vampires from the end of the twentieth century. He is flawed, infected even, but tries with all his might to resist his "true" nature. When Dan first meets D, he says that there are two types of men who don't talk much: "Men who are too busy planning something wrong to have time to say much and good men who believe their actions speak louder than words and only talk when they have something worth saying." Dan believes that D is the second type of man, a good man.

As has been shown, D is certainly not alone in his struggle as a half-breed. But it is not just vampires who can be half-breeds. The television show *Inuyasha* (2000–2004) also deals with a half-breed trying to determine his place in medieval Japan. In this show, Inuyasha is half demon and half human. In the first episode — "The Girl Who Overcame Time" — a flashback shows Inuyasha as he tries to steal the Jewel of Four Souls so that he can be all demon. Later in Season One it is learned that he originally wanted the Jewel so that he could be human and live happily ever after with the Jewel's keeper Kikyo. Thanks to a trap set by the evil Naraku, Inuyasha is led to believe that Kikyo betrays him and wants revenge on her. To rescue the Jewel, Kikyo — who believes Inuyasha always wanted the Jewel to become a demon — shoots him with an arrow and pins him to a tree for fifty years, but she is wounded in the process and dies. Kagome, the reincarnation of Kikyo, unpins Inuyasha and then proceeds to accidentally shatter the Jewel. Inuyasha and Kagome end up working together to find the Jewel shards before the demons can get them.

Throughout the seasons, Inuyasha is constantly torn between his lust for the Jewel and his feelings for Kagome. He believes that it is his demon side that makes him strong. However, early on it is explained that his human side is truly the more powerful side. In one story arc, Inuyasha must find Tetsusaiga, the sword made from one of his demon father's fangs, before his demon brother does. It turns out that only someone who is at least part human can wield Tetsusaiga. As Inuyasha learns, even his demon father had some level of humanity because he truly loved Inuyasha's human mother. As a result of his father's humanity, the sword only truly works when Inuyasha is trying to protect a human. In addition, there are times throughout the series when Inuyasha must make a choice between his human and demon sides. In the end, he always chooses the humanity in him over the monstrosity.

In both of these examples, half-breeds try to find their place in the world. Like other contemporary monster hunters, these characters are neither human nor monster which means that they cannot necessarily always control their monstrous natures. The characters demonstrate that no one is ever truly one way or the other, something the many readers and viewers of these texts already know. Contemporary monster hunters are not Stoker's Van Helsing, yet at different times throughout the texts, they do demonstrate his intellect and knowledge, iron nerve, temper of the icebrook, resolution, self-command, and tolerance. And while the contemporary monster hunters may not always have the kindliest and truest hearts, they try to do the best they can. They know they cannot ever actually defeat the evil and restore humanity, but they never stop trying to help those around them. So far, the monster hunter — whether he has always been on the side of good or is a relatively new recruit — has mostly triumphed, at least for a brief moment until the sequel or next week's episode appears.

Chapter 2

Humanity and the Contemporary Vampire

"The vampire with a soul, once he fulfills his destiny, will become human."
— Shanshu Prophecy in *Angel*

Of the three horror archetypes — Frankenstein's Monster, the vampire, and the werewolf — the vampire has traditionally been the least sympathetic. There can be no doubt that readers of Mary Shelley's novel felt sorry for her monstrous creation. In addition, because the werewolf is human most of the time, people can overlook, or at least excuse, its several nights of mayhem, especially when the human side takes over and feels nothing but remorse. However, no Victorian reader would feel sorry for Count Dracula because Bram Stoker never actually fleshes out the character. And while Tod Browning's 1931 Count may wish — albeit briefly — that he were truly dead, his monstrous intentions overshadow his moment of sympathy. But, as I mentioned in Chapter 1, sympathy has been creeping ever so slowly into the contemporary vampire narrative. It is love which has been the predominant means by which readers and viewers have witnessed the softer side of the undead. In the 1970s, love becomes a major motivating factor that causes significant changes in the vampire myth, as seen in several *Dracula* adaptations including *Blacula* (1972), *Dracula* (1979), and *Bram Stoker's Dracula* (1992). These changes not only make the vampire more sympathetic, they also cause the traditional monster hunter's power to diminish.

According to Nina Auerbach, "In retrospect, the 1970s seem [...] a decade of reintegration, full of hope for new beginnings" (132). While that hope may not have manifested itself in the slasher subgenre, it abounds in the *Dracula* adaptations with their integration of a love story between the vampire and female lead. When love appears in the vampire's life, the monster seems to regain a small amount of his lost humanity. Once Dracula appears human, he also becomes sympathetic and threatens society's patriarchal homogeneity by presenting an alternate view of masculinity: a man who is both monstrous and loving. If the demasculinized male suddenly becomes a film's hero, traditional gender roles shift: men are suddenly feminized while, in some cases, women are masculinized. The old-fashioned, white, educated, upper-class, male protector becomes lost, inept, and even comical. If Paul Wells is right in claiming that 1950s horror films help to destabilize "movie-made masculinity" (62), vampire films of the 1970s certainly continue the trend.[1]

The first example of a love-struck vampire is William Crain's *Blacula*, which begins sometime during the years of the Middle Passage. After dining with Dracula (Charles Macaulay), the African Mamuwalde (William Marshall), and his wife, Luva (Vonetta McGee), anger the Count, who bites Mamuwalde, renames him Blacula, and locks him in a coffin (the ultimate statement regarding patriarchy, slavery, and colonization). He then locks Luva in the room with the coffin, but chains her to the wall so she cannot reach her husband and leaves her to die. When Blacula is finally released from his coffin in 1972, he meets Tina (also played by Vonetta McGee), the reincarnation of Luva. Realizing that love is eternal, Blacula tells Tina that he is a vampire and that she is Luva reincarnated. Tina recognizes their bond and falls in love with the vampire. The two spend the remainder of the film trying to be together, but are pursued by Tina's brother-in-law, Gordon (Thalmus Rasulala), the film's monster hunter. In an unexpected turn of events, Gordon and his detective friend do not kill Blacula. Instead, after witnessing Tina's death, Blacula walks into full daylight, committing suicide.

Blacula and Tina want nothing more than to be left in peace to pursue their relationship. However, Gordon will not allow this. It is the monster hunter's responsibility to uphold the status quo and a relationship between a vampire (the monster) and a beautiful woman just is not "normal." Tina should be with a man whom Gordon and society approve of. Beyond trying to discover the vampire in his midst and prevent an unnatural coupling, however, Gordon is not a central character to the film's action. He is always just a few steps behind the two lovers, and, in the end, he has nothing to do with Blacula's death. It is not so much that Gordon is an ineffectual monster hunter, he is just unnecessary because the film's focus is on the eternal love between Blacula and Tina. Blacula does not want to create vampires and take over the world; he just wants to spend eternity with the woman he loves. Because there is no great plot to foil, there is no need for a monster hunter. Gordon functions as a figurehead, a throw-back to the traditional need for a vampire to have a nemesis, nothing more. *Blacula*, then, becomes one of the first vampire films of the 1970s to move the love story to the front and the monster hunter to the sidelines.

John Badham's adaptation of the Stoker tale also focuses on love between vampire and female lead. Often considered to be the feminist adaptation, because it features a strong woman attempting to break through her patriarchal family structure, Badham's storyline sees Lucy Seward (Kate Nelligan) falling in love with Dracula (Frank Langella). She wants to be bitten and wants to be with Dracula, yet the men in her life try their very best to keep the lovers apart. Other than Roman Polanski's parody, *The Fearless Vampire Killers* (1967), a viewer would be hard-pressed to find a more inept group of monster hunters than those found in Badham's film. As Auerbach argues, "In this breathtaking if confusing movie, Stoker's good men are villains; Stoker's vampire is a hero; the women, victims no more, embrace vampirism with rapture as the sole available escape from patriarchy" (140). Van Helsing (Laurence Olivier), Dr. Seward (Donald Pleasence), and Jonathan Harker (Trevor Eve) only deter Dracula through sheer luck. When Van Helsing tries to stake Dracula, the vampire turns the stake back on him and impales him. In his dying moments, Van Helsing manages to send a hook flying at Dracula, thus enabling Jonathan to raise the vampire into the sunlight. However, Dracula successfully flies away, leaving Lucy with a happy look on her face, knowing the two of them will eventually be reunited.

Some might argue that Langella's Count is nothing more than an updated version of Christopher Lee's hyper-sexed vampire. However, there is a significant difference between the two. As was mentioned in Chapter 1, Lee's vampire goes to England to replace the lover who was taken from him. In other words, his motive is simply revenge. Langella's vampire, by comparison, apparently has no such motive, at least not that is mentioned in the film. Instead, everything Badham does as a director points to the belief that when Dracula meets Lucy, it is love at first sight, a mutual attraction in fact. Langella's Dracula is certainly seen as a savior in this film; his goal is to save Lucy from her oppressive life and unhappy engagement. By having a woman who wants to break free from the status quo and a monster in love, Badham presents a radical shift in what can be deemed "human." Van Helsing cannot let his friend's daughter, Lucy, remain involved with a man deemed inappropriate by society's standards. Both Van Helsing and Dr. Seward want her to be with the "typical" Jonathan, which is why the three men — like Gordon in *Blacula*— do everything to keep the lovers apart. Yet, at the film's conclusion humanity has not been restored to its pre-film status quo. Dracula has escaped, Lucy is clearly expectant of his return, and the most important monster hunter in the genre is dead (or at least dying). Badham refuses his audience their closure and their comforting return to normality.

The next significant *Dracula* adaptation moves us ahead thirteen years to *Bram Stoker's Dracula* in which Francis Ford Coppola provides a thorough back story for his solitary Count, beginning with a voiceover explaining that the vampire is the real-life Wallachian Prince, Vlad the Impaler, thus giving viewers an authentic historical person with whom to associate his monster. Here, Vlad (Gary Oldman) dearly loves his wife, Elisabeta (Winona Ryder). When he returns home after fighting the Turks in the name of Christianity, he finds that Elisabeta has killed herself out of grief because she has been tricked into thinking Vlad is dead. Because she committed suicide, his priests inform Vlad that Elisabeta will never find peace, even though her husband has been a champion for Christianity. In his anger, Vlad renounces God, destroys an altar, and pierces a cross with his sword. As blood pours from the cross's wound, Vlad scoops it up in a chalice and proceeds to drink it, thus becoming a vampire. It is not until many centuries later that he realizes his beloved Elisabeta has been reborn in Mina Murray (also played by Winona Ryder). Keeping Jonathan (Keanu Reeves) imprisoned in his castle, Vlad rushes to England to court Mina. He opens up his heart to her—both literally and figuratively—in the hopes that she will love him back. It is this love that, in the end, saves Vlad. While Vlad lies dying before his damaged altar, Mina—in an act that reciprocates his love—pulls his sword from the cross, thus symbolically healing his wound with God. He is restored to his youth and, presumably, dies at peace. The last shot pans to the ceiling above the altar where Vlad and Elisabeta are painted together in what appears to be Heaven. Their love will most certainly live forever, just as the film's tagline claims.

Like Blacula and Langella's Dracula before him, Oldman's Dracula is not motivated by social domination or revenge but by love. Because everything Vlad has done has been a direct result of his love for Elisabeta, he is the film's sympathetic character. Even Vlad the Impaler becomes more sympathetic because his beloved Elisabeta has been taken from him through treachery. Coppola's viewers are to feel pity and even a sense of understanding when Vlad pierces the cross and renounces his Christianity. Dracula becomes less a monster and more a victim of lost love. But, if Dracula becomes, in a way, this film's hero, what happens to Van Helsing? In Coppola's film, the monster hunters seem more like macho thugs trying their best to keep Mina in the home where they think she belongs than they do the narrative's heroes. In fact, the viewer is meant to cheer when Mina rushes to Dracula's side.

The audience first recognizes Van Helsing (Anthony Hopkins) not by seeing him but by hearing him. His is the voice-over at the film's beginning that retells the story of Vlad the Impaler. This voice-over lends Van Helsing credibility as someone who knows the history of Count Dracula; he is clearly the film's expert. When the viewer first sees Van Helsing, this sense of his knowledge is further enforced. The Professor is lecturing a room of students on sexually transmitted diseases, and, when he meets her, immediately recognizes that Lucy (Sadie Frost) has been bitten by a vampire. However, there is a turning point in the film where Van Helsing's expertise starts to move from respectable to oddly maniacal: to convince Arthur Holmwood (Cary Elwes), Dr. Seward (Richard E. Grant), and Quincey Morris (Bill Campbell) that the supernatural and vampires do indeed exist, Van Helsing relies on tricks. One moment Van Helsing is speaking with the men, the next moment he disappears, only to reappear in a different section of the garden. In past films, Van Helsing has not needed such parlor tricks to convince his students. This use of "magic" both damages Van Helsing's credibility as a learned scholar and emphasizes his own connection to the supernatural; it also alerts the viewer to the fact that Van Helsing is someone to be wary of but not necessarily respected.

In addition, the direct connection between Van Helsing and Dracula is gone. As I discussed in Chapter 1, in past adaptations directors have used cinematography and editing to emphasize the ways in which Van Helsing and Dracula are linked in their eternal battle. The closest Coppola comes to such a scene occurs immediately after Mina leaves England to marry Jonathan. Alone in a room of candles, Dracula is distraught and summons the winds. The camera pans up and out and the scene cuts to Van Helsing, who is also in a room of candles. He is sitting at a desk reading his book on vampires. All of a sudden a wind gusts in and causes the candles to flicker and blow out. Van Helsing recognizes that it is Dracula —"the foe I have pursued all my life"— who has caused the winds and is destroying Lucy. This one sequence is the closest Van Helsing and Dracula get to facing one another in Coppola's film, doing virtually nothing to set Van Helsing up as an expert. Instead of steadfastly trying to protect society, it actually seems as if Van Helsing is pursuing Dracula for personal reasons.

Nowhere is Van Helsing's role reduction more prominent than at the film's end. While Van Helsing takes Mina to Dracula's castle to be used as bait for the Count, Harker, Holmwood, Seward, and Morris pursue Dracula and his Gypsies. When Van Helsing and Mina are attacked by Dracula's brides during the night, Van Helsing can do nothing to destroy the three female vampires. All he can do is form a circle around him and Mina to keep the vampires back. Van Helsing cannot even control or help Mina. Knowing that her beloved Count is vulnerable, Mina jumps up on a wall of the castle and calls on the winds and snow to force Harker and his friends back. The camera shot from a high angle focuses on Mina while below her, on the ground, Van Helsing does nothing to stop her. He merely looks on in a mixture of awe, shock, and helplessness. The traditional white, educated stereotype is truly done in by this film, with Van Helsing actually seeming more of a madman than a professor.

Based on such adaptations, it would seem as if the monster hunter would now be a useless aspect of the horror narrative. *Blacula*'s Gordon is utterly unnecessary, Badham's monster hunters are inept but somewhat lucky, and Coppola's film proves that the monster hunter has been usurped by the monster. If the monster hunter is truly useless, then why is there a resurgence in monster-hunter narratives in the mid and late 1990s? What we need to remember is that directors like Crain, Badham, and Coppola only succeed in ridding the vampire narrative of the white, educated, upper-class male monster, not the notion of a monster hunter. Once the traditional male monster hunter leaves the scene, a new breed of expert takes his place: the sympathetic monsters who are capable of love. These monsters may be, or have been, despicable, but in their connection with love, they attempt to regain a morsel of humanity. Both Blacula and Oldman's Dracula attempt to literally regain their pre-vampire love via their reincarnated wives. Langella's Dracula may not be quite so obvious in his attempt, but he at least wants to spend eternity with Lucy. Love is a humanizing emotion. Traditionally society has viewed those who can love as human; true monsters are not capable of such emotion. Yet it must also be mentioned that these three vampires do not abandon their monstrous ways. When provoked, they fight back. In addition, they must continue to satisfy their bloodlust. In this way, then, these characters begin a new trend where vampires — traditionally unsympathetic monsters — share both monstrous and human characteristics.

It needs to be understood, however, that this duality is not new to gothic and horror texts. No text better demonstrates this duality than Robert Louis Stevenson's *The Strange Case of Dr Jekyll and Mr Hyde* (1886), in which Jekyll's motivation for creating his serum is to rid himself of those attributes he considers to be socially unacceptable in Victorian England. He cannot abide his self-proclaimed base instincts and comments, "And indeed the worst of my fault was a certain impatient gaiety of disposition, such as has made the happiness of many, but such as I found it hard to reconcile with my imperious desire to carry my head high, and wear a more than commonly grave countenance before the public" (60). In Jekyll's opinion, he cannot have improper feelings and still maintain the persona of an upstanding Victorian doctor. In separating the two sides of his personality, however, Jekyll makes a huge mistake; Mr. Hyde is truly a beast: "This familiar that I called out of my own soul, and sent forth alone to do his good pleasure, was a being inherently malign and villainous; his every act and thought centered on self; drinking pleasure with bestial avidity from any degree of torture to another; relentless like a man of stone" (65). Both the human and the monstrous sides of Jekyll battle it out for dominance.

Unfortunately, Jekyll's punishment for his experiment is the complete loss of himself to Hyde. Yet, in the end, even Hyde cannot survive. When Jekyll's friend Utterson breaks into his laboratory, he finds Hyde dead on the floor: "[T]he cords of his [Hyde's] face still moved with a semblance of life; but life was quite gone; and by the crushed phial in the hand and the strong smell of kernels that hung upon the air, Utterson knew that he was looking on the body of a self-destroyer" (49). Along with its other nineteenth-century counterparts—Mary Shelley's *Frankenstein* (1818) and Bram Stoker's *Dracula* (1897)—*Dr Jekyll and Mr Hyde* cannot end with the monster still at large. Both Jekyll and Hyde are punished in Stevenson's story. Because Jekyll dares to release such a monster upon society—despite his original good intentions—he must die, taking with him the monster who cannot be allowed to roam freely around London. With death as the punishment for transgressing societal norms, *Jekyll and Hyde* works as a warning to those who seek to live outside Victorian homogeneity.

While this ending does suggest that monstrosity cannot live within Victorian society, Stevenson leaves the ending's specific details up to the reader, thus forcing him to think about what Jekyll/Hyde's death symbolizes. In doing so, the reader is forced to determine what truly happened in Jekyll's lab that fateful night. Did Jekyll finally manage to kill Hyde by committing suicide? If Jekyll was able to feel the change coming on, could he have taken his own life quickly enough to stop Hyde? If this did, indeed, occur, it could mean that Jekyll, as a monster hunter, predates even Van Helsing. By making the choice to kill himself, Jekyll hopes that he can finally stop Hyde from terrorizing London. Although it is Hyde, and not Jekyll, who is left on the laboratory's floor, this could simply imply that Jekyll turned into Hyde either during or after death.

However, for our purposes, the ending to *Jekyll and Hyde* works on another level as well, one which anticipates the concerns of contemporary horror. Stevenson could be implying that Hyde *chooses* to commit suicide. It is true that there is no indication why Hyde feels that he should kill himself, especially considering the fact that he seems to enjoy wreaking havoc without remorse. As Jekyll's base self, the reader gets no sense that Hyde has a conscience, but, in this alternate reading of the ending, he makes the choice to commit suicide. Is it possible that a little bit of Jekyll's humanity is still deep within Hyde? Is it possible that this most villainous of Victorian monsters feels a tinge of remorse? These questions are not answered in Stevenson's text, but they certainly manifest themselves in other contemporary horror texts. The significant difference, however, is that in today's texts, the monster is not necessarily forced to die. More attention is given to that small spark of remorse until in some cases it becomes a flame driving the monster to seek penitence and forgiveness. Given the right conditions, even the most fiendish of contemporary monsters can become monster hunters. When this happens, readers and viewers are forced to rethink their humanizing ideologies. They must begin to agree with the posthumanists in that there can no longer be a definite duality of monster and monster hunter. As such, there can be no definite distinction between monster and human. There are three significant vampire texts from the end of the twentieth and beginning of the twenty-first centuries that ask and attempt to answer the questions put forth by Stevenson's novel: *Forever Knight*, *Buffy the Vampire Slayer* and its spin-off *Angel*, and the *Blade* trilogy. In continuing the discussion of vampires as humane monsters—characteristics traditionally assumed to be at odds—these three television series and one film trilogy demonstrate the conditions needed to move a vampire from Stoker's Dracula to the sympathetic lover and then to the monster hunter so desperately needed by contemporary society.

The Reformed Ones

Forever Knight is the creation of Barry Cohen and James D. Parriott. This Canadian television show was first a 1989 television movie starring Rick Springfield and then was made into a television series which premiered in 1992, running three seasons until its final episode on May 17, 1996. The series follows the life of Nick Knight (Geraint Wyn Davies), an eight-hundred-year-old vampire, as he tries to regain the humanity he lost when he became a member of the undead. He is aided in his quest by Natalie Lambert (Catherine Disher), a coroner who uses her medical knowledge to help wean him away from blood, which both believe keeps Nick from achieving mortality. In addition, Nick feels that he must atone for his past wrongs by helping rather than killing humans. He does this by becoming a detective. Almost every episode features Nick pursuing a criminal; there is also almost always a flashback to Nick's previous vampire existence linking his current investigation with a past mistake, thus allowing him to right his past wrong. However, Nick is not without temptation. His thoughts and actions are constantly tainted by his vampire sire Lacroix (Nigel Bennett).[2]

In many ways, Nick is a forerunner of two of the most popular vampires-turned-monster hunters: Angel and Spike from Joss Whedon's *Buffy the Vampire Slayer* and *Angel*.[3] Buffy and her friends first hit the popular culture scene in 1992 in a film starring Kristy Swanson as Buffy, Donald Sutherland as Buffy's watcher Merrick, and Rutger Hauer as the vampire Lothos. The film is a campy look at the life of slayer Buffy Summers as she comes to terms with her supernatural, vampire-fighting abilities. Led by Merrick, Buffy learns how to harness her abilities and is eventually able to defeat Lothos. Unfortunately, the end product did not please its creator. In an interview with *The Onion*, Joss Whedon comments, "It didn't turn out to be the movie that I had written. They never do, but that was my first lesson in that. Not that the movie is without merit, but I just watched a lot of stupid wannabe-star behavior and a director with a different vision than mine — which was her right, it was her movie — but it was still frustrating" (Robinson). Whedon did not expect to ever resurrect Buffy, but a few years later he received a call from producer Gail Berman who asked if he would like to turn his original concept into a television show for The WB. Whedon agreed and *Buffy the Vampire Slayer* premiered on March 10, 1997.

The television show both picks up where the film left off and, in some ways, rewrites the film. In the premier, Buffy Summers (Sarah Michelle Gellar) is starting her sophomore year at Sunnydale High in California, having been expelled from her Los Angeles high school the prior year for setting the gymnasium on fire. (Although the film's slayer does not set it on fire, the gymnasium is where the final showdown occurs between Buffy and Lothos.) Buffy wants nothing more than to ignore her slayer powers, but, unfortunately, she is the Chosen One of her generation; until Buffy dies, she will remain a slayer. Once in Sunnydale, Buffy is assigned a new Watcher, Rupert Giles (Anthony Stewart Head) who is also conveniently Sunnydale High's new librarian. In addition, Buffy befriends Willow Rosenberg (Alyson Hannigan) and Xander Harris (Nicholas Brenden). In the series premier, the four are able to stop the vampire master from rising and killing the townsfolk. Thus begins the work of the Scoobies. Each week, the

Scoobies fight demons and vampires who embody and represent the very real dangers faced by typical high school students.

Of the many differences between the film and the television show, none is perhaps more important than the addition of the mysterious Angel (David Boreanaz) and the charismatic Spike (James Marsters). Angel appears in the very first episode of *Buffy*, where he offers Buffy some advice and gives her a silver cross. Buffy does not learn his secret until several episodes later: Angel is a vampire, and, most surprisingly, he has a soul. Spike first appears in the second season episode "School Hard" and becomes the season's "Big Bad" (the evil that must be defeated to save Sunnydale). He reappears in future seasons and tries to regain his Big Bad status, but it is slowly chipped away from him until he becomes a reluctant Scoobie.

Finally, the comic-book-turned-film icon Blade needs to be analyzed within this chapter.[4] In the *Blade* trilogy (1998, 2002, 2004), Blade (Wesley Snipes) is a half-breed born to a vampire father and a somewhat mortal mother. (Blade's mother is bitten either immediately before going into labor or during childbirth and Blade is born before she dies and becomes a vampire herself.) During his teen years, Blade is discovered by Whistler (Kris Kristofferson), a mortal monster hunter whose family was killed by vampires. Whistler helps Blade become an efficient monster hunter both by providing weapons and training and also by providing Blade with serum that fends off the half-vampire's need for blood. While it is not Blade's primary goal to become human — he is actually offered that possibility in the first film and turns it down — he refuses to give in to his vampiric nature. Like Nick Knight, Blade wants to keep the world safe from monsters, and like Angel and Spike he wants to quell the monster within.

Although each of these four monster hunters differs drastically in personality and history, each maintains the same goal: to make the world just a bit safer for the time being. In doing so, they hope to regain some level of humanity. Of the four, Angel and Spike are the most developed by virtue of having the longest-running shows and thus the most time to grow. However, that does not mean that either Nick or Blade are less important to the development of the vampire-turned-monster hunter. Each monster hunter plays an important part in understanding the path a vampire takes to become a monster hunter — a path which includes a soul, love or a community, and a purpose. Pamela Church Gibson claims that "one of the interesting phenomena to be traced within the 1980s and 1990s films is a gradual blurring of boundaries between pursuer and pursued" (180). Nick, Angel, Spike and Blade are excellent illustrations of this blurring. Each vampire has a different path to travel, but, as will be seen, each path is surprisingly similar.

The Soul

If ever there was an abstract term, "soul" would have to be it. What is a soul? The answer is certainly open to interpretation. Since it cannot be easily defined, we must think about the common perceptions of what a soul does. For many, the soul is the moral compass in the ethical center of a person; it usually works in conjunction with a person's conscience. If someone is considered to be a "good" person—a humane person—it might be said that he has a good soul or a big soul. If someone is considered to be "monstrous" he is usually said to be soulless. Whatever mystical configurations go beyond this simple duality depend on cultural, religious, ethical, moral, or spiritual beliefs. Suffice it to say, for the purposes of this chapter we will think of the soul as an either/or identity that connects with whether a person is humane or monstrous.

In the Buffyverse, the soul is a significant aspect of the narrative and is often at the center of discussion and debate. A vampire loses his soul upon changing from human to monster. As Diane Dekelb-Rittenhouse comments in her essay "Sex and the Single Vampire," "In *Buffy*, then, the distinction between the human, evil or not, who existed and the vampire who took it over is very clear: the soul is removed entirely and is not involved in the crimes perpetrated by its demonically animated body" (148). Angel explains to Buffy, "When you become a vampire the demon takes your body but it doesn't get your soul. That's gone. No conscience, no remorse, it's an easy way to live" ("Angel"). Because they are soulless, and thus without consciences, vampires always give in to their base natures. They kill for pleasure and care nothing for the consequences. When Buffy asks Giles, in that same episode, if vampires can be good, he responds, "A vampire isn't a person at all. It may have the movements, the memories, even the personality of the person that it took over, but it's still a demon at the core. There is no half-way." Vampires in the Buffyverse can never be good and are always inhuman; thus, Angel is a complete anomaly. (Spike's transformation occurs later in the show's run and he becomes the only other vampire with a soul.) Because the two series ran longer than *Forever Knight*, the audience gets to learn more about the development of these two monster hunters. What *Forever Knight* begins in regards to a redemptive monster, the Buffyverse continues by truly exploring the consequences of humanity within monstrosity.

In Whedon's supernatural realm, the soul is a tangible object which can be both taken and given, if a character can complete the necessary magic.[5] When Angel tells Buffy that the vampire's soul is gone, he never says that the soul is destroyed. Rather, the soul goes to another place, perhaps a different plane of existence or an alternate universe. It can be moved from that other place and put into a vampire, or it can be stored in a container, as occurs in *Angel*, Season Four.[6] In this respect, Whedon conceives of the soul very much like the primitive tribes studied by British anthropologist Sir James George Frazer:

> Unable to conceive of life abstractly as a "permanent possibility of sensation" or a "continuous adjustment of internal arrangements to external relations," the savage thinks of it [the soul] as a concrete material thing of a definite bulk, capable of being seen and handled, kept in a box or jar, and liable to be bruised, fractured, or smashed in pieces [774].

Vampires may lose their souls, but other characters can bargain theirs away. Charles Gunn (J. August Richards), one of the main characters on *Angel*, sells his soul for a "tricked-out" truck, which he then uses to hunt vampires in Los Angeles. Similarly, without even realizing it, gamblers at a Las Vegas casino, in the *Angel* episode "The House Always Wins," have their destinies removed by the casino's management, thus making them nothing but empty shells. These destinies are then represented as poker chips and sold to the highest bidder. Although a character's destiny is not exactly a soul, the capability to lose both demonstrates that the "essence" of a human being can become tangible and can then be moved from one place to another, if desired.

For Whedon, having a soul does not necessarily make a character good, but lacking a soul definitely marks a character as evil. All vampires are inhuman, and they allow that side of themselves to rule their every move — in fact, there is no other side to them. Because they spend their time destroying life, when a vampire is suddenly given a soul, a conscience, the emotional pain can be excruciating. For, in the Buffyverse, like in the real world, the soul is also synonymous with the conscience. After cursing Angel with his soul, the gypsy woman tells him, "It hurts, yes? Good. It will hurt more. [...] You don't remember everything you've done, for a hundred years? In a moment you will. The face of everyone you've killed — our daughter's face — they will haunt you and you will know what true suffering is" ("Becoming, Part 1"). The gypsy returns Angel's conscience with his soul, thus forcing him to remember, and mourn, every human he ever harmed. It is no surprise, then, that Angel refers to his soul as a curse rather than a gift.

A person's conscience is as much a humanizing apparatus as law and religion. Our conscience helps us make decisions. Making a "wrong" decision by a culture's humanizing standards (i.e. stealing or lying) will often cause a person to experience the pangs of a guilty conscience, thus helping to keep him from pursuing the course of action or at least pursuing the course of action more than once. A vampire does not have this humanizing apparatus; there is no little voice inside his head questioning the inhuman choices he makes. When Angel's soul is returned, his little voice returns and brings with it a very guilty conscience. In fact, Angel feels so guilty about his past crimes that he spends almost an entire century living in back alleys, entirely removed from society, eating rats.

In the Buffyverse, a soul can also be mechanically duplicated, at least to some degree. To prove this, *Buffy* has an entire multi-season storyline involving a microchip that acts as a pseudo-soul. After leaving Sunnydale in Season Three, Spike returns in Season Four to once again wreak havoc and try to kill Buffy. However, before he gets the chance, a covert government agency takes him prisoner and inserts a microchip in his head. Now, every time Spike tries to harm a human, let alone bite one, he is shocked into great pain. For the first time in his vampire life, Spike must think about his actions and realize that there are painful consequences. Although it does not turn him into the monster hunter he will later become when he receives his actual soul, the chip does force Spike to carefully consider his actions and to rethink his purpose in Sunnydale. In giving Spike the microchip, Whedon recognizes that even the most monstrous of beings can be somewhat controlled. However, in consistently highlighting the fact that Spike has not chosen to do good, Whedon reminds viewers just how fragile our humanizing apparatuses are. Prison and rehabilitation—both of which seem quite similar to Spike's chip—can keep the monsters in a controlled environment for a time, but they may not actually change their lifestyles. Spike constantly reminds the Scoobies he will kill them just as soon as he has his microchip removed.

In creating Spike's pseudo-soul, Whedon illustrates a point made by Michel Foucault in his *Discipline and Punish*: "Rather than seeing this soul as the reactivated remnants of an ideology, one would see it as the present correlative of a certain technology of power over the body. [...] [I]t exists, it has a reality, it is produced permanently around, on, within the body by the functioning of a power that is exercised on those punished [...] [T]he soul is the prison of the body" (29–30). While Angel's soul is a metaphorical prison, causing him the powerful guilt of past torture and murder, Spike's prison is much more physical since he feels actual pain every time he even thinks about harming a human. Despite their differences, however, both souls bring about the same outcome: they force their bearers to reevaluate their lives and, in the process, help their bearers move away from their monstrous pasts and back to humanity.

The possibility for redemption and forgiveness has long been a prominent aspect of many religions. In many cases, redemption is achieved by having the suffering person confess his sins in some way so as to achieve absolution through some type of act of contrition. In his "Technologies of the Self," Michel Foucault argues that "technologies of the self [...] permit individuals to effect by their own means or with the help of others a certain number of operations on their own bodies and souls, thoughts, conduct, and way of being, so as to transform themselves in order to attain a certain state of happiness, purity, wisdom, perfection, or immortality" (18). Foucault traces this care of the soul from the Greeks up through to the Christian concept of conscience and confession. What he shows in his historical trace is that, traditionally, when humans have realized that they have entered the realm of monstrosity, they must try to pull back and then do something about it. According to Foucault, "Penitence of sin doesn't have as its target the establishing of an identity but serves instead to mark the refusal of the self, the breaking away from self. [...] It represents a break with one's past identity" (43). This break is exactly what the contemporary vampire-turned-monster hunter hopes to achieve. These vampires are not necessarily seeking any religion's promise of eternal life; instead, they want to break with their past lives and become a part of some aspect of society. They no longer want to remain beyond the boundaries of humanity. Their bearers may even be able to achieve the golden ring some day: forgiveness.

Joss Whedon's concept of the soul is both tangible and representative of a person's conscience, but there is one more aspect of the soul that is vital in both the Buffyverse and monster hunting in general: choice. It is this choice which connects these monster hunters most strongly with Foucault's discussion in "Technologies of the Self." This is where Nick Knight and Blade are like Angel and Spike. Although the soul is not discussed in either *Forever Knight* or the *Blade* trilogy, it is clear that both vampires possess a conscience which has led them to choose monster hunting. From his flashbacks, viewers learn that Nick did not always care for humans. In his early centuries he happily preyed on the helpless with Lacroix and Janette (Deborah Duchene). However, something made him change (although viewers never know exactly what the something is.) There are moments when he holds back or even sympathizes with his victims. For example, in "For I Have Sinned," Nick flashes back to his friendship with Joan of Arc. When she is sentenced to death, Nick offers her immortality and is confused when she chooses her fate due to her strong belief in Heaven and immortal life after death. It is moments like this one that seem to cause Nick to rethink his own existence to the point where his flashbacks show him saving rather than killing humans. In "Father Figure," his flashbacks show him, Janette, and Lacroix living in London during World War II. They save an orphaned boy but Janette wants to turn the child into a vampire, a thought which bothers Nick. To save the boy, Nick hypnotizes him and tells him to run. Unfortunately, the child is found and made a vampire anyway. Nick's guilt for losing the boy motivates him to protect Lisa (Chantellese Kent), a young girl who witnesses a murder. Nick's own perceived inadequacies and mistakes haunt his conscience — his soul — and drive him to protect mortals. In addition, his conscience drives him to seek mortality so that he can end his life as a monster.

Blade's own conscience is not a focus of the films — which should come as no surprise because the films focus more on action and special effects than character development — but his possession of a soul certainly pokes through at different times. The most obvious indication that Blade has a soul and a conscience is in his desire to suppress his hunger for blood. Blade does not want to become a full vampire; instead, he wants to maintain his humanity. However, there is more to Blade than just a desire to be somewhat human: he also sees himself as necessary to the balance between monsters and humans. As Whistler explains to Karen (N'Bushe Wright), Blade's love interest in the first film, "There's a war going on out there. Blade, myself, a few others — we've tried to keep it from spilling over onto the streets." In the first film, Karen finds a way to cure humans who are bitten by vampires. As a hematologist, Karen possesses the knowledge needed to fix vampirism, which is a genetic defect. Whistler hopes that this knowledge will help them create a stronger serum for Blade, an injection he must take regularly to control his vampiric urges but which he is starting to build up a tolerance for. Although Karen might be able to cure Blade, the vampire only insists that she make him a better serum. This monster hunter knows that the lurkers are just outside the door and he is the only thing standing between humanity and total vampire infiltration. He recognizes that the world needs him and makes the choice to remain a monster hunter.

Each of these four monster hunters possesses a vital human characteristic: a soul. In each text, the soul acts as a conscience, a prison for the body. These four vampires must constantly fight their vampiric urges and focus on what their souls tell them to do. And the soul can be a very powerful element in monster hunting because the monster hunter needs to be willing to lay down his life for the good of humanity. After all, Stoker requires his own famous monster hunter to have "self-command and toleration exalted from virtues to blessings" (129). What is a soul if not the part of a person which allows for "self-command" and "toleration"? But just having a soul will not immediately make one a monster hunter. It takes time for all four vampires to actually take up the monster-hunting call. At the beginning of this chapter, I argued that while love can create a more sympathetic vampire, it is not enough to turn a vampire into a monster hunter. For Nick, Angel, Spike, and Blade, a soul is not enough to make them monster hunters. There needs to be more, a reason to fight. For these four vampires, that reason is based heavily on love and community.

Community Connection

Although the soul and conscience are vital elements of turning a vampire into a monster hunter, nothing is more important than community. Of all the things a monster should avoid, alienation is the biggest because it is community which leads to humanity. For good or bad, those being shunned as monsters must live on the periphery of society. Their refused entry often causes problems. For example, Frankenstein's Monster wants more than anything else to be accepted by the De Lacey family. When he learns that no members of society will accept him due to his outward appearance, he demands a companion. When Dr. Frankenstein denies the Monster a companion, the Monster realizes he is utterly alone in the world and seeks revenge against his maker. We see this with Dr. Jekyll as well. As long as he continues his experiment in isolation, there is no one to assist him when things get out of hand. Had he confided to his friends sooner, perhaps they could have helped him. While we can only surmise what would have happened to these two characters had they connected with the outside world, we do see a trend at work here. The alienation occurring in these gothic texts implies that community is a vital element of humanity. This sentiment is certainly echoed by Dennis H. Barbour who says the following about Mel Gibson's role in the *Mad Max* trilogy (1979, 1982, and 1985): "It is through his [the postmodern hero's] reluctant heroism, through the need to serve others, that he finds his role in life. Like the Fisher King and other modern archetypes of the lone, suffering individual, he can only find his redemption through connecting with others and abandoning his elitist isolation" (30). Like their monstrous predecessors, Angel, Spike, Nick, and Blade begin life in isolation from humanity—either alone or within a community of monsters. But like other postmodern heroes—and other monster hunters—they must connect with a community of monster hunters to move back into the realm of humanity.

For Nick, this shift in community is the most difficult to achieve because he is torn between his vampire and his mortal communities. Nick's former community consists of Lacroix and Janette (although flashbacks show Nick interacting with other vampires as well). His new community is his mortal partner Schanke (John Kapelos) and his mortal love interest Natalie. Unlike how Angel and Spike move on by severing all ties with vampires, Nick does not do this, although he does try to break Lacroix's hold on him in the show's pilot, "Dark Knight." In this episode, Nick comes face-to-face with Lacroix, who is trying to bring Nick back into the vampire community. Nick refuses and the two engage in a battle where Nick ends up killing his mentor.[7] While Lacroix may be physically dead for at least part of the series, he remains an active part of Nick's memory and psyche. For better or worse, Lacroix's words and actions continue to haunt Nick throughout the episodes and help to inform Nick's decisions—often by Nick doing the exact opposite of what he did when he was with Lacroix. Janette, on the other hand, is less of a bad influence on Nick. In fact, she often proves useful by hiding witnesses in her bar or telling him the word on the street. Yet, despite being helpful she still tries to keep Nick within the vampire community. In the episode "False Witness," Nick comments, "We spend our whole lives running away. I don't want to do that any more. I want to fit in." However, Janette reminds Nick that he is neither vampire nor human: "You're pathetic. You want to belong? You belong to no one. Not us; not them." Like Angel, Spike, and Blade, Nick is not sure of his place in society. He is neither truly a vampire nor yet a human.

To off-set the vampire community, Nick has his law enforcement community. While Schanke does not know of Nick's secret, his friendship is an important link to humanity for Nick. However, it is Natalie who rivals Janette for Nick's affection and attention. For as much as Janette tries to keep Nick in the vampire community, Natalie tries to help him over into mortality and humanity. In "Only the Lonely," viewers experience a flashback to Natalie and Nick's very first encounter where she learns he is a vampire. Nick has been brought into the coroner's office because while trying to prevent a crime and he in an explosion. Natalie is surprised to find that her dead patient is not really dead at all. After learning who and what he is, Natalie offers to help Nick, to which he responds, "Are you serious? No one can help me. My immortality is a curse, a fall from grace. Evil is a metaphysical condition." But Natalie believes otherwise and replies, "You're not evil." She makes it her goal to try and help Nick regain his mortality so that he can join the human community for good.

Ultimately, Nick attempts to synthesize both communities in a way that Angel, Spike, and Blade will not. In *The Self After Postmodernity*, Calvin O. Schrag comments, "The self that has nothing to remember and nothing for which to hope is a self whose identity stands in peril [...] without past and future there can be no meaningful, life-affirming present" (37, 65). It is Nick's attempt to live in both worlds that illustrates Schrag's comment. Nick has found a way to remember and use his brutal past for good. While he regrets what he has done over the centuries, he vows to learn from his mistakes. By constantly remembering those past mistakes, Nick is able to have a new and different future where Natalie may just be able to help him obtain his mortality. For Nick, both communities share an important part of his role as monster hunter.

While Nick moves somewhat seamlessly from one community to another, Angel and Spike both travel different paths to secure a place within a monster-hunting community. For Angel, that path actually begins with total alienation from both communities: monstrous and human. For one hundred years after becoming a vampire, Angel travels the world with his sire, Darla (Julie Benz), wreaking havoc. Eventually, he sires Drusilla (Juliet Landau) who, in turn, sires Spike. The four make a ferocious community based on death, destruction, and chaos, not unlike Lacroix, Nick, and Janette. But then Angel is cursed with a soul and the community falls apart. After he is cursed, Angel's guilty conscience actually drives him away from humanity. He spends his energy removing himself from temptation, living in alleys and sewers and eating rats. In one flashback from *Angel*, the vampire saves a woman's dog from an approaching car. When the woman offers to thank him, he says, "Take a hike, Betty. Scram" ("Orpheus"). He in no way wants to put himself in a position where he can harm someone. It is not until a flashback from Manhattan, 1996, that viewers really know what drives Angel out of the sewers and to Sunnydale. The "Powers That Be," the higher beings who govern the universe, send a good demon, Whistler (Max Perlich), to guide Angel away from his own self-pity, since Angel is at risk of following in Blacula's suicidal footsteps. Whistler explains to the vampire that at this point in his life, Angel can go either way: "You can become an even more useless rodent than you already are, or you can become someone, a person, someone to be counted." Angel responds, "I just want to be left alone." Whistler answers, "Yeah, you've been left alone for what, ninety years already? And what a package you are: the stink guy" ("Becoming, Part 1"). Despite his soul, Angel is nothing—neither monster nor monster hunter at this point. Whistler takes Angel to L.A. and there the vampire sees a teenage girl who has just learned that she is a slayer. Angel watches as Buffy fights her first vampire. Because of Buffy, Angel chooses to help, telling Whistler that he wants to be someone. Whistler responds, "This isn't gonna be easy. The more you live in this world, the more you see how apart from it you really are." For the first time in his entire immortal life, Angel is willing to take that chance. His instant connection with Buffy moves Angel out of self-pity and into the beginning stages of monster hunting. As Stacey Abbott claims in her essay on Angel, "These flashbacks demonstrate that it was not the curse and the return of his soul that set Angel onto the path of goodness, but rather it was Buffy. Through her, his mission was clear" (par. 17). From the very first episode of *Buffy*, Angel is there offering help.

Angel's choice to assist Buffy is an important step towards the construction of his self-identity as a monster hunter. First, Buffy becomes a point of contact for him; she brings him into a society he has been avoiding for almost a century. Second, in helping Buffy, Angel must use his vampiric power and knowledge. He is even more of a vampire expert than her Watcher Giles and he has superhuman power, both of which make him an important ally. His love for Buffy and her need for his expertise allow Angel to both remember his past and hope for a future, a future with Buffy. As long as he has her and, by proxy, the Scoobies, Angel spends less time brooding and remains on the path of monster hunting.

For Angel, the soul comes first and love comes second; once Angel sees Buffy, he is able to take that important first step towards monster hunting. Spike, however, is quite the opposite. Remarkably, Spike has some level of humanity before he even receives his pseudo-soul. His humanity comes from his love for Drusilla. In this respect, Spike is very much like Louis from *Interview with the Vampire* (1976): he is capable of some level of humanity, but he chooses to ignore it most of the time. He and Drusilla do, indeed, love one another, as opposed to something like lust or animal magnetism. This fact is confirmed on several different occasions. For example, when the duo resurrect a demon who can detect humanity, the demon comments, "You two stink of humanity. You share affection and jealousy" ("Surprise"). Several seasons later, Drusilla returns to Sunnydale for Spike and tells Buffy, "Oh, we can, you know. We can love quite well, if not wisely" ("Crush"). But it is not just in his love for Drusilla that Spike's humanity shines through. Although he is the Big Bad for part of Season Two, Angelus usurps his power.[8] It is Angelus's idea that they should awaken the demon Acathla, thus sending Earth into a hell dimension. However, Spike disagrees with the plan and goes to Buffy to offer his help. When Buffy asks why he would do this, Spike explains that he likes the world: "You've got dog racing and Manchester United. And you've got people, billions of people walking around like Happy Meals with legs. It's all right here" ("Becoming, Part 2"). Nobility cannot necessarily be attributed to Spike at this point, but the viewer does see that Spike is not, like Angelus, entirely evil. According to Michele Boyette, "[T]hough supposedly soulless, there's something soulful in this [Spike's] character" (par. 7).

But, like the vampires before him, Spike is no monster hunter (his involvement with the Scoobies in Season Two is only a selfish anomaly). According to Claire Fossey in her essay on Spike, "we could say that humanity has always been present in him in the form of a hairline crack which with time and events has grown in size until it could no longer be shrugged off with a flippant, 'Yeah, what of it'" (par. 11). Indeed, it is his combination of a pseudo-soul and his love for Buffy that increases his hairline crack to a sizable canyon. Like Angel, Spike is smitten with the slayer. Drusilla recognizes it immediately following their Season Two escape from Sunnydale, but it takes Spike until Season Five to admit his love. Now possessing his pseudo-soul, Spike has time to contemplate feelings which go beyond his base vampiric instincts. When he tells Buffy that he has changed, she responds, "What, that chip in your head? That's not change. That's just holding you back. You're like a serial killer in prison" ("Crush"). But Spike is beginning to change. The chip is forcing him to make a choice between his past self and the self he could become. He is not yet ready to seek penitence, but he is moving ever closer to wanting redemption.

Despite the fact that he knows she can never love him, Spike truly wants to be a better person for Buffy's sake. In fact, his subconscious desire to be more human than monster leads him to seek out his real soul, though he does not yet understand what he is truly seeking. Having left Sunnydale angry with Buffy, Spike believes that he wants only to be the monster he was before he received the microchip. When he finally comes before the demon who has the power to remove the chip, he demands, "You give me what I want. Make me what I was so Buffy can get what she deserves" ("Grave"). To this monster who has thought only of his primal instincts for so long, destroying the woman he loves will release him from the pain that love brings. In addition, he feels that Buffy has used him — which she has — and now he wants revenge. Both Spike and the audience members truly believe that the vampire only wants his chip removed so that he can once again be the Big Bad. However, the demon is capable of understanding Spike's subconscious and the true reason the vampire wants the chip removed and responds, "Very well. We will return your soul" ("Grave"). The shocked impression on his face shows that Spike is not expecting to have his soul returned, nor did he intentionally imply that request in saying "give me what I want." From this point on, Spike must face the agony of a guilty conscience, much as Angel has done for over a century, and he does it all for the love of a woman and the desire for a new community, something he admits to Buffy when she learns about his soul.

Alienation is always a danger for both Angel and Spike because when they are isolated, they face the possibility of drifting back towards monstrosity. Susan Nelson cautions, "[A]lienation from one's true way of being a self in the world would mean the erosion of one's very own soul" (99). Before Angel and Spike had souls, they traveled together but were never really a community. Every group of vampires in Sunnydale and beyond has been more akin to a tyrannical hierarchy than to a community: one head vampire tells the others what to do; those others obey out of fear. There is no sense of community in such a social structure. It is not until Angel and Spike regain their souls that they are able to disconnect themselves from the tyranny they once imposed and reconnect with both a community and, in a larger context, humanity. It is acceptance into the Scoobies and Angel Investigations—Angel's L.A. detective agency created to help the hopeless— that finally gives each vampire a sense of identity. Connected to a band of monster hunters, they are able to see that the path of what is morally right is better than any other path. According to Schrag, "[C]onscience is able to supply the requisite authority and direction for responsible moral deliberation and action within the community of actors. [...] To exist ethically with other selves is to respond in a fitting manner to their discourse and action" (98). When Angelus, Darla, Drusilla, and Spike ravaged much of Europe and Asia, they did not have any sort of moral compass; the four were equally monstrous. The Scoobies are at the complete opposite end of the moral spectrum. This band of Sunnydale monster hunters always knows what is right and wrong, even if they do not always obey their own set of ethics. Angel and Spike are at their closest to being human when they are with the Scoobies because the two vampires recognize and mimic the humanistic qualities their fellow monster hunters uphold.

Just like his contemporaries, Blade must also commit to a community before he can truly call himself a monster hunter. While Blade has always been a vampire, he is not immediately a monster hunter. In the first film, Whistler explains to Karen how he found Blade: "I found Blade when he was thirteen. He'd been living on the streets, feeding off the homeless. Apparently the Thirst manifested itself at puberty—I took him for one of them at first, almost killed him, too. But then I realized what he was." Whistler then becomes a father figure for Blade. It is he who trains Blade how to fight. Whistler is everything to Blade: he builds weapons, helps with the serum, and monitors the vampire community. But he is also the only family Blade has ever known. Unlike other vampires, Blade is almost able to make a complete break from the vampire community. Part of this is because he is so unlike other vampires and, because he never knew either his mother or father, he has no connections to them. In fact, when he finally learns of his vampire family, he is able to completely reject them. Deacon Frost (Stephen Dorff) is Blade's main adversary in the first film, and the two are connected even more closely than just as foes. Blade is, in fact, Frost's vampire son since it was Frost who bit Blade's mother and passed his genetic make-up on to the unborn child. When Blade is finally reunited with his mother (surprisingly, she survived Frost's bite — thus becoming a vampire — and has been living with him ever since), Frost comments they are "one big fucking family." Blade recognizes in Frost a great threat to humanity and takes it upon himself to destroy that threat. Even though Blade has always known he had a vampire father, there are no familial emotions or feelings between Frost and Blade. In fact, given Blade's heightened hatred of Frost after this revelation, it can be said that his revealed paternity makes Blade hate Frost even more.

When Whistler dies at the beginning of *Blade: Trinity*, it appears that the half-breed monster hunter has lost his community. However, Whistler has always recognized the importance of Blade's connection to humanity. A group calling themselves the Nightstalkers rescues Blade from jail. One of the group's members is Abigail Whistler (Jessica Biel), Whistler's daughter. As Hannibal King (Ryan Reynolds) — the group's spokesman — tells Blade, "We're all part of Whistler's 'contingency plan.'" That contingency plan seems to be twofold. First, it appears that Whistler has created a huge network of monster hunters to fight the battle if Blade is elsewhere or if he fails. Second, the group needs to be a base for Blade, a reason to care. A man — or woman — on a revenge mission is not a monster hunter and without perspective, Blade could easily become a single-minded vigilante. Yet Blade is not ready to accept his new community. When Blade asks King how many Nightstalkers there are, King responds, "Enough. We operate in sleeper cells. When one goes down, a new cell activates to pick up the slack. Consider us your reinforcements." Blade scoffs at this comment and clearly believes the group is nothing but a bunch of inept children running around. In the beginning Blade is not impressed with his new community, but over the course of the film he comes to accept them.

In his discussion of Kierkegaard's work, Schrag comments, "self-constancy as it is achieved throughout a life of commitment is the highlighting of the bonding of self with other selves" (65). Bram Stoker knew this when he created the monster hunter prototype. Community is a vital element of success for Van Helsing and his protégés. Even Stoker's choice to reveal the narrative through journal articles and newspaper clippings emphasizes the importance of community. Only when Van Helsing, Jonathan and Mina Harker, Seward, Morris, and Holmwood come together and share knowledge can they truly defeat Dracula. The same certainly holds true for today's vampires-turned-monster-hunters. These new creations are vital to defeating today's evils because they once themselves embodied those evils. Traditional monster hunters cannot defeat monsters like Freddy Krueger and Jason Vorhees, but these two slasher villains certainly have the know-how to defeat each other — something they do attempt in *Freddy vs. Jason* in 2003. The vampires' personal experiences make them invaluable to the monster hunters around them, whether those monster hunters face mortal threats like in *Forever Knight* or supernatural threats like in *Buffy the Vampire Slayer*, *Angel*, and *Blade*. Yet that very background also makes them potentially dangerous. While humanity may be the ultimate goal of these new monster-hunting recruits, their past is never truly behind them. Each vampire still yearns for blood and still feels the pull of his past, no matter how much he tries to ignore or suppress that yearning. Despite a strong community of monster hunters, these vampires always risk losing their way.

In his maxims, Friedrich Nietzsche warns, "He who fights monsters should look into it that he himself does not become a monster. When you gaze long into the Abyss, the Abyss also gazes into you" (466). Each of these contemporary vampires slides into the abyss at some point or another, even if it is only briefly. For example, several episodes of *Forever Knight* show Nick dealing with his bloodlust. In fact, in "Feeding the Beast" Nick goes undercover and joins a support group for addicts which shows the viewers that Nick's need for blood is an addiction he just cannot seem to overcome. Again and again Nick falls off the wagon and gets drunk on blood (he keeps wine bottles of blood on hand in his refrigerator, the bottles being another indication that blood is like alcohol for vampires). Luckily, these moments occur while Nick is alone and he soon moves on and returns to work. While Nick's slips into the abyss seem relatively minor, they remind the viewer that no matter how committed this vampire is to helping humanity, he is not entirely human. (After all, addicts are deemed somewhat monstrous in contemporary society, even when they are mortal.) His monstrous nature is always there waiting to come out at the first sign of weakness and this weakness usually occurs when Nick is alone and at his most vulnerable.

For Blade, his one significant slip into the abyss occurs at the end of the first film. Frost uses Blade's blood to start the process that will bring about La Magre, the Blood Monster. Blade weakens as his blood pours through the walls and ceiling of the vampire sanctuary until Karen finally discovers and saves him. Because he is the only one who can stop the process begun by Frost, Karen has him drink her blood. Blade drinks while Frost anxiously awaits the coming of La Magre. The two scenes occur simultaneously, with cross-cutting used to enhance the mirroring that both men are monsters. As Blade drinks, Frost cranes his neck to watch the blood pooling on the ceiling. At one point, one of Frost's cohorts rips open his shirt, giving the two men yet another commonality as Blade is also shirtless. The scene comes to a climax when Frost throws open his arms and watches the first drop of blood plummet to his forehead. The shot finally then cuts to Blade tossing Karen aside and throwing his head up to growl at the ceiling.

The implication is clear: Blade and Frost are identically matched, which is even more marked when the viewer realizes that Blade has given in to his vampiric side—making him, for the moment, a monster—and Frost has literally become the monster La Magre. In the end, of course, the two fight and Blade destroys Frost. As a result, Blade's slip is forgivable because it is necessary for him to destroy Frost. In addition, Blade does not kill Karen; he only takes what is necessary from her. Once Blade's strength is restored and Frost is dead, Blade returns to his previous serum-taking existence.[9] Blade's abyss, like Nick's, does not seem overly treacherous. However, the implication in both texts is that Blade and Nick must remain committed to their communities and their causes or they will revert back to their monstrous ways.

Angel and Spike, however, experience slips much more dire than either Nick or Blade. Angel's very love for Buffy threatens his humanity.[10] To try and maintain his identity as a monster hunter, Angel moves to L.A., but, in the process, he loses his community and his hope for the future. In "Walking the Fine Line Between Angel and Angelus," Stacey Abbott claims, "[W]ith the launch of the new series, the character Angel is introduced as being alone, stripped of the community to which he briefly belonged on *BtVS* and [...] the character is intensely aware of this loss" (par. 9). Although he goes to L.A. to help people, he does so alone and falls prey to Whistler's warning that he is not necessarily a part of the human world. Just as Buffy propels Angel to monster hunting, Angel is approached in L.A. by another who helps him reconnect: Doyle (Glenn Quinn). When Doyle first meets Angel, he tells the vampire a story which ends, "[The vampire] goes to L.A. to fight evil and atone for his crimes. He's a shadow. A faceless champion of the hapless human race" ("City Of"). That is all Angel is, a shadow. It is only a matter of time before he slips back into darkness and obscurity, again living off rats in back alleys. As the episode continues, Doyle reminds Angel that disconnection is not healthy, even for an immortal vampire; connection, Doyle says, is about "[R]eaching out to people. Showing them that there's love and hope still left in this world. [...] It's about letting them in your heart. It's not just saving lives, it's saving souls. Hey, possibly your own, in the process." What Doyle is really telling Angel is that through community, one can avoid the monstrous abyss and possibly even achieve redemption. In L.A., Angel must find new people with whom he can connect, which he achieves by opening a detective agency with Doyle and Cordelia (Charisma Carpenter), another ex-Scoobie who is trying to reconnect. More importantly, however, when Angel is in L.A. he learns about the Shanshu Prophecy: "The vampire with a soul, once he fulfills his destiny, will become human" ("To Shanshu in L.A.").[11] Being the only vampire with a soul at this point, Angel now has a very clear future for which to hope: if he works hard enough and avoids the abyss, he may become human.

Spike, on the other hand, wavers between his past life as a vampire and future possibility as a monster hunter much more than Angel does. For a long time after receiving his pseudo-soul, Spike cannot decide with which side he wants to align himself, and this indecision causes him to constantly move between the abyss and humanity. Xander immediately recognizes that with his microchip, Spike is unable to reclaim his position as Big Bad. In the Season Four episode "Doomed," Xander points out, "I hate to break it to you, oh impotent one, but you're not the Big Bad any more. You're not even the kinda naughty. You're nothing but a waste of space." Even Buffy recognizes Spike's lack of community as she taunts, "Look at you, you idiot. Poor Spikey. Can't be a human, can't be a vampire. Where the hell do you fit in?" ("Smashed"). For Buffy, a microchip is not a soul; it is nothing more, in fact, than a muzzle. In these episodes, both Xander and Buffy point out that as long as Spike is facing an identity crisis— and facing it alone — he has no purpose. Eventually Spike will realize he wants to fit in with Buffy and the Scoobies, thus moving him away from the abyss. Although it takes some time for the Scoobies to accept him, in the end Spike's new community of monster hunters will help him become the man he could be; that man will sacrifice himself to save Sunnydale and the world.

Despite their connections to a community, Angel and Spike both experience one significant slip into the abyss, an abyss of hopelessness. For a brief time these two vampires totally alienate themselves from their communities and must experience some type of epiphany before they can finally transcend the abyss. In *Angel*, Season Two, Angel severs his ties with Angel Investigations after taking steps towards becoming a lone vigilante. Seeking revenge against Wolfram & Hart — the evil law firm that is the proverbial thorn in his side — Angel locks a group of the firm's lawyers in a room with Darla and Drusilla, sentencing the lawyers to death for he knows that the vampires will kill them. Following this escapade, his friends comment,

> **Wesley (Alexis Denisof):** Angel, while it's certainly true that these lawyers brought this on themselves, what you did is...
> **Cordelia:** ... is wrong
> **Gunn:** You went too far. [...]
> **Cordelia:** You have to change the way you've been doing things. Don't you see where this is taking you?
> **Wesley:** Listen to her! Right now the three of us are all that's standing between you and real darkness.
> **Gunn:** Best believe that, man.
> **Angel:** I do. You're all fired
>
> *"Reunion"*

Angel feels that nothing he does matters any more. He sees his monster hunting as something akin to putting a finger in a leaking dam: he cannot make a difference; he cannot save everyone. At this point, he feels a vigilante crusade would be a more effective direction, or at least would make him feel better about himself.

When Angel removes himself from his established community, he also removes himself from the ethics and morality associated with that community. In doing so, Angel breaks the community's moral code: he takes the law into his own hands by sentencing humans to death. Compassion is always a significant humanistic aspect of both the Scoobies and Angel Investigations. In addition, there is a clear line where humans are concerned: "Humans [...] have a special status in Buffy's moral system. This special status makes them exempt from being seriously harmed by her, even if they do harm others" (Greene and Yuen par. 3). No matter how immoral human beings may be, in the Buffyverse monster hunters do not pass judgment on them. As a vigilante, Angel crosses a very clear line between humanity and monstrosity. As Schrag claims, "Responsibility, nurtured by the call of conscience, supplies the moral dimension in the narrative of the self in community" (100). It is not until Angel realizes that he needs Angel Investigations, and asks Wesley, Cordelia, and Gunn for forgiveness, that he can return to his monster-hunting duties. During this story arc of Season Two, Angel moves as far away from humanity as he can without actually reverting to Angelus.

To get to the point of forgiveness, though, Angel must journey to a higher understanding of why he is a monster hunter. During his time as a vigilante, he confronts Wolfram & Hart and demands to visit the "Home Office." Holland (Sam Anderson), one of the lawyers Angel locked in the room with Darla and Drusilla, beckons the vampire to an elevator which then proceeds down into what seems to be the fiery pits of Hell. Holland explains to Angel, "We're in the hearts and minds of every single living being and that, friend, is what's making it so difficult for you. See, the world doesn't work in spite of evil, Angel. It works with us, it works because of us" ("Reprise"). When the elevator stops, Angel finds himself back on the street in L.A. at the same moment he left. Holland continues, "You see, if there wasn't evil in every single one of them out there, why, they wouldn't be people. They'd all be angels." Angel has found Wolfram & Hart's home office: Earth. Rather than depress Angel, however, Holland's elevator monologue actually gives the vampire hope. Up until this point, Angel has been trying to save himself and fulfill the Shanshu Prophecy; he is acting on a selfish motivation. After talking with Holland, Angel has an epiphany:

> The greater scheme, the big picture, nothing we do matters. There's no grand plan, no big win. [...] If there's no great, glorious end to all this, if nothing we do matters, then all that matters is what we do. Cause that's all there is; what we do now, today. I fought for so long for redemption, for a reward, finally just to beat the other guy. But I never got it. [...] All I want to do is help. I want to help because I don't think people should suffer as they do because if there's no bigger meaning, then the smallest act of kindness is the greatest thing in the world ["Epiphany"].

After all these years, Angel finally understands what Whistler was trying to tell him. Instead of saving himself, Angel is now ready to make the world a safer place. He has finally reached the ultimate definition of a monster hunter: one acting in selfless service for the greater good of humanity.

While Angel may feel relieved after his epiphany, Spike is not at all happy when he comes to the same realization. In the very last episode of *Buffy*, Spike sacrifices himself to save the world from the First Evil, only to find himself rematerialized during the first episode of the next season of *Angel*. However, he is not entirely himself. Spike is non-corporeal, not quite a ghost but not quite human either; once again, Spike cannot seem to find where he belongs. As he tells Angel, "I save the world, throw myself on the proverbial hand grenade for love, honor, and all the right reasons, and what do I get? Bloody well toasted and ghosted is what I get, isn't it. It's just not fair" ("Just Rewards"). For his self-sacrifice, Spike should receive redemption. But things do not always work out that way in the Buffyverse. Angel knows that and, in the following episode, explains it to Spike:

>   **Angel:** You save the world, you end up running an evil law firm.[12]
>   **Spike:** Or playing Casper with one foot in the fryer.
>   **Angel:** Do you think any of it matters? Things we did, lives we destroyed, that's all that's ever gonna count. So yeah, surprise, you're going to Hell. We both are.
>   **Spike:** Then why the bother? Try to do the right thing, make a difference?
>   **Angel:** What else are we gonna do?
>
>   "Hell Bound"

What Angel and Spike decide to do is make the world safer for those around them. In doing this, the two vampires actually achieve a level of redemption akin to the Jewish belief of *tikkun olam*, translated as "repairing," "mending," or "improving" (Shatz 1). As David Shatz argues, "In the most general sense [...] *tikkun olam* is associated with the thesis that Jews bear responsibility not only for their own moral, spiritual, and material welfare, but for the moral, spiritual, and material welfare of society at large" (1). After their epiphanies, both vampires take on this responsibility. Although humanity may be the final goal of Angel's and Spike's existence—for the Shanshu Prophecy can now be applied to both, or either, of them—they also learn that it is not the end result that matters, but, rather, what they do on a day-to-day basis that makes a difference. Angel and Spike have chosen to become monster hunters and now do the only thing they can: they fight the good fight for as long as possible. This choice leads them to a certain level of redemption. They may be going to Hell, but they can try to make the world a little better on their way down.

In the end, Angel and Spike do everything that they can to make the world a little safer for humanity. Angel creates a plan in which the members of Angel Investigations kill L.A.'s major demonic players. But this last battle is most likely a losing one. Angel explains that even if they succeed in killing the Big Bads, Wolfram & Hart will send an army to kill them, and he is correct. His community of monster hunters does, indeed, succeed in killing the bad guys, but when they regroup they are set upon by a vast demonic army, including a dragon or two. There is no way that Angel Investigations is going to survive this battle.

As the season and series comes to an end, Spike asks Angel for his plan. Angel merely smiles and says, "Well, personally, I kind of want to slay the dragon. Let's go to work" ("Not Fade Away"). This is all Angel and Spike can do. Since neither believes that complete redemption is possible—although they both harbor some small hope that the Shanshu Prophecy will come true—it is not about clearing their own personal balance sheets any longer. Instead, it is about slaying just one more dragon. They may die in this battle, but they have once again made the world a little bit safer for those around them.

In his work on resurrection and suffering, Henry A. Williams comments, "The ultimate challenge of life is squarely to face our capacity for evil and destruction and by receiving and assimilating it to transform it into what is positive and creative, so that the dynamic of our evil potential becomes harnessed to what within us is constructive and good" (156). These four vampires do just that: they face their inner demons and, in some very special cases, defeat those demons and work for the greater good of humanity. Nick's, Blade's, Angel's, and Spike's contribution to contemporary horror is the formula through which a monster can become a monster hunter. When all the elements are there — a soul, love, a community, and for some an epiphany — even the most villainous of monsters can come back from the abyss to humanity.

What is possibly even more important here is that these four vampires offer contemporary audiences some semblance of hope, a hope that was lost during the 1970s. These monsters are able to overcome their pasts — no matter how evil — to become heroes. In his essay on redemption, Christopher Deacy makes the following argument:

> Since the Enlightenment [...] there has generally been a shift in emphasis away from the role played by God and Christ in the redemptive process, and a concomitant tendency to concentrate more on the manner in which each individual human being has the capacity to undergo redemption *within themselves* [...] each individual person is believed to be capable of attaining his or her *own* redemption, by consciously and authentically responding to the potential for goodness that is intrinsic to each person [52].

Angel, Spike, Nick, and Blade demonstrate that actions do speak louder than words, or at least personal histories. These vampires are not perfect, but they do try to tap into whatever goodness they have left by whatever means possible. By coming to love and care about these vampires, contemporary audiences recognize that even monsters can be humane. After experiencing the aftermath of both the Vietnam War and Watergate, it is possible that contemporary audiences can begin to forgive their leaders and military just as they can begin to forgive their fictional monsters. This does not mean that contemporary audiences are suddenly becoming optimistic about the world they live in, but it does mean that they are becoming a bit less pessimistic. Even though there is no guarantee that the hard-won safety will be sustained, it is still a break from everyday worries and the unknown.

These characters are certainly not perfect; we may not even consider them to be heroic all of the time. They certainly do not have quite "the kindliest and truest heart that beats" like their ancestor (Stoker 129). They are flawed and they know it. However, they want to reform and atone for their transgressions. Whether or not they truly become human is really irrelevant. As the posthumanists agree, we cannot even define humanity. Perhaps these vampires' actions are human, perhaps not. No matter what, though, these four men are working as monster hunters. While they recognize that the world cannot truly be saved — and maybe they cannot be saved either — they try to make the monsters remain in check so that humanity can continue on just a little bit longer. With the advent of vampires like Nick, Angel, Spike, and Blade, the monster hunter is no longer in his grave.

Chapter 3

Vigilantism and the Graphic Novel's Monster Hunters

"Anarchy wears two faces, both creator and destroyer. Thus destroyers topple empires; make a canvas of clean rubble where creators can then build a better world."

— *V for Vendetta*

 One may wonder why there is a chapter on graphic novels within a work on the monster hunter in traditional horror and gothic texts. At first glance, the graphic novel does appear to be of another genre, perhaps even its own genre. Yet, the graphic novel fits firmly within the same larger literary genre as horror and gothic: fantasy, or, as Rosemary Jackson calls it, the literature of subversion. According to Jackson, "Literature of the fantastic has been claimed as 'transcending' reality, 'escaping' the human condition and constructing superior alternate, 'secondary' worlds" (2). She continues, "In this way, fantastic literature points to or suggests the basis upon which cultural order rests, for it opens up, for a brief moment, on to disorder, on to illegality, on to that which lies outside the law, that which is outside dominant value systems" (4). Just as the posthuman theorists want to analyze society's humanizing apparatuses, so too does fantasy literature. Just as horror and gothic seek to question dominant ideologies, so too does the graphic novel.

 The graphic novel grew from the dissatisfaction comic book creators had over censorship. For the early part of the twentieth century, comic books were left alone by critics and enjoyed by young boys. In the 1940s and 1950s, comics grew in popularity and became mass produced. At the same time, Americans became increasingly aware of and concerned over juvenile delinquency. Unfortunately, certain members of the government linked the two cultural events. In 1954, Senator Estes Kefauver led the Senate Subcommittee on Juvenile Delinquency. This subcommittee spent some time discussing comic books' influence on juvenile delinquency. As a result of these Senate hearings, the comics industry began self-censoring its material. This time of self-censorship did not prove to be a positive one overall. The "good" guys always had to triumph over anything that was not approved by America's dominant ideology. Each comic book looked like the one that came before.

Luckily, not all comic book creators believed in self-censorship. In the 1960s a movement of underground comics began called the Underground comix. These comics criticized the dominant ideology — including censorship — with their extreme subject matter — such as sex and drugs— and their graphic artistry. According to Mila Bongco, in his book *Reading Comics*, "They defiantly opposed the sanitised views and values of middle class society proffered by their traditional counterparts. Instead, they offered biting parodies and satires of media and social customs as alternatives" (6). After a decade, the Underground comix movement fell by the wayside. However, this group of artists showed their readers what comics could be and that censorship was unnecessary. In addition, the Underground comix were the first batch of comics written for an adult readership; these comics creators realized that comics were not just for children and chose a more mature subject matter. It is out of this change in attitude that the graphic novel appeared.

Their link to subversion is what allows the graphic novels in this chapter to fit with the horror and gothic texts previously discussed. As has been argued, the contemporary monster hunter is a reaction to the traditional hero of the Victorian gothic novel: the Van Helsing character. As the attitudes of today's readers have changed, so too have the attitudes of today's heroes. In horror, the pure and goodly hero cannot hope to challenge the chaos of the contemporary monster. With its focus on heroes and villains, the comic book industry has also needed to change its heroes. Traditionally, the superhero, the comic book's protagonist, has appealed to young readers (mostly male) by being strong, fast, smart, and handsome, all the traits desired in youth. To help uphold the dominant ideology, those with these acceptable traits had to trounce those deemed monstrous: the villains. Just like Stoker's Van Helsing, the superhero was a humanizing apparatus.

However, just like in horror and gothic texts, the very fact that the monster exists reminds readers that human and monster are not so far apart. As Bongco comments,

Even in a "classic plot" involving rather uncomplicated protagonists, there are at least two problematic elements: a) the depicted society is always in danger and its institutions for law enforcement are deficient, otherwise it would not need a superhero; and b) the restoration of peace and order is only temporary since recurring threats to a superhero's domain are intrinsic to the genre [93].

These two points could easily be applied to any gothic or horror text, even ones from the Victorian Era. Bongco's quote also reflects the purpose of the contemporary monster hunter. Further he argues, "It is possible to perceive the genre as actually dealing with the transgression of the law, portraying the play between breaking and restoring the law, or at the very least, showing an ambivalence about law and order" (93). Just as horror and gothic narratives seek to push consumers out of their comfort zone, so too do some comic books. Although order is restored at the plot's end and "good" triumphs over "evil," there exists the sense that law and order are not static boundaries. This line of questioning continues right on to present-day graphic novels. In contemporary graphic novels, superheroes are no longer so "super." As Bongco comments, "[T]he new comics dealt simultaneously with something very familiar and very strange: heroes who have ceased to be superhuman, who sometimes have problems with drugs, alcohol and sex, and above all, who grapple with notions of authority, power, and evil that are not always clear and against which they do not always win" (141). Again, this certainly sounds like the vampires discussed in Chapter 2. In addition, "Also noticeable is the hint of amorality which started to surround some superheroes as they worked more and more on the borderlines of the law" (145). All of these quotes from Bongco's book succinctly characterize what is going on in contemporary monster-hunting narratives as well as what is going on in contemporary comic books. The texts discussed below all continue to question the dominant ideology and move beyond the dichotomy of good and evil and into the domain of the monstrous monster hunter.

But graphic novels share more with horror and gothic than just a tie to subversive fantasy literature. The graphic novels discussed in the following pages all contain various gothic conventions and typical gothic issues. In *Nightmare on Main Street*, Mark Edmundson claims, "In Gothic novels readers discovered, or were reacquainted with, the night side of life" (8). While this is a prominent feature of gothic and horror texts, it also appears in the works of both Frank Miller and Alan Moore, the two writers discussed in this chapter. The contemporary graphic novels chosen for this chapter mostly take place either at night or in the gloomy city life of places like New York and London. They feature characters who battle the evils of the night — those creeps who strike fear into all the law-abiding citizens of these cities.

In addition, Edmundson says, "Gothic works invite the audience to acquaint themselves with, and to fear, the shadow that dwells within" (11). From the dual personality of Bruce Wayne and Batman to the egomaniacal scheme of Ozymandias in *Watchmen*, readers of these graphic novels learn that the darkness within can appear in many forms. That said, these graphic novels share another important characteristic with the gothic: "No Gothic narrative can work unless the villain is in some way an admirable figure" (11). No matter how extreme their actions may be, the monster hunters within these graphic novels all hold admirable long-term goals; like their monster-hunting contemporaries, the protagonists in this chapter all hope to make their worlds safe for the time being. Unfortunately, like their horror contemporaries, they must act a bit monstrous to achieve this end. Bongco argues, "The implicit high moral of these avenger-type heroes provides a critique of the customary institutions of law and order in society, and expresses a desire for a fiercer and purer authority that would arise to punish evil, without the delays and corruption of constitutional law" (103). This same sentiment can be applied to all contemporary monster hunters. Today's legal system just is not providing enough safety for people. The lurker has already gotten by. Until a new system appears—if that would even be possible—contemporary readers are left with the ambiguous monster hunter.

The Dark Knight

Considered to be one of the most influential graphic novels of the late twentieth and early twenty-first century, Frank Miller's *Batman: The Dark Knight Returns* (1986) presents readers with a truly ambiguous monster hunter. The story begins with a newspaper clipping by James Olson about old villains who spend their time in a seedy Metropolis bar. They talk about the old superheroes: "But they never talk about the mean one. The cruel one. The one who couldn't fly or bend steel in his bare hands. The one who scared the crap out of everybody and laughed at all of the rest of us for being the envious cowards we were. No, they never talk about him" (7). From the very beginning, Miller wants his readers to understand that his hero is not remotely heroic in the traditional notion of the term. Miller's version of Batman is called the Dark Knight for a reason. In this case, "dark" is not so much referring to the fact that he works at night or that he wears a black suit. Instead, the "dark" here refers to the soul of the Caped Crusader which may or may not be every bit as tainted as those he captures. In an interview with Christopher Sharrett, Miller comments, "Batman doesn't work when he's a figure of authority. He'd would [sic] be a tyrant" (43–44). Batman's unapologetic use of vigilante means would never be wholly accepted in society. If policemen suddenly acted without rules there would be more damage done than good. Miller recognizes this fact. Yet, people may believe that one lone vigilante could be a good thing if he would only go after the worst villains in society. His enemies recognize Batman's darkness and they begrudgingly accept and possibly admire the trait. Bruce Wayne, however, does not.

Miller's novel finds Bruce Wayne an older man who has, he thinks, managed to retire Batman. Since Batman's disappearance, Gotham has fallen into violence and ruin. Despite what he may believe, Bruce's dark side is not ready to retire. As Bruce says within the story's opening pages, "As we part, Jim squeezes my shoulder and grins. 'You just need a woman,' he says.... While in my gut the creature writhes and snarls and tells me what I need" (12). Batman haunts Bruce's dreams and Bruce tries admirably to stay on top:

> I was only six years old when that happened. When I first saw the cave... Huge, empty, silent as a church, waiting, as the bat was waiting. And now the cobwebs grow and the dust thickens in here as it does in me—and he laughs at me, curses me. Calls me a fool. He fills my sleep, he tricks me. Brings me here [the cave] when the night is long and my will is weak. He struggles relentlessly, hatefully, to be free—I will not let him. I gave my word. For Jason. Never. Never again [19].

Bruce cannot manage his dark side any better than his fellow male monster hunters. When asked about Batman's evil side, Miller responds, "Anyone can be a victim. This is exactly what makes him a good character. It's how one uses the evil inside. It's how we use our rage, our venom. [...] Batman makes his devils work for the common good" (Sharrett 44). As the novel progresses, Bruce realizes that Batman is stronger than he is, just as Angel and Spike realize that evil will always be with them and Blade and Nick Knight know their hunger will only be sated for a short time. What all these men have in common is their desire to, as Miller says, use the inner evil to "work for the common good." This is the decision that makes these characters so important to contemporary society. Bruce must once again don his cape and cowl because it is what he does; he is not a useful member of society until he accepts his place as, and among, other monster hunters.

In Chapter 2 I discussed how being both vampire and human (a term I use loosely) causes the vampire-turned-monster-hunter to be a posthumanist creation. Although Bruce is not actually a supernatural monster, he is still no less a posthuman monster hunter because he must deal with being both monster and human. Although the bat within him does not give him special powers, it does give him a monstrous side. As Batman, Bruce Wayne fulfills Nietzsche's prophecy that one who looks too much into the abyss will become the abyss. Batman uses his nemeses' toys and techniques on them. He is not afraid to fight fire with fire and this makes him appear to his society every bit as monstrous as the monsters he fights. Because Batman appears to have few, if any, scruples when it comes to fighting villains, he lives on the outskirts of his society's dominant ideology. It is the discussion of Batman's own vigilantism that forms much of the reason Miller's graphic novel deserves a place within this chapter.

One of the main storylines in *Batman: The Dark Knight Returns* is the heated debate over Batman's vigilantism. For example, in one set of panels Batman is described as "A ruthless, monstrous vigilante, striking at the foundations of our democracy— maliciously opposed to the principles that make ours the most noble nation in the world" (65). Because he refuses to follow the dominant legal ideologies, Batman becomes a threat to Gotham. However, just as the Buffyverse, Blade's world, and Knight's Toronto need an ex-monster to help fight crime, so too does Gotham. The police are not able to defeat the city's very real villains because they follow the law; instead, they need someone who is willing to break some rules for the greater good, a need understood by the contemporary monster hunter. Miller admits that he purposely went against the comics' traditional world of good-vs-evil:

> The code through which most comics still pass insists on a benevolent world where authority is always right, policemen never take bribes, our elected officials always serve our best interests, and parents are always good and sound people. They don't even make mistakes. The world we live in does not resemble the world of the censors. I simply put Batman, this unearthly force, into a world that's closer to the one I know. And the world I know is terrifying [Sharrett 38–39].

Miller recognizes what horror fans had known for decades: the lurkers have arrived and there are no longer adequate heroes to fight them back.

The discussion of vigilantism is most prominent in the television panels which feature an ongoing debate between Dr. Bartholomew Wolper, popular psychologist and social scientist, and Lana Lang, managing editor of Metropolis' *Daily Planet*. Dr. Wolper, resident psychologist at Arkham Asylum, is obviously against Batman, having made his career rehabilitating the villains Batman has captured. Dr. Wolper believes that Batman's violent tendencies are what cause super-villains like Harvey Dent (Two Face) and the Joker to exist, not that Batman is there as a reaction to these villains. Yet this is a very naïve view for the characters within the novel and serves to remind the readers without that life is neither easy nor entirely good, nor is it even black and white. Dr. Wolper's best-selling book is entitled *Hey — I'm Okay*, a very misleading belief for contemporary society. Not everyone in the world is okay. Sociopaths, psychopaths, and other extremely disturbed individuals need to be separated from others so as to make the world safe. In some ways, Dr. Wolper is like the Victorian readers of gothic tales: both believe that evil can be done away with. For Wolper the evil can be psychoanalyzed. By creating such a naïve self-help guru, Miller nods to the idea set forth by Andrew Tudor that by the 1980s the lurkers had already crossed the threshold into popular consciousness. Wolper then becomes a parody of those people who still believe that their leaders can do no wrong and that all is right with the world. As Angel learns when Holland explains that evil is within every human being, so too are Miller's readers reminded that sometimes life is dark and scary and everything is really not okay. It is just such a realistically frightening society that needs monstrous heroes.

In this debate, then, Lana is set up as the voice of reason. When asked how she condones "behavior that's so blatantly illegal? What about due process—civil rights?," Lana responds, "We live in the shadow of crime, Ted, with the unspoken understanding that we are victims—of fear, of violence, of social impotence. A man has risen to show us that the power is, and always has been, in our hands. We are under siege—he's showing us that we can resist" (66). This is a much more realistic take on Batman's violence and one that mirrors Miller's comment on individual will. As opposed to Dr. Wolper's belief that evil Batman begets evil super-villains, Lana sees the reverse happening: evil super-villains beget evil Batman. But despite the reader's probable alignment with Lana's view of Batman, we must look more closely at this argument as it will be the crux of the other graphic novels in this chapter and relates to the quandaries raised by other monstrous monster hunters. The reporter interviewing both Wolper and Lana responds to Lana's view by saying, "You haven't exactly answered my question" (67). He is correct. Lana has dodged the bullet on illegal punishment of criminals, due process, and civil rights. These are serious issues and ones that certainly pertain to the twenty-first century reader. It is all well and good that Batman can take the law into his own hands. Readers applaud it and love his brand of vigilantism. But what happens when this blatant disregard appears in everyday "real" life? What happened when, post 9/11, Homeland Security began stringent checks on travelers of Middle Eastern descent? Or when the public learned that the government wanted to monitor library users? The American public suddenly became less than happy with this new type of government-sanctioned vigilantism. If the American government was simply responding to what we can label as contemporary super-villains, why were their actions criticized? Why were they not held up as modern Batmen? Why did the supporters of Lana Lang suddenly become the supporters of Bartholomew Wolper?

What makes Batman's actions acceptable? Why is it that we can get beyond his own villainy and applaud the way he tries to clean up Gotham? I would argue that it is because, as readers, we are privy to what goes on in his head. We understand Bruce's own conflicts so we sympathize with him. It is an understanding that Commissioner Gordon has and one that newly chosen Commissioner Ellen Yindel refuses to attempt. While Gordon worked with Batman—understanding that the law cannot always do what needs to be done—Yindel believes in a world of right and wrong, black and white, something no effective contemporary monster hunter can do. This belief causes her to immediately discuss the issue of Batman by saying, "I'm surprised there is a controversy. His actions are categorically criminal. I will have him brought to trial. [...] My first act as Police Commissioner will be to issue an arrest warrant for the Batman on charges of assault, breaking and entering, creating a public hazard" (72). But if there is one thing contemporary monster hunter fans know, it is that nothing is black and white. This comes as a hard lesson for Commissioner Yindel, who eventually realizes that Batman is "too big" (176). His vigilantism is, unfortunately, successful. Whether Gotham's residents love him or hate him, he is a mythologically effective monster hunter who can get the job done. Whether she agrees or disagrees with his tactics, there is evidence that Yindel accepts the Dark Knight, for in her final panel of the story the news reports, "Commissioner Yindel refuses to comment on the charge that Gotham's police have been lax in pursuing the murder charge against the Batman" (187).

Batman's ambiguity is a central issue for Miller's graphic novel. From the first pages to the last, Batman is a villain, a monster, a hero, a saint, among many other things. It is the duality of Bruce Wayne and the Dark Knight that aligns him with characters such as Blade, Nick Knight, Angel, and Spike. Like these other characters, Bruce also manages to eventually find a space for his abilities. As the graphic novel ends, Bruce appears to have finally let Batman die. However, unlike when the tale begins, Bruce has not gone cold turkey from monster hunting. Instead, the final panel shows Bruce surrounded by a new generation of monster hunters. The closing dialogue features him saying,

> He'll [Batman] leave me alone now. In return, I'll stay quiet. So will Robin ... and the rest ... we have years—as many as we need. Years—to train and study and plan ... here, in the endless cave, far past the burnt remains of a crimefighter whose

time has passed ... it begins here — an army — to bring sense to a world plagued by worse than thieves and murderers ... this will be a good life ... good enough" [199].

Miller explains, "The key transition would be his [Bruce's] recognition that he's no longer part of authority. That's really the transition at the end of *Dark Knight*, this knowledge that he's no longer on the side of the powers that be anymore, because the powers that be are wrong" (Sharrett 39). Instead, Bruce does what all effective, long-term monster hunters do: he has found a community of like-minded individuals who will assist him on his quest. Bruce has managed to find a happy medium for his knowledge as Batman with his conscience as Bruce. It appears that for the remainder of his life he will work outside the law to help keep Gotham safe both now and in the future.

While Miller's incarnation of the monster hunter preceded the men mentioned in Chapter 2 by almost a decade, the issues Bruce faces in terms of using monstrous actions to protect the people of Gotham — if only for a short time until a new evil arrives— are ones which will continue on into the twenty-first century. Given the popularity of the most recent Batman film — *Batman Begins*, as of October 2005, made over $205 million in box office grosses alone and the sequel *The Dark Knight* broke box office records in Summer 2008 — it appears the monstrous monster hunters are still very much in vogue. Miller recognized the power of monstrous monster hunters as early as 1986 when he commented, "Anytime a hero is done even reasonably well there's a *tremendous* popular response. Modern art and literature have so diminished the idea of the hero, at least up until a few years back, that there was a crying need" (Sharrett 35). More importantly, it is the conflicted monster hunters— those who are both monstrous and heroic — that appeal to contemporary audiences. But Frank Miller is certainly not the only comic book writer to grapple with issues of ambiguous monster hunters. His own contemporary, Alan Moore, deals with these same issues in his very popular and influential graphic novel, *Watchmen*. But whereas Miller dealt with the schizophrenic nature of one monster hunter, Moore takes apart all sides of the contemporary monster hunter and places those sides into several different characters.

The Watchmen

Traditional superheroes— no matter what their motivation — manage to transcend dominant ideologies just by being larger-than-life and having superhuman qualities. Because they are themselves above the law, the vigilante discussion of Batman in *The Dark Knight Returns* is important; he does not care about the law and wants only to save Gotham, no matter what that means. Because he can best the law, who is there to stop him? According to Jamie Hughes, in "'Who Watches the Watchmen?': Ideology and 'Real World' Superheroes," "They [superheroes] are unlike us, and because of this, they are impossibilities." The article goes on to say, "By placing these characters on pedestals as champions of justice and perfection, their creators also positioned them outside of the realm of ideology" (546). Law, religion, and education mean practically nothing to traditional superheroes in that they know what they are doing is "right." Their goals are lofty — to save the world — and most are beyond reproach. More importantly, most are supernatural, superhuman, or alien in some way. These traditional superheroes are somewhat posthuman in that they — even those like the X-Men who are human genetic mutations — are beyond and above human ideologies. They are not of this Earth so they are not held to human rules. Again, this is what makes Batman's existence so problematic in Miller's story. He is human so he is expected to adhere to human ideologies, despite the fact that he believes in ideals that cannot be obtained through traditional "humane" means. Batman tries to be the human version of his superhuman contemporaries.

In *Watchmen* (1986), however, the superheroes are normal people wearing costumes who are, for various reasons, motivated to help those around them. Unfortunately, unlike the ideal superheroes, the superheroes of *Watchmen* are, as Hughes asserts, entirely caught up in ideology. These characters are superheroes for "money, power, fame, or to promote their own ideology" (548). Their goal is never to transcend "the repressive state" (550), which the traditional superheroes — even Batman — attempt. Adrian Veidt (Ozymandias), the smartest man on Earth, truly believes that the world's problems can be fixed through intellect alone, but he is also very concerned with his own fame. Laurie, the Silk Spectre, is pushed into crime fighting by her mother, the first Silk Spectre, but is not invested in any specific cause. Rorschach, the most vigilante of all Watchmen, sees the world as good or evil and wants only to destroy all the evil. Dan Dreiberg, the Nite Owl, takes over the role from his hero, Hollis Mason, when Hollis decides to retire; Dan is probably the most pragmatic yet idealistic of all the group. Yet he seems to enjoy the fun and thrill of fighting crime rather than having an overriding desire to save mankind. Each of these characters, and the other Watchmen, come to crime fighting with different agendas. While most of them truly want to help, they almost all do it for selfish ends. Nowhere in the group will one find a truly altruistic hero like Superman.

Despite the good the Watchmen accomplish (albeit on a smaller level than a group like the Justice League who are superhuman), the American government begins to disapprove of their actions. After a House Un-American Activities Committee outlaws the Watchmen, most of them remove their costumes and go about their lives. All, that is, but Rorschach. Of all the Watchmen, Rorschach is most like Miller's Batman in terms of forcing the reader to question the legitimacy of vigilantism. However, whereas Miller seems to approve of Batman's actions, Moore has not set up Rorschach to be a hero. In fact, Moore commented in an interview with *Entertainment Weekly,* "I originally intended Rorschach to be a warning about the possible outcome of vigilante thinking" (Jensen par. 24). The major difference between Batman and Rorschach is that Batman never sees the world in terms of black or white, while that is exactly Rorschach's dominant ideology.

Rorschach's history is a complex web of pain and abuse. Moore tells this history in Chapter VI: "The Abyss Gazes Also." Students of Nietzsche certainly understand Moore's nod to the German philosopher; he is referring to the maxim I quoted in Chapter 2: "He who fights monsters should look into it that he himself does not become a monster. When you gaze long into the Abyss, the Abyss also gazes into you" (466). So far, I have interpreted this maxim as a warning to monsters-turned-monster-hunters; these characters must be careful not to fall back into the abyss. With Rorschach, such an interpretation is not quite so clear-cut. As readers learn, Rorschach is beaten by his mother, who is a prostitute. He is raised in squalor and constantly picked on. At ten years old he is called a "whoreson" and attacks the boy who calls him that, putting a lit cigarette in the boy's eye. As a young man he reads a story in the newspaper about a woman who is "Raped. Tortured. Killed. Here. In New York. Outside her own apartment building. Almost forty neighbors heard screams. Nobody did anything. Nobody called cops. Some of them even watched" (Chapter VI 11). Rorschach honestly believes that humans are evil. He has looked into the abyss and sees it to be nothing more than humanity's mirror. He tells his psychologist, "Existence is random. Has no pattern save what we imagine after staring at it for too long. No meaning save what we choose to impose. This rudderless world is not shaped by vague metaphysical forces. It is not God who kills the children. Not fate that butchers them or destiny that feeds them to the dogs. It's us. Only us" (26).

Because Rorschach firmly believes that humanity is useless, he frees himself in some ways of dominant ideology. However, in its place he creates his own ideology, one of black and white. As Hughes comments, "Like the mask he believes is his true face, there is no gray in his judgment of society, and because society is cruel and merciless, so is he" (552). Rorschach is so driven by his own ideology that he is no longer even an objective observer of the world around him. This lack of objectivity would appear to make him truly monstrous and unsympathetic. Although Moore intended him to be the least desirable Watchman, Moore says, "But an awful lot of comics readers felt his remorseless, frightening, psychotic toughness was his most appealing characteristic — not quite what I was going for" (Jensen par. 24). You see, for every bad person Rorschach mercilessly kills, he saves at least one other person. To some readers, this type of crime fighting is appealing because it is so effective. But this vigilante ideology also leads to Rorschach's death because the world cannot tolerate a person who cannot accept a gray area. While Batman and Rorschach both employ vigilante means, their motives are significantly different. Batman, like Rorschach, sees evil that needs to be stopped. However, unlike Rorschach, Batman understands that there are shades of gray; those who at first seem evil can be reformed to help battle those who are truly evil. This is a sentiment that both Angel and Spike must come to when they move beyond their own self-pity and see the world in a new light. Rorschach is unable to achieve this enlightenment. This is exactly why he works as Moore's warning against vigilantism. If the contemporary monster hunter has been broken into its parts in *Watchmen*, Rorschach represents what happens when a monster hunter falls into the abyss and remains there, possibly even liking it.

Although Rorschach is the only Watchman to openly continue his fight against crime, there is another who secretly plots to save the world: Ozymandias, who sees humanity on the brink of complete annihilation. As he explains to Rorschach and Dan, "For the first time, I genuinely understood that Earth might die. I recognized the fragility of our world in increasingly hazardous times" (Chapter XI 21). Referring directly to the nuclear arms race, Ozymandias continues,

> I saw East and West, locked into an escalating arms spiral, their mutual terror and suspicion mounting with the missiles, making the possibility of disarmament progressively more remote. [...] Both sides realized the suicidal implications of nuclear conflict, yet couldn't stop racing towards it lest their opponents should overtake them [21].

To try and scare both sides out of this race to destruction, Ozymandias creates the world's biggest hoax. He convinces a group of writers and artists to create a large alien for him. Then, using teleportation technology, he sends the creation to New York City, hoping that the alien will force humanity out of imminent destruction and onto a path of enlightenment. Unfortunately, the technology is unstable and the alien blows up, killing three million New Yorkers. Yet, out of this tragedy comes some hope: weapons are put down and truces are called. In Ozymandias, Moore shows readers the personification of the fine line between good and evil that the contemporary monster hunter must walk. This line is certainly not new. The male monster hunters mentioned in Chapter 2 all run the risk of falling over to the villainous side. In Chapter 4, we will see that the female monster hunters also occasionally walk this line. What makes Ozymandias especially interesting is his misguided view of saving the world on one grand and all-encompassing scale, something which none of the previous monster hunters have had to face.

Despite his seeming nonchalance over killing three million people, Ozymandias still manages to get to an epiphany like that of his fellow male monster hunters. As he sees Dr. Manhattan — a fellow Watchman — for the last time, he says,

> Jon ... I know people think me callous, but I've made myself feel every death. By day I imagine endless faces. By night ... Well, I dream about swimming towards a hideous ... no. Never mind. It isn't significant. What's significant is that I know. I know I've struggled across the backs of murdered innocents to save humanity ... But someone had to take the weight of that awful, necessary crime [Chapter XII 27].

For all his misguided, egotistical moments in the graphic novel, Ozymandias does, in the end, care about the world. He tries to do the right thing, even if it ends in a monstrous action. While Rorschach refuses to acknowledge the dominant ideologies of his place and time, Ozymandias attempts to create a new ideology: he wants the world to unite in their awe of an alien race and instead gets a world unified in its despair and fear.[1] Does this make Ozymandias any less of a monster hunter? That depends entirely on one's perspective of the monster hunter. If we think of monster hunters in the traditional manner, Ozymandias is a beast. Van Helsing would never risk the life of another — let alone millions — to get to Dracula unless he absolutely had no other choice. In fact, when Mina suggests they use her to help track down the vampire, Van Helsing is at first hesitant. However, if Ozymandias is examined within the context of the contemporary monster hunter, his actions are somewhat justifiable because mass death was not his initial goal and he has, indeed, managed to save the world from itself for a short period of time.

While Rorschach and Ozymandias face concerns similar to, yet more extreme than their fellow monster hunters, there is one member of the Watchmen who faces a completely different conundrum: Dr. Manhattan.

Dr. Manhattan was an atomic physicist. Unfortunately, he accidentally got locked in a test chamber and was ripped into pieces on an atomic level. Although everyone assumed him to be dead, Dr. Manhattan learned how to put himself back together atom by atom. As he does, he learns that he has superhuman powers such as the ability to teleport, play with space and time, and grow to incredible sizes. While some may think this atomic recreation would make him the perfect superhero, Moore actually goes in a different direction.

In losing his life to nuclear energy, Dr. Manhattan also loses his humanity. As Mark Bernard and James Bucky Carter claim, "Throughout the graphic novel, Manhattan struggles with his humanity; he seems to be losing touch with human experience as we know it due to his amazing ability to never age and to be aware always of the past, present, and the future" (par. 17). Eventually, he quits the Earth entirely, preferring to reside on Mars. He is so far above all prevalent ideologies of education, race, religion, and law that he needs nothing and can only remove himself from everything. Yet, like Rorschach, even Dr. Manhattan becomes sympathetic. It takes his ex-lover Laurie's very birth to remind him that thermo-dynamic miracles can occur. As he explains to her,

> In each human coupling, a thousand million sperm vie for a single egg. Multiply those odds by countless generations, against the odds of your ancestors being alive; meeting; siring this precise son; that exact daughter ... until your mother loves a man she has every reason to hate, and of that union, of the thousand million children competing for fertilization, it was you, only you, that emerged [Chapter IX 26–27].

It is this realization that makes Dr. Manhattan care again. As he comments, "But the world is so full of people, so crowded with these miracles that they become commonplace and we forget ... I forget. We gaze continually at the world and it grows dull in our perceptions. Yet seen from another's vantage point, as if new, it may still take the breath away" (27). When Rorschach looks into the abyss, he sees nothing but evil; when Dr. Manhattan looks, he sees hope. He is able to remember that Earth is, indeed, worth saving. In fact, when Rorschach leaves to tell the world of Ozymandias' plan, it is Dr. Manhattan who stops him. In his actions, Dr. Manhattan represents the epiphany that the contemporary monster hunter must experience in order to be effective.

Alan Moore has influenced a wide variety of graphic novelists, artists, and writers, including Joss Whedon, who commented to *Entertainment Weekly*, "I learned at Alan Moore's feet" (Jensen par. 41). It is not surprising that Angel and Spike would experience many of the same quandaries that the Watchmen characters embody. Because the Watchmen are human, their lofty goals are compromised by their human ideologies; these men and women are not above ideologies like their superhero counterparts. As a result, the Watchmen cannot save the world forever. Before bidding adieu to Dr. Manhattan, Ozymandias says, "Jon, wait, before you leave ... I did the right thing, didn't I? It all worked out in the end." Dr. Manhattan responds, "'In the end'? Nothing ends, Adrian. Nothing ever ends" (Chapter XII 27). Like all contemporary monster hunters, Dr. Manhattan understands that ideologies are very difficult to completely overthrow. In his article on the ubermensch and Ozymandias, Matthew Wolf-Myer comments,

> Thus there are those heroes who "go under" in an attempt to radically affect humanity, marginalized and few, and the larger society of heroes who simply preserve what has already come to be. And necessarily there is tension between these two factions, the first appearing lawless and as vigilantes, while the latter retain their heroic stature and as such are lauded, when, in fact, they are acting against humanity, rather than for it, retaining the hegemonic capitalism they defend, rather than promoting utopia [501].

Sadly, the majority of the Watchmen are preserving what has come to be. Rorschach may be a slight exception, but he is only after an immediate satisfaction in knowing the bad guys are dead; he does not seek to change ideologies. Even though Ozymandias changes the course of history, there is no sense that humanity as a whole has been affected. In this respect, the contemporary monster hunter must understand that his actions come with no guarantees; there is only the hope that he can defeat the next evil. This sentiment will be one carried through Moore's other popular works.

V for Vendetta

Fans of Alan Moore's *V for Vendetta* (1988) may wonder about its inclusion in a work on monstrous monster hunters, and for good reason. V is clearly not as monstrous as, say, Angel. Nor is his vigilantism on the same level as Rorschach's unforgiving nature. Yet V is an important character in this chapter's analysis. Readers of *V for Vendetta* must struggle with the same question posed by Ozymandias: When is it acceptable to sacrifice a few for the purpose of saving the many? No monster hunter wants to see a sacrifice and many times he will sacrifice himself before another. But the contemporary monster hunter is often faced with such a dilemma, whether or not he is consciously aware of it.

V for Vendetta was originally published in 1988, but Moore actually started writing the story in 1981. The story itself begins on November 5, 1997, and concludes on November 10, 1998. Sometime in the not-so-distant-past, nuclear war was fought. While readers do not get specifics, they do know that Africa and Europe are both gone. Chaos rules in England until a few fascist groups calling themselves Norsefire get together and take over. Undesirables like blacks, homosexuals, and foreigners are sent to concentration camps. Much like in an Orwellian world, England is ruled by a group of people who watch the citizens' every move. Each branch of the government—the Eye, the Nose, the Finger, the Ear—all tie into one main computer named Fate. Because of their strict laws and complete monitoring, the citizens live in constant fear. Out of this fear comes the story's monster and monster hunter: V. He has no actual name. The "V" comes from his room assignment—Room V—in Larkhill Resettlement Camp, one of the regime's concentration camps. As the reader learns, V was chosen for a hormone research project and, along with four dozen other inmates, is given an injection of a pituarin/pinearin mixture. All inmates die a gruesome death except for V. For some reason, the injection affects him mentally but not physically. Over time, he is allowed to work in the camp's garden. He is even given access to fertilizer, which he eventually uses to blow up the camp and escape.

From the opening pages, V is set up as both monster and monster hunter. The story begins with a sixteen-year-old girl, Evey, propositioning a man so that she can earn some money. Unfortunately, the man is a Fingerman, a sort of secret policeman. He and his squad begin to push Evey against the wall so that they can rape and then, presumably, murder her. Before they get too far, a man in a Guy Fawkes mask and cape shows up. Using tear gas, he helps Evey escape the Fingermen, leaving behind a bomb that kills several of the squad. Saving a young woman from certain death would seem a heroic act reminiscent of superheroes. However, the reader soon learns that V is not like traditional caped crusaders. Only five panels after the escape, readers see that Parliament and Big Ben are blown up.[2] When Evey asks, V admits to being the arsonist. It is made very clear from the story's beginning that V's intention was never to save Evey from the Fingermen. Instead, he happened to be at the right place at the right time. Of course, having saved and befriended her, V uses her in his vendetta, which again brings up questions as to whether V is a monster or a monster hunter.

It seems that in V, Alan Moore has contained the vigilante sensibilities of Rorschach with the hopeful thinking of Ozymandias. V's vigilante nature is based on his desire for revenge. The first act of revenge attributed to V—although not the first he has committed—is the punishment of Lewis

Prothero, the voice of Fate. While riding on a train, Prothero is kidnapped after V kills the Fingermen guarding him. Prothero is taken to a mock-up of Larkhill Resettlement Camp where his doll collection stands in for the prisoners. Because Prothero was in charge of the camp's ovens, V sets fire to the collection, driving Prothero insane. Although still alive, all Prothero can say is "ma-ma," just like his dolls. V could have simply killed Prothero and, in light of what happens, death seems like a more humane option. Instead, V seeks to work out the worst punishment on Prothero possible. He possibly wants Prothero to experience the same insanity he himself now deals with. V does not just kill Prothero, he tortures him. Other than Rorschach, no contemporary monster hunter gets enjoyment out of torture. Yes, the vampires of Chapter 2 did, but only when they were clearly the monsters. Therefore, when V is monstrous for personal means—like Prothero—he is the villain.

One of the most problematic sequences in *V for Vendetta* occurs when V tortures Evey. Evey, and the readers, believe she has been captured by the Fingermen to snitch on V. She is tortured repeatedly but never tells the Fingermen what they want to know. She stays strong because she learns of the life led by the woman in the next cell. Written on toilet paper and shoved through a hole in the wall, the woman's life story finishes with the following: "I shall die here. Every inch of me shall perish ... except one. An inch. It's small and it's fragile and it's the only thing in the world worth having. We must never lose it, or sell it, or give it away. We must never let them take it from us" (159–160). Evey takes this point to heart and decides to face a firing squad rather than tell the government about V. At this point, Evey is set free by V both physically and emotionally and readers learn that it was V who set the whole thing up. Evey realizes what V gives her and soon forgives him. However, for the reader the sequence is troubling. The gift of freedom from fear is huge, but so is the price tag. V does not seem to show remorse for torturing and fooling Evey. In fact, he comments that she was in a prison and now, "The door of the cage is open, Evey. All that you feel is the wind from outside. Don't be afraid" (171). Just because V had to go through hell and back to gain his freedom does not make it right. Evey's torture is a monstrous act just as Ozymandias' destruction of three million New Yorkers is a monstrous act. By including such a sequence, Moore is reminding his readers that V is not an altruistic hero. He is very flawed and his actions toward Evey prove that. No monster hunter is entirely pure in this day and age and V is another character who must negotiate between the monstrous and human spheres and, just like his contemporaries, he occasionally gets it wrong.

In addition to his occasional bursts of monstrosity, V often crosses the line to Rorschach's side of vigilantism. However, there is one time when a kind of humanity appears through V's vengeance, something that never happens with Rorschach. The final Larkhill tyrant to die is Dr. Delia Surridge. As readers learn after her death, Dr. Surridge was the one to administer the genetic testing. She used the inmates at Larkhill as her own personal guinea pigs; she created V. Because she now works in the city's morgue, Dr. Surridge has learned of V's murderous rampage and has figured out who he is. When he arrives to kill her, Dr. Surridge is waiting and the two have a very civilized chat. When V arrives in her bedroom, Dr. Surridge says, "It's you, isn't it? You've come ... you've come to kill me" (70). When V says yes, she responds, "Oh thank god" (70). Then, he asks if she is afraid. She says, "No. I thought I would be, but I'm not. I'm ... relieved. Oh god, all these years. All this waiting ... You see, I always knew you'd come back" (73). Dr. Surridge even goes so far as to say, "We deserve to be culled. We deserve it..." (73).

When she gives V permission to kill her, Dr. Surridge unintentionally moves him from Rorschach's realm of black and white vigilantism to Batman's realm of killing the great evils of his world. For, in V's world, the people of Larkhill, and by extension the government who sanctioned the experiments, are super-villains like the Joker and Two Face. The parallel to the Nazis and their extermination of the Jews is not by any means subtle. Just as the world had little sympathy for Nazi doctors like Josef Mengele and Horst Schumann, the readers of *V for Vendetta* are to have little sympathy for the people from Larkhill tortured or killed by V. Because we know the backstory, we are to applaud V, or at least understand his need for revenge. Thanks in part to Dr. Surridge, at this moment in the graphic novel we treat V not as a vigilante, but as his society's monster hunter. This sympathy is even greater when we learn of Dr. Surridge's last moments. When she learns that V has already injected her with poison, Dr. Surridge asks, "Is there any pain?" (75). V tells her no. Moments before she dies she asks to see V's face and tells him, "It's beautiful" (75). This compassionate death is far removed from either Prothero's insanity or Bishop Lilliman's death where he is forced to eat a communion host filled with cyanide. It is Dr. Surridge who reminds the reader that although he may be teetering on insanity and cruelty at times, V is righteous in his vengeance and in truly removing the monsters from his society.

V believes that only by removing Adam Susan, the Norsefire Leader, can he truly create change. However, this change will come at a price V is willing to pay: the death of innocent Londoners. At the story's beginning,

V is seen talking to a statue of Madame Justice. V explains to her that once upon a time he worshipped her. But then he accuses her of an adulterous fling and says, "You always did have an eye for a man in uniform" (40). For V believes that Madame Justice has been in bed with the Leader and Norsefire. When she does not respond, V comments, "Very well. So you stand revealed at last. You are no longer my justice. You are his justice now. You have bedded another" (41). Now V has another love: anarchy. As he explains to Madame Justice, "She has taught me that justice is meaningless without freedom. She is honest. She makes no promises and breaks none" (41). As he leaves, Old Bailey blows up, taking Justice with it. Like Ozymandias, V feels that he is above the law. Moore makes clear to the reader that V refuses to buy into his culture's dominant ideology because he has been betrayed. In refusing justice and accepting anarchy, V frees himself from ideological constraints. He has no qualms about destroying London's landmarks—landmarks of justice—presumably killing people in the process. In his mind, V is actually on the way to freeing the people of London from their prison and their monsters. He is more of an ubermensch than Ozymandias. He has "gone under" to "radically affect humanity" (Wolf-Meyer 501). He is trying to be the ultimate monster hunter by freeing the people from Norsefire's ideology. At the end of *V for Vendetta*, V explains to Evey, "Anarchy wears two faces, both creator and destroyer. Thus destroyers topple empires; make a canvas of clean rubble where creators can then build a better world" (222). V is the self-appointed destroyer.

As she sends V to his final task, Evey reflects on what he has taught her. By this point, V has been killed by Edward Finch, the head of the Nose, the police unit. V asks Evey for a Viking funeral, which means that Evey will place him in a subway car filled with explosives so that he can blow up the Leader's headquarters on Downing Street. In addition, the Leader has been murdered (although neither V nor Evey appear to know this) by the desperate widow of Derek Almond, the leader of the Finger, whom V had earlier killed. As she realizes V's plan, Evey comments,

> You came out of an abattoir unharmed, but not unchanged. And saw freedom's necessity. Not just for you, but for all of us.... You saw, and seeing, dared to do. [...] Your foes assumed you sought revenge upon their flesh alone, but you did not stop there ... you gored their ideology as well. The people stand within the ruins of society, a jail intended to outlive them all... The door is open. They can leave, or fall instead to squabbling and thence new slaveries. The choice is theirs, as ever it must be [260].

Like his fellow contemporary monster hunters, V understands that he can only do so much. While monster hunters like Angel and Spike recognize that they have made things better only for a short time, V and his fellow comic book monster hunters, like Ozymandias, realize they have simply opened the door. These men manage to defeat the monsters of their time, but that does not necessarily mean chaos has been squelched and the status quo will be restored. In fact, these monster hunters do not want the status quo to return. These men are simply trying to give their society hope, hope that a better time can arise. For V, that hope is achieved when Evey dons his mask and cape and becomes a symbol for a new society.

While V is the dominant monster hunter in *V for Vendetta*, another character — the aforementioned Mr. Finch — deserves mention. As was discussed in Chapter 1, monsters and monster hunters were clearly defined as evil and good, respectively, in early horror and gothic texts. It was not until the 1970s that the monster hunters took on monstrous tendencies, or were monsters themselves, to help defeat the monsters bent on wreaking chaos. In the character of Finch, Alan Moore embodies this transition. At the beginning of the story, Finch is clearly out to get V. For Finch, possibly the only respectable member of the Leader's team, V is breaking the law and must be stopped. In this way, he has the good vs. evil mentality that plagues Rorschach, except he never employs Rorschach's vigilante ways and always has the law on his side. In other words, Finch utterly and completely buys into his society's humanizing apparatuses.

However, when Finch reads Dr. Surridge's journal — he and the doctor had been friends and occasional lovers — his sympathies begin to waiver. He becomes obsessed with finding and stopping V. To do so, Finch feels that he must get into V's mind and learn his motivations. To that end, Finch gets LSD and takes it at Larkhill, or at least in the ruins of Larkhill. His drug-induced hallucinations allow him to experience the realization that he, not someone else, is in control of his life (a realization that both V and Evey painfully achieve through torture). In freeing himself, Finch finally learns how to kill V and where to find him. Finch tracks V underground via Victoria Station's closed subway entrance and fatally shoots him. When Finch notices V's blood on the ground, he exclaims, "Flesh and blood after all ... I killed you, you monster" (237). It is important that Finch refers to V as a monster here because it demonstrates that Finch believes himself to be the monster hunter. By taking the LSD and learning why V is the way he is, Finch gains the knowledge of the enemy so important to the early monster hunters. In his mind, Finch becomes Van Helsing.

Yet, despite his intentions, Finch is not a traditional monster hunter. His time and culture will not allow him that. Like the other contemporary monster hunters, Finch comes to a very important epiphany when he realizes that V could have killed him but did not. He explains his epiphany to his partner Dominic:

> They're still there. Not doing anything, mind. Just waiting. It's funny.... They're not the terrorist's [V] followers or anything. They're just rioters.... But he's become some sort of all-purpose symbol to them, hasn't he? People need symbols, Dominic. He understood that, we've forgotten it. Those people outside lost families during the war. We've kept the lid on their bitterness for years, but we haven't helped them deal with it. Maybe he didn't either, but he certainly took the lid off" [252].

Unlike his fellow monster hunters, Finch will not be spurned on to monster hunting by this epiphany. Instead, he decides to leave London. He turns his back on the crumbling society and, like V does, leaves the chaos to the creators. In fact, the last four panels of the graphic novel are devoted to Finch as he 1) climbs a hill to the freeway; 2) stands beneath the M1 sign to Hatfield and the North; 3) lights a cigarette; and 4) starts walking. The reader is unsure what will happen to Finch, but knows that he takes an understanding of his supposed monster with him. Perhaps Finch will become the next monster hunter, when and if the need arises.

It is interesting to note that both Angel—as was discussed in Chapter 2—and Finch tell their epiphanies to younger monster hunters. Angel tells his realization—"The greater scheme, the big picture, nothing we do matters. There's no grand plan, no big win. [...] If there's no great, glorious end to all this, if nothing we do matters, then all that matters is what we do"— to Kate, a detective he has come to trust and respect ("Epiphany"). Because Kate leaves the show, viewers never know if Angel's epiphany helps her like it helped him. Angel's motivation for explaining himself may be just to hear himself say it out loud. However, Finch tells Dominic his epiphany in the hopes that the younger detective will also leave London. Unfortunately, in the novel's final pages, a character who looks suspiciously like Dominic is abducted into an alley. A few pages later, this character is awoken by Evey, dressed as V. She has chosen this young man to help her create the new world; readers are left with the sense that Finch's epiphany and Dominic's apparent goodness—he has never been shown doing anything illegal or unethical—will make him an excellent partner for Evey. Like Evey, Dominic will become a creator of a (hopefully) new ideology. It is interesting that both Angel and Finch choose members of the legal establishment as their protégés. Perhaps this is a hold-over from the traditional horror and gothic stories when Van Helsing imparted his knowledge to a younger group of followers. More importantly, perhaps this is meant to give viewers and readers hope that their ideological educators can be trained to be good monster hunters.

The League of Extraordinary Gentlemen

In *The League of Extraordinary Gentlemen*, Volumes I and II — released as a collection in 1999 and 2002, respectively — Alan Moore bands together Captain Nemo, Allan Quatermain, Hawley Griffin (the Invisible Man), and Jekyll/Hyde under the leadership of Mina Murray. These fantastic creations come together — albeit begrudgingly — in the first volume to rescue cavorite — a concoction used for flying — from Dr. Fu Manchu. However, they soon learn that they are working for Arthur Conan Doyle's villainous James Moriarty who uses the cavorite to start an air raid over the Limehouse district in London. The group then goes after Moriarty's main ship and recaptures the cavorite, thus stopping the air battle. Afterwards they are kept on by the government for future jobs. In Voume II, the group is used to help combat Martians from H. G. Wells' *War of the Worlds*. Nemo and Hyde manage to keep the Martians at bay while Mina and Quatermain get a biological weapon from Dr. Moreau. (Griffin has since defected to the Martians). Once again the group succeeds.

Of the five League members, Hyde is the one I wish to analyze because he fits perfectly within the current trend of ex-monster monster hunters in that he makes a conscious choice to help humanity. There is no doubt that Moore intends Hyde to be the League's resident monster.[3] When readers first meet Hyde, he is terrorizing Paris; more importantly, he is being portrayed as a brutal monster because he is behind a series of prostitute murders in the Rue Morgue. In his discussion of the current murders, the detective Auguste Dupin explains the murder of a fifty-year-old to Mina: "The older woman, Madame L'Espanaye, had been almost decapitated with a razor, then hurled from that window. Her daughter, Camille L'Espanaye, had first been throttled, then thrust feet-first up a chimney" (20). When Mina asks about the man who did it, Dupin responds, "It was no man, mademoiselle. It was an ape, an ourang-outang escaped from the sailor that had owned it" (20). The new Paris murders — so similar in their viciousness to those of the Rue Morgue — are a puzzlement to Dupin. For the readers, though, Moore is connecting Hyde to an ape, thus putting forth the idea that Hyde is no mere man.

Going undercover as a "demi-mondain," Mina is kidnapped. Quatermain and Dupin track her down, but instead of the timid doctor who propositioned her, they find the beast Hyde. As drawn by Kevin O'Neill, Hyde is a brute of a creature who is taller than the doorway he is stepping through and who has the strength to lift Quatermain off of the ground. His face is sinuous with large, white eyes and sharp teeth. When Dupin shoots off half his ear, Hyde just gets angrier and more ferocious. It is only when Quatermain forces a bottle of laudanum in his mouth that the three manage to sedate Hyde. From the first moment — in his appearance and actions — Hyde becomes the most monstrous of the team. Although Griffin's actions are deplorable — the League members first find him raping a young woman — Hyde's remain worse as he seems not to care about anything, a characterization taken directly from Stevenson's novel.

As in Stevenson's novel, Hyde is consuming Jekyll. To get his assistance, Mr. Bond — the League's connection to the government — has his man offer Hyde a cure. Hyde responds, "A cure? You'll cure me, will you, like a wart on Jekyll's arse?" (47). Clearly Hyde has absolutely no desire to be Jekyll again. And why not? When speaking of Jekyll, Nemo comments, "What of Jekyll? He did not seem an evil man" (46). To which Bond replies, "Oh, Dr. Henry Jekyll is a highly moral individual, you may be sure" (47). To members of the League, Jekyll seems very human, and not only in his looks. He is "moral" so he must follow the dominant ideology of the time. He is an acceptable member of society. In fact, he creates Hyde to get rid of his inhuman characteristics. And if Jekyll is human, does that make Hyde inhuman? His apparent enjoyment in killing would certainly imply an inhuman character, as would his outward appearance. Because Hyde revels in his monstrousness, he would not be moved by a cure; Hyde does not believe a cure is necessary because he does not see a problem with his lifestyle choices.

This inhumanity really surfaces when Hyde is fighting. In Hyde's very first fight scene as a League member, he is shown graphically ripping apart his foes, both with his teeth and with his arms. In the first panel Hyde tears off one man's arms while biting off what appears to be the other man's hand. In the next panel he is holding the forearm of a man in one hand while putting the rest of the other man into a wall. In the third panel Hyde's back is to the reader; blood, arms, and legs are all flying and the victim is screaming, "EEEAAGH!" (84–85). The other battles in which Hyde participates look similar to this first one. There is always blood flying through the panel along with body parts. Moore and O'Neill clearly want to portray Hyde as a sadistic monster who enjoys utter annihilation.

Since the monstrous side of Hyde is so dominant, what happens to Jekyll? In the graphic novel, Jekyll is portrayed as a weak, frightened man. He is always pictured with eyes seeming to dart left and right as if looking for something worrisome and usually he has sweat running down his forehead, thus implying that he is always nervous and unsure of both himself and his surroundings. When Jekyll first faces the League members, he states, "W-well, for my part, I'm prepared to help the cause as much as possible.

It's just that.... Well, sometimes I'm not myself. I'm not sure I can always be relied on" (51). A few pages later he echoes this sentiment: "I hadn't thought about him [Griffin]. To be honest, I've more pressing worries of my own.... The thing is, I don't trust me with myself" (54). The doctor is not a useful member of the League. His abilities as a monster hunter appear non-existent. He is worried all the time and has no confidence in himself at all. In this way, it appears that Moore is trying to put more stock in Hyde's inhuman monster rather than in Jekyll's human man. In fact, when Jekyll and Quatermain go to speak with some men about Dr. Fu Manchu's whereabouts, Jekyll almost loses control and gets both him and Quatermain into trouble. In the panel's foreground the reader sees Jekyll trying to keep from changing into Hyde. Meanwhile, the man Quatermain is questioning asks, "And what ails your friend there?" (63). Quatermain responds, "H-he's sick. He needs opium badly, and he ... *uh* ... he ate the tar by mistake" (63). When Quatermain asks Jekyll what is wrong, Jekyll says, "I-I was scared that they might kill us. I'm afraid I ... I almost lost control. I had to will myself to remain calm" (64). Quatermain is thankful Jekyll did not turn into Hyde for that would have caused them a lot of trouble in trying to keep a low profile.

Once again, we are shown that the contemporary monster hunter is useless without an element of monstrosity. Jekyll's presence is pointless; he does little to help the League. It is Hyde who is required. But, like his fellow contemporary monster hunters, Hyde is not without some level of humanity. And, like his fellow monster hunters, this humanity appears in relation to a woman: Mina. I recounted the following scene in Chapter 1, but it bears discussion here within the context of the graphic novel's entire analysis. During their final battle in Volume I, Mina begins hitting Jekyll in an attempt to make him become Hyde. When he finally turns, Hyde says, "I told you to stop it!" and grabs Mina's hand. Quatermain tries to step in but Mina says, "That will not be necessary, Mr. Quatermain. Mr. Hyde, you are hurting my hand, sir, and I will not allow that. I should be grateful if you would release me" (134). In the next panel the two simply stare at each other. In the following panel Hyde lets go of Mina and she thanks him. This may seem like an unusual action for a monster who has no qualms about killing prostitutes and stomping on little girls, but in Volume II readers learn why Mina has some level of control over Hyde:

> **Hyde:** Sometimes I think I should just rape you and behead you. But a voice in me still fiercer than my own tells me if I did that, I must next take my life. It's puzzling. Perhaps it is that I would then have killed the only living thing that did not fear me. D'you think that's it?

Mina: Y-you would be quite mistaken, sir. I fear you very much.
Hyde: Perhaps. Perhaps you do. But not like all the others. I believe you do not hate me. I believe you have perhaps met someone worse than me. Would that be right?
Mina: Yes.
Hyde: I thought as much. Miss Murray, though I am a beast, do not think that I am stupid. I know that I am hideous and hateful. I am not loved, nor ever hope to be. Nor am I fool enough to think that what I feel for you is love. But in this world, alone, I do not hate you ... and alone in this world, you do not hate me [44–45].

If love does, indeed, soothe the savage monster-hunting beast, as was discussed in Chapter 2, then it makes sense that Hyde's humanity would come out when he is around Mina, the only woman he could possibly ever love.

Although Moore takes certain liberties with Hyde to make him fit the role of the contemporary monster hunter, there is one important interpretation that both links Moore's Hyde to Stevenson's and gives Hyde a sure place within the league of contemporary monster hunters: Hyde's death. In Chapter 2 I suggested that one could read the ending of *Jekyll and Hyde* with Hyde choosing to commit suicide rather than wreak more havoc on London. At the end of Volume II, Moore picks up this very interpretation and has Hyde kill himself to help save the world. The Martians are approaching and the government needs more time to get the biological weapon in place. Hyde decides to single-handedly take on the advancing creatures. His fellow League members ask him to reconsider because they know it is a suicide mission. Mina tells him, "Edward, I can't allow this. You'll be killed." Hyde responds, "Yes, I suppose I shall. And ending up looking rather noble, when all I really want is to slaughter something, eh?" (135). Hyde does, indeed, manage to stop the Martians long enough for the government to use the weapon to kill them; however, he dies in the process. Yet, he has sacrificed himself to protect humanity, at least for the time being.[4]

There can be no doubt that Hyde is the most ruthless member of the League. Yet, as has been seen throughout this study, ruthlessness does not necessarily mean that someone cannot be a monster hunter. In fact, it is Hyde's very ruthlessness that makes him an asset to the League. His brute force and willingness to jump into the heat of battle make him almost noble. This is not to say that Hyde's actions are in any way excusable. In fact, he is more heinous in Volume II than in Volume I. When he learns that Griffin betrays the League and beats up Mina, Hyde goes after him. (Hyde has always been able to see Griffin's outline from the heat his body gives off.) He explains to Griffin that he is cross "because your treatment of Miss Murray was uncivil" (111). Rather than just kill Griffin, Hyde rapes him first, thinking nothing wrong of his actions. Moore is certainly quick to point out that Hyde should not be applauded, but then neither should many of his fellow monster hunters. It is these very actions that make him the flawed being so popular in today's horror fiction.

Hollywood's Take on Moore's Contemporary Monster Hunters

When a text is adapted for the silver screen, fans often complain that the film does not do the original text justice. What these fans forget is that adaptation is not just about putting the original text into a visual medium. Many good adaptations refuse to be exactly like the original because that is not the point. To make a good adaptation, the filmmaker must adhere to the original intention of the text, but with his own interpretation of that intention. For example, James Whale's 1931 adaptation of *Frankenstein* may not initially seem to be a particularly honest adaptation, especially considering the fact that his Monster shares little in common with Mary Shelley's eloquent creation. However, the idea that the Monster is lost and looking for love and acceptance still comes through in Whale's vision. The film may not be exactly what the novel's reader envisions in his mind, but the underlying themes and ideas are still present, which makes the film a successful adaptation. With Hollywood's adaptations of Moore's *V for Vendetta* (2005) and *The League of Extraordinary Gentlemen* (2003), this is not the case. In each adaptation, the complexity and ambiguity of the main monster hunters are diminished. In fact, in *League*, this complexity is almost entirely erased and it is no secret that Moore hated the *League* adaptation. Hollywood has managed to sidestep the intriguing questions Moore presents about monster hunters, leaving the viewer with a different, more palatable, text. Hollywood's inability to deal with ambiguity is nothing new. In his interview with Kim Thompson, Frank Miller comments on the *Superman* films: "The success of the first *Superman* movie demonstrates that, now that the world is good and fucked, the super-hero could be revitalized, could encourage us on a fantasy level to find the strengths we need" (66). However, he continues, "The dwindling box office at its two sequels demonstrates that Hollywood has no idea what to do with it, quickly turning it into ingenuous self-parody, focusing on all the parts of the character that are sentimental and outdated" (66). This is exactly what happens in the two films discussed below. In both instances, Hollywood latches on to the sentimental—and palatable—parts of the story and almost completely ignores the questions of humanity and monstrosity. In doing so, the films demonstrate that some writers and filmmakers think the contemporary monster hunter is still unsure of its place in popular culture.

Although *League* was adapted first, I want to begin with *V* because Director James McTeigue and Screenwriters Andy and Larry Wachowski stayed somewhat true to Moore's vision. That said, V (Hugo Weaving) becomes much more humane in the adaptation than in the graphic novel. In the novel, Moore points out again and again that V's true mission is to create anarchy in England. In doing so, V does hope that something new and better can come about. However, he is not deluded enough to think it will immediately happen. As was previously discussed, V tells Evey, "This country is not saved" (245). V sees himself as the man who would topple the old to usher in the new. He does this by creating utter chaos.

In the film version, V is something else entirely. He is not merely the bringer of anarchy; he is a rallying point. This is made clear from the first moments of the film when V's broadcast asks the population to stand beside him on the following November 5th: Guy Fawkes Day. In creating a bond with the people of England, V becomes a hero, something he never truly achieves in Moore's graphic novel because he is too monstrous. The film's V is also more optimistic about the future and the people of England. When Evey (Natalie Portman) asks him why he would blow up a building, V responds, "The building is a symbol, as is the act of destroying it. Symbols are given power by people. Alone, a symbol is meaningless, but with enough people, blowing up a building can change the world." V talks about change here, not anarchy. In fact, the only time anarchy is mentioned, it is by a man robbing a store who says, "Anarchy in the UK!" In the film, V's focus is always on giving the people power. While he is killing those members of Larkhill who destroyed him — yes, he is being spurred on by vengeance, as in the graphic novel — that vengeance is a tool of power for the people. His own vendetta will bring about freedom from oppression. In fact, the most famous line of the film — "People should not be afraid of their governments. Governments should be afraid of their people"— is never in the graphic novel. This sentiment makes V heroic, not monstrous. In addition, there is a subplot involving a young girl's support for the terrorist V.[5] She is shown fascinated by his television broadcast. This may be V's most sympathetic fan. Evey even catches her in a cape similar to V's, spray-painting a "V" over one of the Party's posters. When the young girl, who at the time is wearing the Guy Fawkes mask and cape, is shot by a Fingerman, an angry crowd rallies around her murder and kills her murderer. This action proves that V is changing England's power dynamics through the symbol he has become. The people are giving him power. He is a man trying to bring about revolution for the people and that overshadows the personal vendetta he has against the men and women currently in power.

That said, he does still torture Evey in order to give her freedom from her fear, so Hollywood has not made him entirely sympathetic and heroic. Previously I mentioned that this torture adds to V's monstrosity in the graphic novel. Because he cares for Evey, this section of the book is disturbing. In the film, the torture is given another angle because the Wachowski brothers imply a love between V and Evey from the very beginning and this constant presence of love makes V a much more humanized monster hunter. For one, Evey never believes V to be her father; this is one of the underlying implications Moore makes for part of the graphic novel. Because the relationship begins with this implication it never really moves into a more sexualized love. In the graphic novel, the two remain predominantly platonic as teacher and student. Once that incestual implication is gone, as it is in the film, there is nothing barring V and Evey from falling in love. When Evey returns to V on the night of November 5th for a dance, V tells her, "I must confess, every time I heard a siren, I worried about you." This V clearly has feelings for Evey that go beyond Moore's platonic relationship. As V leaves Evey to go to his death, Evey tells him to stay; she claims that the two of them can run away together. V actually considers this for a brief moment. His true feelings come through even though he wears a mask and viewers cannot see the emotion on his face. It comes as no surprise, then, that when V is dying he tells Evey, "For twenty years I sought only this day. Nothing else existed until I saw you. Then everything changed. I fell in love with you, Evey, like I no longer believed I could." In contemporary monster hunter narratives, it is typical that a monster would become a monster hunter through love. In this adaptation, love does more than that. Evey's feelings for V actually make him far less monstrous than the graphic novel's V.

There is one scene that does try to make V into more of a monster. This scene is worth noting, for no other reason than it actually makes V less of a monster than perhaps anticipated by the filmmakers. After Evey realizes that V has been behind her torture, she asks him why he did it. V responds, "You said you wanted to live without fear. I wish there'd been an easier way but there wasn't. [...] I know you may never forgive me but nor will you understand how hard it was for me to do what I did. Every day, I saw in myself everything you see in me now. Every day, I wanted to end it." To this Evey comments, "You're sick! You're evil!" V agrees and tells Evey, "What was done to me was monstrous." Evey replies, "And they created a monster." With this brief exchange, the filmmakers try to set up an excuse for V's actions. But it does not work because underlying all of V's actions is his apparent love for Evey. It is true that this scene takes its inspiration from the graphic novel. In the graphic novel, when Evey comes out of V's prison, V tells her his rationale for the torture: "Because I love you. Because I want to set you free" (167). To some extent it is true that V loves Evey. But her anger at V and, again, her original transference of her father onto V, preclude a sexual love between the two. While Evey is, after her lengthy tirade, able to break out of her "prison" and be reborn under the rainy night sky, she still does not come to the same sexualized love for V that is expressed in the film. In addition, in the graphic novel Evey never calls V a monster at this point. She does not have to because the reader already understands that V is a monster. He is, to an extent, selfish and uses Evey because he sees in her his opposite: the creator. He recognizes that Evey has a place in the society he is about to usher in, if she only wants to take it. Their love can never be realized to the extent that Evey's love is in the film. In fact, as if to further push the idea of love in the film, the filmmakers choose for Evey to absolve V of the monstrosity she imposed upon him. As they stand together at the film's end on the Underground's platform and Evey tells V to come away with her, he says, "No. You were right about what I am. I have no tree[6] waiting for me. All I want, all I deserve, is at the end of that tunnel." Evey tells V it is not true and kisses him (or at least kisses the mask's lips). In this kiss—something which never occurs in the graphic novel—Evey forgives V, understands V, and loves V.

Just as V becomes more humanized in the adaptation, so too does Mr. Finch (Stephen Rea). From the very beginning, Finch has a grudging respect for V. When the viewer first sees Finch, he admits to Chancellor Sutler (John Hurt), the Party's leader, that V is "very good." As the Chancellor chides Finch, the detective appears to be frustrated or even fed up with the Party. From the very beginning, Finch is set up as a V sympathizer and a man about to forego his party connections. As he digs deeper and deeper into V and Larkhill, he is repeatedly told to leave it alone and focus his attention on V. The pressure even gets so bad that he uses a mechanism in his office to interfere with the Party's evident bugging. But the pivotal point in Finch's change of heart is when V chooses him as a messenger of sorts. V meets with Finch—although Finch believes V to be Rookwood, a man Finch is searching for—and tells him that the Larkhill biological tests created a biological weapon which the Party then chose to test on England itself. Finch is appalled but not surprised. As previously stated, Finch has always been portrayed as being at odds with the Party. While he does go to Larkhill, he does not take LSD in an attempt to think like V. Like the rest of England and the viewers, he has already seen in V a possible way out of the oppressive military state England has become; he has already sided with the terrorist. It is not Finch who kills V, nor does he run away from London at the film's end. Instead, Finch makes his way to the Underground and tries, half-heartedly, to stop Evey from sending the train to blow up Parliament. When he decides not to stop her, he is left standing by Evey as the train rolls away. As it goes, Evey tells Finch that blowing up Parliament will bring the people hope. The two are left to witness V's final victory and his completed vendetta. Even though there is no strong sense of rebuilding here, as in the graphic novel, there is the sense that Evey and Finch will help usher in a new era of hope.

This analysis is not to say that the film version of *V for Vendetta* is bad. On the contrary, the movie is quite spectacular and did manage to gross more than $130 million worldwide. The film certainly reflects many postmillennial fears. But it distills Moore's original intentions as to V's monstrous behavior. While still a character somewhat ambiguous, the film's V is much more palatable to a worldwide audience than the graphic novel's V. But the adaptation could have been worse. In fact, there is a far worse adaptation of Moore's work and that is *The League of Extraordinary Gentlemen*. When James Robinson wrote the screenplay for Director Stephen Norrington's film, he completely destroyed the ambiguity so prevalent in Edward Hyde and created a heartwarming group of monster hunters who have little in common with Moore's League.

One of the most interesting aspects of Moore's *League* (the graphic novel), at least for my purposes, is that all five League members are in some way morally ambiguous. Because of Mina's encounter with, and subsequent bite from, Dracula, she is, by Victorian standards, a fallen woman. Not only that, she has chosen to divorce her husband; although legal, this action would have been scandalous for Victorian society. The fact that she has sex with Allan Quatermain in the second volume implies a "looseness" to her, meaning that she is far from the impeccable "Angel in the House" so important to Victorians. Likewise, Allan Quatermain is certainly not the hero worshipped by Victorian boys. When Mina first finds Quatermain, he is holed up in an opium den, high out of his mind. His addiction gets the best of him in Paris and he leaves his post to get a bottle of laudanum from a pharmacy across the street; thus allowing Mina to get taken by Hyde. Griffin, as was mentioned previously, is found raping young women. Nemo, probably the least ambiguous of all the members, is still considered to be a pirate. And, of course, Hyde has been fully analyzed already for his ambiguity. When these five characters come together, they are begrudgingly helping the government, but that does not mean they are good people. Griffin and Hyde are taking part in the group for their own selfish ends and Quatermain really does not want anything to do with England any more.

In the film version, the five original League characters are nothing like their graphic novel counterparts in terms of ambiguity. Instead, these characters are pure of heart, even Hyde (Jason Flemyng). The most significant change is to Allan Quatermain (Sean Connery). When a government agent finds Quatermain in Africa, he is far from the opium-addicted Quatermain in the novel.[7] Instead, he is still a ferocious hunter, as is shortly proven when the Phantom's (Richard Roxburgh) agents come to kill him and he takes on all of them single-handedly. Most of this battle requires brute force and Quatermain is up to the task. Here is England's greatest hero and it comes as no surprise that Quatermain becomes the leader of this League, as Hollywood could not have the hyper-masculine Sean Connery taking orders from Mina Harker (Peta Wilson).

In this film, Griffin has died but a "gentleman thief" by the name of Rodney Skinner (Tony Curran) has stolen his invisibility formula. Skinner is not found raping young women. Instead, he comes to the League for an antidote because he has found that being invisible has its drawbacks. In fact, it is Skinner who will prove vital to finding the Phantom. When his fellow League members believe he has betrayed them — something he does in the second volume of the graphic novels — he follows the true betrayer, Dorian Gray, to the Phantom's lair and then provides Nemo (Naseeruddin Shah) with the coordinates. He also risks his own life to save another added member, Tom Sawyer (Shane West). Skinner is much more heroic than his invisible counterpart in Moore's tale.

Mina is still a vampire, but there are three significant changes made to her character. First, the men learn she is a vampire early on and then both respect and fear her. In the graphic novel, at least in Volume I, there are hints to a suspicious bite from an Eastern European nobleman but no one outwardly asks Mina about it. Second, she is a chemist, which immediately earns her a begrudging respect from the male members of the League. Finally, she is not divorced, but widowed. This is a significant change because it makes Mina sympathetic in a way she never is in the novel. In addition, her status as both a widow and a scientist imply a certain respectability and goodness to her. Even though she may viciously suck the blood from her enemies, she is not ever thought to be monstrous by the viewers. That said, there is a level of sexuality to her that the Victorian Era would find offensive. When she meets Dorian Gray (Stuart Townsend), she speaks of an affair the two had. Indeed, this affair becomes a point of contention with both characters and is often mentioned. Whether this affair happened before or after her marriage to Jonathan is never discussed. It is there to add a sexual element to the film. Even so, Mina still comes off to the viewer as a respectable, integral member of the League, even if it takes her fellow male members a while to have the same reaction.

While Nemo remains virtually the same in the film as in the novel, Hyde's transformation is once again worthy of discussion. As was previously mentioned, Hyde is a despicable creature who eventually manages to suppress his counterpart Jekyll. In the film, the two characters actually work together, surprising though that may sound. At first, this cooperation is something Hyde would never do. Once he is captured by Quatermain and Sawyer, he fights his chains. But when he realizes he has no other option, he changes back into Jekyll and both agree to work for the League. However, Hyde does not go quietly. At one point he taunts Jekyll. It appears that Jekyll finds Mina attractive. When he looks in a window Hyde appears and claims that she would never look at the doctor but would look at the beast. This mirrored image of Hyde appears quite a bit. Rather than one consuming the other, the filmmakers have chosen to allow both personalities to inhabit the same body. They can communicate with one another through mirrors and windows and, presumably, any other reflective surface. But other than this moment, Hyde is rather heroic. After bombs are set off in the Nautilus, a section of the ship must be closed off, thus risking the drowning of several sailors in that section. Jekyll looks in a reflective surface and Hyde says, "We can do it Henry. [...] You know we can do it. Together." Jekyll turns into Hyde and the two risk their life to save the men. Hyde looks in a window and Jekyll compliments him: "Bravo, Edward. Bravo." The two have formed a symbiotic relationship that is certainly not present in the graphic novel. And although Jekyll remarks, "Let's not make a saint out of a sinner. Next time he may not be so helpful," the truth is that Hyde will be that helpful again. He will prove an invaluable member of the League. He never suppresses Jekyll in this narrative and the result is a very tame monster hunter. In fact, the complexity of Hyde's character so prevalent in Moore's tale — a complexity that is at the forefront of Moore's work in general — is completely missing.

To compensate for this lack of ambiguity in the original League members, the filmmakers have thrown two new members into the mix: Tom Sawyer[8] and Dorian Gray. It is difficult to say why Tom is added to the text, other than to take the place of Quatermain's son and add a father-figure dimension to the character. However, Dorian Gray is clearly added to be the film's assistant villain. (The Phantom acts as the key villain.) Dorian is to spy on the group; thus filling Griffin's role in the graphic novel's second volume. As was mentioned, he also provides a sexualized subplot with Mina. But even this character cannot be truly evil. He is working for the Phantom because the Phantom has stolen Dorian's picture, an object that is very valuable to Gray and dangerous. That said, Dorian Gray is never a moral character in Oscar Wilde's novel, so there is no indication that he would be in this film. He is working for the highest bidder, in a sense, and cares nothing of the Phantom's cause. In fact, once he has his picture, it appears that he will return to England to continue his lifestyle. That is until Mina kills him by stabbing his portrait. By adding Gray, a character for the viewer to despise, the filmmakers can create a League of good people.

Hollywood is continually distilling the contemporary monster hunter into a palatable character. Even when original material makes for villainous heroes, Hollywood just cannot seem to bring itself to adhere to the original intent. Something must be added to either make the monstrous monster hunter more sympathetic or human — like in *V for Vendetta* with the focus on a sexual love between V and Evey — or other characters must be added who are more monstrous so that the monstrous monster hunter is better by comparison. It is no wonder that Moore would despise the *League* adaptation; the filmmakers have certainly not adhered to his original intentions for the characters. At the time of this writing, *Watchmen* is being filmed, a task various studios and filmmakers have tried over the years. When it finally comes to the screen what will fans see? Will Rorschach be a good guy? Will he be a sympathetic monster hunter? Will Ozymandias be less selfish? Who will be added as a villain to make these characters more humane? What will Hollywood require to make these monster hunters more acceptable to contemporary society's ideologies? It is hard to say but one thing will be sure: fans of Moore's work will be warily optimistic to see what happens. Hopefully Hollywood will finally get it right.

Graphic novels are accomplishing exactly what the gothic/horror genres are: giving contemporary readers an ambiguous monster hunter to think about. More importantly, these graphic novels themselves are joining the discussion of what it means to be a contemporary monster hunter. Dr. Wolper and Lana will never come to a consensus about Batman just as the Watchmen are forced to police themselves and decide when it is okay to ignore ideological mandates (Ozymandias) and when it is not (Rorschach). With the graphic novels mentioned in this chapter, we begin to discuss the complexities of vigilantism. It certainly would be nice to see a drastic change in the world — à la *V* — but we must remember that every change comes with a price. What if something worse than Norsefire takes over? The graphic novels in this chapter remind readers that vigilantes are dangerous as well as heroic. This dualism is one that must never be forgotten when analyzing the contemporary monster hunter. These graphic novels show that the character can easily fall into the abyss and cause more bad than good, even if Hollywood would prefer to ignore this small fact in its adaptations. However, these graphic novels also offer the possibility that when done right, the vigilante monster hunter can make a difference, at least for the immediate future.

Chapter 4

THE ADVENT OF THE FEMALE MONSTER HUNTER

"She Saved The World A Lot"
— *Epitaph on Buffy Summers's Tombstone*

For the first three chapters, I have been focusing on male monster hunters. This is not because I believe they are more worthy of discussion, but because women have not, until quite recently, been true monster hunters. Women in horror texts have always been problematic. In a patriarchal culture, women are told to occupy a specific role, usually wife and mother. If a woman refuses to occupy such a place, she is either "reprogrammed" to accept her place or done away with in some respect. This societal view also holds true in the horror genre. Traditionally, women have fallen into two roles within horror: the victim and the vixen. The victim is present to uphold the traditional feminine role and be rescued by the hero. The vixen is considered monstrous and needs to be done away with by the text's conclusion. For the most part, a victim should never be a vixen and vice versa. A victim cannot have any agency — else why would she be a victim — and a vixen must be punished for her agency. Because the monster hunter has agency in a horror text, the character has been male. However, attempts have been made to create female monster hunters in the past. Bram Stoker's Mina can be considered the grandmother of the contemporary female monster hunter and the Final Girl from the 1970s and 1980s can be considered her mother. But it took major cultural shifts in attitudes towards women to allow both of these female characters. And both gave birth to today's monster hunters from such texts as *Alien*, Laurell K. Hamilton's Anita Blake series, and Joss Whedon's *Buffy the Vampire Slayer*.

Much like the posthumanists do with humanizing apparatuses, feminist film critics look for those places in film and literature where the boundaries of patriarchy are at their weakest. As Constance Penley argues, feminist film criticism is first and foremost an "attempt to find ruptures, gaps, contradictions, and other points of resistance in the apparently seamless patriarchal fabric of the classical film" (5). Although it represents a society's repression, or perhaps because of this, horror is often criticized for being antifeminist. However, as many horror critics have shown, horror contains as many ruptures, gaps, contradictions, and resistance as other types of film. Feminist criticism in general is a necessary lens to use with horror texts because it helps us better understand the seeds of the female monster hunter movement as well as why it took so long to have a female monster hunter. Most feminist film criticism — and certainly most feminist horror film criticism — takes its cues from Laura Mulvey's seminal text, *Visual Pleasure and Narrative Cinema*. In this text, Mulvey argues that women have no agency in film and are only present to be looked at by the male viewer. With its continual reliance on such cinematic techniques as the I-camera and the steadicam, horror relies on the gaze, or lack thereof, to enhance the viewer's fear. It is only natural, then, that horror critics would focus on Mulvey's argument to enhance their own, both agreeing and disagreeing with her.

One of the most important texts to use Mulvey as a starting point in feminist horror film criticism is Linda Williams' "When the Woman Looks." Williams agrees with Mulvey's assertion but then explains how women do have a sense of power when they finally do the looking in a horror film. At first, Williams is not surprised that women often look away from horror films or cover their eyes. Often, a woman is asked to "bear witness to her own powerlessness in the face of rape, mutilation, and murder" (15). Williams comments that even when the woman is permitted to look, it is usually through an on-screen vixen who is always punished for her audacity. Yet, even though the woman — both within the horror film and, by proxy, within the viewing audience — has little to no agency in horror films, there is a bond between her and the film's monster. According to Williams, "The female look [...] shares the male fear of the monster's freakishness, but also recognizes the sense in which this freakishness is similar to her own difference" (21). When the woman does look, she encounters a being who, like her, has little power within the patriarchal framework and who must be punished for looking. However, Williams argues, "[T]here is a sense in which the woman's look at the monster is more than simply a punishment for looking or a narcissistic fascination with the distortion of her own image in the mirror that patriarchy holds up to her; it is a recognition of their similar status as potent threats to a vulnerable male power" (23). For Williams, then, women may not hold the power in horror films, but they are not completely demeaned either. For perhaps one brief moment, women in the horror film — and those in the audience — understand that they and the monster are threats to patriarchy and in that realization is a bit of strength. Unfortunately, women in early horror films almost never maintained either power or agency. In the rare cases where they did, they were eventually punished. Part of this lack of power certainly stems from gender stereotypes.

Heroes have traditionally been male. Their "maleness" implies a certain group of gendered traits such as strength (both physical and emotional), aggression, and risk-taking. None of these are considered feminine traits. In his discussion of comic book superheroes, Mila Bongco has this to say about masculinity: "Masculinity, however, is a social concept that goes beyond being muscular and excelling in brute strength. Being male and masculine manifests itself more in how effectively a superhero uses mind and/or muscle to resolve various power struggles, thereby displaying authority and self-sufficiency, and gaining public recognition" (115). In subversive literature, whether it be film, television, or graphic novels, women have traditionally been seen as the opposite of these characteristics. Women are often physically weaker so they cannot actually fight back. In addition, in early texts women may be smart, but are rarely smarter than the men. And, of course, women are mothers, which means that nurturing is a characteristic seen as weak (as opposed to something like aggression). All of these feminine qualities are ingrained in society and make it very difficult for early female characters to be heroes. Bongco even goes so far as to analyze the female superhero's inability to be equal to the male superheroes: "The intervention of female heroines seldom seems to evoke the deference from lawmen or terror from criminals (regardless how reluctantly) that herald the arrival of male superheroes in critical situations" (111). Frustrating though these quotes may be to the contemporary feminist, they have traditionally been true. And women in horror and gothic tales have fared only slightly better than their comic book contemporaries. However, there have been a few women who have briefly broken free of traditional gender stereotypes. It is these women who led the way for the contemporary female monster hunter.

The New Woman and Mina Harker

Bram Stoker's Mina is the grandmother of the contemporary female monster hunter,[1] a type of new woman who is credited with a vast store of knowledge: she memorizes train schedules, knows shorthand, and types up the diary entries of the novel's monster hunters. Although pure and noble, she is not the typical Victorian "Angel in the House" whose primary role was to tend the house and raise the children. Mina can think for herself and wants to help her husband and the other monster hunters any way she can. Due to her unusual abilities and strengths, many critics have faced great difficulty in analyzing her. While most agree that Mina Harker represents Bram Stoker's reaction to the New Woman of Victorian England, no consensus has yet to be reached as to whether Mina is a positive or negative reaction. Examining this critical quandary a little more will lead us to better understand how Mina is both the first female monster hunter and, simultaneously, not quite a monster hunter.

One thing many critics agree on is that Stoker's writing often contains strong women. According to Jean Lorrah, in her article on *Dracula* and the New Woman, "While Bram Stoker never took a public stand in favor of feminism, his mother was an advocate of what little women's movement there was in Ireland, and there is evidence in Stoker's other works that he was interested in the relationship between men and women, and was an admirer of strong women" (31–32). This admiration is clear in Van Helsing's description of Mina. It is Mina who essentially puts together all the pieces of the vampire hunt by transcribing the various diaries so that all members of the monster-hunting team have access to all of the information. This action is praised by Van Helsing: "Ah, that wonderful Madam Mina! She has a man's brain — a brain that a man should have were he much gifted — and woman's heart. The good God fashioned her for a purpose, believe me, when He made that so good combination" (Stoker 240). This passage has long given critics trouble. Lorrah sees the compliment as veiled sarcasm on the part of Van Helsing and comments, "Now Mina, even if quietly and in a womanly way, begins to direct the affair. Soon Van Helsing's dominance is threatened as everyone is well-informed and thus on an equal footing" (38). I disagree with this reading; I believe that Van Helsing, and by proxy Bram Stoker, is not as threatened by Mina's abilities as Lorrah believes. Instead, Stoker is almost attempting to create a new woman himself: one with both feminine and masculine attributes. More importantly, Stoker chooses the best attributes of both: a man's brain and a woman's heart. The traditional gender characteristics come together to create a vital member of Van Helsing's team. Rather than being fearful of Mina's dominance in the group, Van Helsing applauds her ability to embody the best both sexes have to offer.

Yet Mina is still sheltered from the majority of masculine monster-hunting duties. When it comes time for the men's first attempt to track down and kill Dracula, they decide to keep Mina in the dark about their plans. She is permitted a place taking notes and giving schedules, but when the hunting begins, Van Helsing tells her, "When we part tonight, you no more must question. We shall tell you all in good time. We are men, and are able to bear; but you must be our star and our hope, and we shall act all the more free that you are not in danger, such as we are" (Stoker 246–47). Van Helsing further explains to Dr. Seward why Mina should not have a part in their monster hunting: "Mrs. Harker is better out of it. Things are quite bad enough for us, all men of the world, and who have been in many tight places in our time; but it is no place for a woman, and if she had remained in touch with the affair, it would in time infallibly have wrecked her" (259). Despite his earlier praise of Mina, Van Helsing will not go so far as to say she is physically and emotionally strong. As Mila Bongco comments in regards to comic books, Mina would not strike fear into Dracula's heart even if she were a member of the team. However, the men soon realize that it is a mistake to keep Mina from their monster hunting; every plan they make without Mina's knowledge seems to fall apart. It is only when Mina is fully permitted into the monster-hunting circle that the band finally has the strength and ability to defeat the vampire. And it is at this point that Mina manages to be both masculine and feminine.

While the men are out trying to destroy the vampire, Dracula enters Mina's mind and begins to infect her, but it is not until Dracula bites Mina, and she, in turn, unwillingly drinks his blood, that she becomes a powerful monster-hunting ally. Mina draws a sort of strength and independence when she becomes part vampire. This strength is exactly what Linda Williams is discussing in "When the Woman Looks." When Mina is an Other on the level of Dracula, she is truly powerful. Only as a monster can she gain equality with the men in the story. Her "man's brain" can be applauded because it does not truly undermine the patriarchal culture Van Helsing is trying desperately to maintain. But when she is "infected" with power — when she gains a psychic bond to Dracula — she becomes a monster hunter in her own right. This monstrosity will be a vital element for contemporary female monster hunters as it will allow them to embrace both their feminine and masculine sides.

Once Mina is bitten, she chooses to put herself in harm's way. Knowing that she has a psychic connection to Dracula, she permits, even encourages, Van Helsing to use that connection for the greater good of the group: "You must take me with you. I am safer with you, and you shall be safer too. [...] I may be of service, since you can hypnotize me and so learn that which even I myself do not know" (Stoker 322–23). The men in her life would happily protect Mina, but she understands the full potential of her connection with Dracula. Even though she may not readily know her new powers, she does understand that she is even more helpful now that she is a monster. Her desire to risk her own life to save her society is certainly indicative of those nurturing instincts. Not only does Mina have a brain and power—both masculine attributes—she has a pure heart and nurturing instincts—both feminine attributes. When these attributes all come together, she is more powerful than Van Helsing or any of his men. Lorrah comments, "It is Mina who directs the final chase, she who maps the itinerary, deducing the route the Count will take from her study of his personality and past habits. And, of course, she continues to keep the records" (41). No matter how she does it—whether hypnotized or actively working with Van Helsing—Mina is a vital part of the final chase and destruction of Count Dracula. Without her, the male monster hunters would not be able to complete their task, as is evident in the men's failure at all their early attempts on the vampire's life—attempts that do not include Mina.

Mina is thus a capable monster hunter in her own right, an ability that appears to stem from Stoker's admiration—albeit ambiguous—of the Victorian New Woman. However, Mina is not a career monster hunter like Van Helsing. Due to Van Helsing's vast knowledge of vampires, the reader assumes that the good doctor has come in contact with the supernatural in the past and may need that knowledge again in the future. Mina, on the other hand, does not appear to be a long-term monster hunter. In fact, the novel ends with Mina happily pursuing the role of mother, not monster hunter, thus fully giving in to her feminine side. At the novel's conclusion, Jonathan praises his wife saying, "This boy [their son] will some day know what a brave and gallant woman his mother is. Already he knows her sweetness and loving care; later he will understand how some men so loved her, that they did dare much for her sake" (Stoker 369). Nowhere does Jonathan recognize Mina's own contributions to their fight. Instead, he embraces her return to the stereotypical female role by claiming that the men risked much for her. Mina's monster-hunting days are over. The end to her careers—both monster hunter and secretary—symbolizes Mina's break from the role of the New Woman. Carol Senf states, "That she [Mina] is *not* a New Woman can be seen in her [...] decision to marry and her subsequent relationship with her husband, [and] her desire to nurture and protect children" (45–46). For Mina Harker, monster hunting is a one-time experience; in the end she chooses the traditional Victorian role of wife and mother. For that choice she is praised nearly as much as she is praised for her "man's mind." But the very fact that Mina breaks through traditional Victorian gender roles—albeit for a brief moment—and is not punished for it makes her the grandmother of the contemporary female monster hunter.

Victims and Vixens

As far back as Bram Stoker's *Dracula*, and really beyond, there have traditionally been two types of women in the horror genre: the victim (Mina) and the vixen (Lucy). The victim is just as one would expect: the virginal or pure girl who is to be rescued by the male hero(es). The vixen, however, is much more complex. She is the women who is obviously linked to the monster; she is monstrous because of her sexuality. According to Rhona J. Berenstein, in *Attack of the Leading Ladies*, "Monsters do not fit neatly with a model of human sexuality. Instead, they propose a paradigm of sexuality in which eros and danger, sensuality and destruction, human and inhuman, and male and female blur, overlap, and coalesce" (27). It is this very link that makes them so dangerous and requires their death and destruction. It is bad enough when a male monster appears to upset the traditional sexual boundaries; however, when a female monster appears, she is even more deadly. A female monster represents not only an affront to traditional gender roles but also an affront to traditional sexual roles. Traditionally, the vixen has been, to some extent, the sexual predator of the film. For a brief moment she manages to remove the man's power; with her comes the fear of castration. As Karen Hollinger claims in her article on *Cat People*, "If the woman is related to the monster in that they both are seen by patriarchy as representing sexual difference and castration fears, then she is allied not to a representation of weakness but to one of power in sexual difference" (299). The male monster may be bad enough, but a female monster is doubly terrifying to a patriarchal culture and must, at all costs, be destroyed to protect the good and pure woman.

In Tod Browning's 1931 film adaptation of Stoker's novel, Mina takes a significant step backwards. Whether we agree that Stoker's Mina is a New Woman or not, she still maintains a sense of strength and agency. She may be the focal point around which the men rally, but she also demonstrates her own abilities as monster hunter. In Browning's film, Mina has absolutely no agency. She is entirely a victim, even when she briefly trespasses into vixen territory. In contrast, very little time is spent on Lucy in Browning's film, thus downplaying the vixen role. Instead, the focus is around Mina's (Helen Chandler) slow descent into vampirism. This descent begins when she tells John (David Manners) her dream about being bitten. John comments, "Darling, we're going to forget all about these dreams." He completely negates her fears—well-founded though they turn out to be—and treats her like a child who has suffered a nightmare. Because he cannot imagine that there is anything amiss, her fears must be foolish. But John is not the only man to treat Mina as a child; her father, Dr. Seward (Herbert Bunston), and Van Helsing (Edward Van Sloan) both tell her to go to her room to rest. Mina cannot be privy to the men's discussion. The implication is that she is neither strong enough nor smart enough to learn about vampires. While the men in Stoker's novel attempt to keep Mina out of harm's way, they never blatantly treat her like a child as do the men in Browning's adaptation.

After Mina is infected by Dracula's bites, she vacillates between victim and vixen but never attains a true sense of power. When she first realizes what is going on with Lucy—Lucy has become the woman in white who is stalking children—she begs Van Helsing, "If you can save Lucy's soul after death, promise me you'll save mine." She recognizes herself as a foul, soiled woman who needs saving. When John protests, she says, "No John. You musn't touch me and you musn't kiss me ever again." She even goes so far as to tell John their life is over because of Dracula's power over her. Even though John still has his doubts about Van Helsing and vampires, Mina knows what she is. As a pure and proper woman, she does not want to infect John, which is why she tells him they can never be together. This moment demonstrates that Mina's nurturing side is what makes her special; she cares more about saving others than she does herself.

It is only when Mina is the vixen that John finally believes in vampires. Mina convinces John to join her on the terrace in the evening. She points out the stars and while John is looking at them, the viewer's gaze is drawn to Mina who is looking longingly at John's neck. She has the same lighting highlighting her eyes as Dracula does when he is in a scene. At this point, the viewer knows what Mina has become. No "pure" woman would wantonly ogle a man's neck. Further along in the scene, Mina tries to convince John to take Van Helsing's crucifix. The camera zooms in on Mina's eyes as she tries to hypnotize John. Mina is clearly in control in this scene. She has power and that power stems fully from her sexuality. Barely veiled, this sexuality is what lures John onto the terrace in the first place. It is only when Van Helsing interrupts by lunging at Mina with a crucifix that she snaps out of her brief moment as the vixen and becomes, once again, the victim. To emphasize this change, she tells John and Van Helsing, "He came to me. He opened this vein in his arms and he made me drink." She is ashamed of this action as if she is to blame for her "rape." She had no choice in the matter just as she currently has no choice in her move to vixen status.

From this point in the film to the end, Mina remains a victim. Dracula hypnotizes her into following him to the Abbey. Once there, he carries her to the ruins in the basement. (Mina cannot even walk there on her own.) John and Van Helsing pursue in their attempt to rescue Mina. After Van Helsing hammers the stake into Dracula's heart, viewers hear Mina scream and watch John as he finds his beloved. Even at this final moment Mina comments that while in Dracula's trance she could hear John but was powerless to do anything, further cementing her role as victim. John then leads her up and out of the basement. Never in this adaptation is Mina given any sense of agency. She is constantly being led by the men in her life who treat her like a child or even a doll. The only time she has power, it is linked with her sexuality and she immediately feels great guilt for giving in. All traces of Stoker's Mina's "male mind" are gone here and Browning's Mina is nothing more than a damsel in distress. Unfortunately, it is this film's characterization of Mina that will shape female horror victims to come for almost fifty years. In most vampire texts, and certainly most films, women are there to give men something to do. If they are not there to be rescued, they are there to sidetrack the male hero with their sexual wiles.

If a woman actively uses her sexuality to get what she wants, she is considered the vixen of the film. Most often, at least in early horror, the vixen is the film's monster, thus reminding viewers that a woman's sexuality is truly monstrous. No film better depicts the fear of a vixen than Lambert Hillyer's 1936 film, *Dracula's Daughter*. With its story beginning only hours after Van Helsing kills Dracula in Browning's film, *Dracula's Daughter* follows the plight of Countess Marya Zaleska (Gloria Holden) as she tries to rid herself of her father's vampiric influence. When she burns Dracula's body, Marya believes herself to be free and tells her manservant Sandor (Irving Pichel) while she plays the piano, "I can live a normal life now, think normal things, even play normal music." At this point the viewer feels sympathy for Marya, but that sympathy quickly disappears—as does the sympathy for Dracula when he tells Lucy he wishes to be truly dead—when Sandor points out that Marya's music has turned dark. Over time, Marya's repeated efforts to live a normal life will come to nothing as over and over her monstrous side wins out and she takes life after life.

Marya hopes that Dr. Jeffrey Garth (Otto Kruger), a psychiatrist, can help her overcome her evil ways. At first Jeffrey is attracted to Marya's exotic qualities and tells her she must fight her unexplained urges. Unfortunately, Jeffrey soon learns what Marya is and goes to confront her. During this confrontation, Marya claims, "I'm leaving London tonight, forever. [...] I know the truth now. There's nothing ahead for me but horror." She begs

Jeffrey to come with her and says, "You're a great doctor — a doctor of minds, of souls. [...] I need you to save my soul." This plea echoes that which Mina makes to Van Helsing in Browning's *Dracula*. There, the plea falls on sympathetic ears as neither Van Helsing nor John can dream of Mina, the victim, becoming a monster. However, in *Dracula's Daughter*, Marya's plea falls on utterly unsympathetic ears. Jeffrey has, at this point, no desire to save Marya because she is a monster. And, as must occur in all early gothic and horror texts, the monster must be killed. For her sexuality and refusal to live within patriarchal boundaries, Marya is punished; Sandor kills her by shooting an arrow through her heart.

If there is a vixen in a horror film, there must be a victim as well to balance out the human and inhuman and to give the protagonist someone to fight for. In this film, the victim is Janet (Marguerite Churchill), although she does not seem much like a victim at first. In fact, Janet has a bit of a vixen in her just as Marya has a bit of the victim. Janet appears to be independently wealthy and is the brash secretary to Jeffrey. She verbally spars with him repeatedly in a flirtatious manner and works more as a personal assistant than a secretary. Janet also has an instant distrust of Marya. However, despite her independence, Janet's role of victim is instantly cemented when Marya kidnaps her as bait to get Jeffrey to Transylvania. In fact, Janet becomes a pawn as Marya uses her life to barter with Jeffrey to get him to become a vampire. Janet desperately needs saving in this film. Although she carries some of the vixen's traits, she can never truly be a vixen. In early horror the victim and vixen must be two completely different beings. In the end, Janet will get Jeffrey and Marya will get eternal peace (one hopes).

Of great importance to early horror films is the fact that female monsters tend to be more sympathetic than their male counterparts. While viewers may feel momentary sympathy for Dracula, his daughter elicits far more sympathy in her continual plight to gain normalcy. Another film which features a sympathetic female monster is Jacque Tourneur's 1942 film, *Cat People*. The main character, Irena (Simone Simon) is worried that she has her people's curse: when she falls in love, she will become a panther and kill her husband. (The film hints that this is what happened to Irena's own father.) When Irena really does fall in love with and marries Oliver (Kent Smith), she avoids kissing him or even consummating the marriage. However, when Oliver confides the abnormality of his marriage to his co-worker Alice (Jane Randolph), her lack of privacy leads to Irena's jealousy and the unwitting release of the panther within.

Like Marya, Irena is set up as the vixen from the film's beginning. Even though she seems innocent enough, there are elements of darkness in her.

First, Oliver meets Irena at the zoo where she is sketching a panther. Later in the film, the zoo caretaker comments that no one comes to visit the panther unless she is depressed, thus implying there must be something wrong with a woman who thinks the beasts are beautiful. In addition, Irena is very forward with Oliver and invites him to tea in her apartment the very afternoon they meet. As it gets dark, Irena comments, "I like the dark. It's friendly." None of these attributes are overly feminine and they set her apart from her fellow women. Finally, Oliver learns that Irena is descended from Satan worshippers and witches, which again places her away from the stereotypical "good" woman.

Although she has a dark side, the viewer still remains sympathetic towards Irena. Part of this sympathy stems from the fact that she wants desperately to be a "normal" woman. She does not choose to be a panther; she is an unwitting victim of a family curse. Whether she will actually become a panther remains unclear for the first half of the film, but Tourneur makes it clear that Irena fears the possible change more than anything else. On their wedding night, Irena begs Oliver to let her have time, "Time to get over that feeling there's something evil in me." Later in the film, after the two have quarreled about Alice, Irena claims, "Never let me feel jealousy or anger. Whatever is in me is held in, is kept harmless when I am happy." Just as Marya wants desperately to be cured, Irena wants desperately to avoid hurting Oliver. Both women need to, nay want to, be human; they want to be normal women by society's standards. Sympathy is a key ingredient in the early horror films when it comes to vixens. As both *Dracula's Daughter* and *Cat People* demonstrate, women—even when they are the film's villains—cannot be truly evil. Unlike the male villains, these women want to be discovered and stopped. Whether they openly admit their monstrosity or not is irrelevant. What is important is that these women did not choose their fate and now do not want to be monstrous. Because they are women, these characters cannot be truly despicable. The dominant ideology of the time could not imagine a purely evil woman, so even the rare female villain is tempered by her own extreme dislike of what she has become.

Another element these two vixens have in common is their deaths. Both Marya's and Irena's deaths can be attributed to men who want to use them. Marya is killed by Sandor who wants to become a vampire. When she refuses to make him one and says she is going to change Jeffrey instead, Sandor gets angry and evil. Irena commits suicide after her psychiatrist, Dr. Judd (Tom Conway), tries to force himself on her because he is both attracted to and fascinated by her. By having aggressive men kill or attack the female villains, both films demonstrate that these women, even though they live on the margins of humanity, must still succumb to a dominant man. Their fate is the exact same as that of their victim counterparts.[2] This imprisonment within patriarchy for both the victim and the vixen will continue well into the 1990s. In fact, it is only with the advent of the female monster hunter that women finally are able to break through their gender stereotypes. It takes a woman who can embrace both her victim (feminine) and vixen (masculine) sides to finally leap towards an entirely new set of gendered ideals.

Before moving closer to this leap, there is one more early female horror film character who deserves discussion: Nina (Greta Schroeder) from F. W. Murnau's *Nosferatu* (1922). Nina comes closer to Stoker's Mina than any other female character of the first half of the twentieth century. At the film's beginning, Nina is shown first playing with a kitten on her windowsill and then doing needlepoint, both of which are traditional feminine acts. In addition, she is clearly distraught when her husband, Jonathon (Gustav von Wangenheim), must leave her to go to Transylvania. Before leaving, Jonathon makes sure that Nina is safe by having her stay with friends. It would seem that Murnau is setting Nina up to be the traditional victim because she is certainly acting like, and being treated like, a child — someone who needs protection.

However, Nina is more aware of Jonathon's dangers than even Jonathon himself. On the second night of his stay in Count Orlok's (Max Schreck) castle, the vampire visits him and Nina enters a trance. The scenes cut between Orlok entering Jonathon's room and Nina sitting up in bed. As Orlok gets closer, Nina walks out on to her terrace. When Orlok leaves the room, Nina falls back on the bed. The intertitle which follows claims, "The doctor laid Nina's trances to some unknown disease. Since then I have learned that she had sensed the menace of Nosferatu that very night. And Harker, far away had heard her cry of warning." At this point, only Nina knows of the danger Orlok poses. Of all the characters, she is the wisest. Her connection to her beloved Jonathon gives her a clear agency that mirrors Mina's own after she has been bitten and infected by Dracula's blood. Despite this mirror, however, it is important to note that Nina's connection is with her husband, not the monster. In making this vital distinction, Murnau emphasizes that Nina is in no way tainted with monstrosity. This purity will be vital for the film's climax and Nina's status as monster hunter.

Nina's knowledge is not confined solely to her psychic bond with her husband. If it were, she would not move slightly into the realm of masculinity. Her knowledge also comes from her reading of Jonathon's *The Book of*

Vampires. Even though Jonathon has asked her not to read it, she does and learns, "Only a woman can break his [Nosferatu's] frightful spell—a woman pure in heart—who will offer her blood freely to Nosferatu and will keep the vampire by her side until after the cock has crowed." When Nina goes against her husband's wishes, she takes on agency and a bit of aggression—both male tendencies in early horror narratives. In fact, only when she embraces both her feminine (her dreams) and masculine (the book) sides can she know how to save her town. As Matthew Brennan states in his article on *Dracula* and *Nosferatu*, "In fact, Nina is the only character in *Nosferatu* to achieve full knowledge of the vampire, and significantly she acquires it through a combination of both conscious research—reading *The Book of Vampires*—and close attention to images of her unconscious" (5). In addition, the purity that was mentioned earlier comes to bear on her ability to be a monster hunter. Had she been linked to the vampire, she would not be able to be the film's savior.

When Nina watches the coffins being carried down the street—thus showing the viewer that Orlok has brought Bremen a terrible plague—she knows that she must become the monster hunter. In this moment she chooses her fate, even it if means her death. During the night Nina is awoken by Orlok calling for her. She struggles between his summons and Jonathon's love. Finally, she wakes Jonathon and sends him for Van Helsing, thus allowing Orlok time to enter her bedroom. As the vampire drinks her blood, the shot cuts to a shot of a rooster crowing. The sun rises over Bremen and Orlok turns to ash. Jonathon arrives and Nina's last words are his name; she dies in his arms. Brennan claims, "[I]f Stoker's Mina becomes a victim of Dracula unknowingly and unwillingly, Murnau's Nina decides consciously to sacrifice herself, and through this willed act she achieves the kind of psychological effect that Jungians and mythographers like Joseph Campbell often ascribe to heroes" (5). Nina is clearly this film's hero and monster hunter. Beyond narrating the film, Van Helsing plays only a small role in the film and Jonathon is virtually useless. Only Nina has the power and knowledge to fight the vampire.

Yet, while she is ascribed such an important role, it comes at a price: Nina must die. Brennan argues, "[S]he dies, in a sense, for opposing society, as happens to many New Woman characters..." (7). Marya and Irena could be considered New Women, as can all vixens, but they must die. Nina is saved from viewers ascribing her death to punishment because of her purity. She selflessly kills herself to save the world and that is much different than being killed because of her sexuality. She never treads too far into the masculine-gendered attributes of power and sexual dominance, so she is rewarded for her femininity with the utmost of motherly sacrifices: she saves an entire town, not just her immediate family. In this case, death may not seem like a reward, but her selfless death is. Nina is only the second female character to achieve a relative balance between feminine and masculine attributes. Like Mina Harker in Stoker's novel, this balance makes her another forerunner of the contemporary female monster hunter.

Women of the Slasher Films

The Final Girl may be one of the most problematic characters in horror and feminist studies. For every critic who sees the character as a strong female there is another who claims that she is a construction of a misogynistic subgenre. To help define the Final Girl and determine her place within the monster-hunting culture, I turn to Carol Clover's oft-quoted book, *Men, Women, and Chain Saws*. I see the Final Girl as the mother of the contemporary female monster hunter; yet, at the same time, I do not see her as an actual monster hunter. Unique to the slasher genre, the Final Girl recognizes the danger she is in and manages to fight back. As Clover explains,

> She is the one who encounters the mutilated bodies of her friends and perceives the full extent of the preceding horror and of her own peril; who is chased, cornered, wounded; whom we see scream, stagger, fall, rise, and scream again. She is abject terror personified. [...] She alone looks death in the face, but she alone also finds the strength either to stay the killer long enough to be rescued [...] or to kill him herself [35].

Clover's own definition demonstrates the problems of this character: she is "abject terror personified" but she also has great strength within her. The Final Girl, then, is one of the first horror women to contain almost equal amounts of both the victim and the vixen within her. This is an important marriage of characteristics and one which makes it so difficult to label the character.

No Final Girl better establishes the combination of victim and vixen than Laurie (Jamie Lee Curtis) from John Carpenter's *Halloween* (1978). I do not want to rehash what Clover has already said of Laurie. Instead, I want to discuss how she is both victim and vixen. For those who may not know, *Halloween*, is about a psychotic killer named Michael Myers (Tony Moran) who chooses Halloween as the day to break out of his psychiatric hospital and attempt to murder his little sister, Laurie. Unaware of this brother and his plans, Laurie has plans of her own for the evening: babysitting. In a sequence of shots that cut between an approaching Michael and

Laurie's day at school, viewers learn that Laurie takes her responsibilities very seriously. While her friends are talking about using babysitting as a cover to be with their boyfriends, Laurie remains quiet. Already the viewer knows who is set up as the obvious victim (Laurie) and who are the obvious vixens (her friends).

Several elements of the victim are at work here in Laurie. First, there is a clear sense that Laurie does what is expected of her as a woman. She will not neglect her duties to spend time with her friends. She is responsible and fits the ideals of a patriarchal culture. As Clover reminds us, viewers identify with the character who holds the gaze. For much of the film, Michael Myers is the character through whom viewers see Laurie. Therefore, Laurie is to be looked at; she is certainly not the one doing the active gazing. More importantly, Laurie is also filling the role of the surrogate mother in *Halloween*. This role is set up immediately within Laurie's first five minutes on screen. On her way to school, Laurie runs into Tommy (Brian Andrews), the boy she is going to babysit. He asks her questions like, "Can we make a jack-o-lantern" and "Will you read me a story?" Laurie answers "sure" to all of his questions, just as the ideal mother would. Laurie even agrees to watch Lindsey (Kyle Richards), one of her friend's wards. Later, she will put both Tommy's and Lindsey's safety before her own. In fact, she refers to them as her "babies" and has them lock themselves in a room while she fights Michael. When she thinks it is safe, she tells Tommy and Lindsey, "I want you to go down the stairs and out the front door. I want you to go down the street to the McKenzies' house. I want you to tell them to call the police and tell them to send them over here." At this point in the film, Laurie is what E. Ann Kaplan labels "The Heroic Mother." She is certainly "suffer[ing] and endur[ing] for the sake of [...] children" and "she acts not to satisfy herself but for the good of the family" (468). What makes Laurie's actions all the more impressive is that she is not the children's biological mother. She is selflessly sacrificing herself for children not even related to her. These actions certainly place Laurie within the ideal framework of a victim.

However, as with all Final Girls, there comes a time when Laurie moves from victim to vixen, when she commands the gaze and controls the action. As Clover comments about this moment, "By the end, point of view is hers: we are in the closet with her, watching with her eyes the knife blade pierce the door; in the room with her as the killer breaks through the window and grabs her; in the car with her as the killer stabs through the convertible top, and so on" (45). For Laurie, this scene occurs when she attacks Michael through the closet door. At this point, Laurie is the monster. She has taken

Michael's role from him, even if it is only for a moment. This move from victim to vixen is vital to the evolution of the female monster hunter. It demonstrates that women can move smoothly, almost seamlessly, between the two gender stereotypes. More importantly, this move is comfortable to the viewers. Whereas viewers of *Dracula's Daughter* may have had difficulties digesting a female vampire — sympathetic though she may be — there is no disgust or backlash for the Final Girl. She is merely doing what anyone in her situation would do. By making this gender transition the norm to horror viewers, slasher films pave the way for the female monster hunter who embraces both gendered attributes at once.

While most horror fans think of movies like *Halloween* and *A Nightmare on Elm Street* when they think of slasher films, there is a sub-genre of slashers that also must be taken into account in the discussion of the evolution of the female monster hunter: the rape-revenge film. These films are certainly not easy to watch and are closer to pornography than horror, but they must be mentioned in a discussion of the Final Girl. When the woman in a rape-revenge film is raped, she is stripped of her femininity. If she survives, what is left for her? Masculinity. These women leave all sense of being a victim behind when they take revenge on their attackers. As Clover comments, "[F]emale self-sufficiency, both physical and mental, is the hallmark of the rape-revenge genre" (143). Self-sufficiency is not typically a feminine trait but a masculine one. Clover goes further, "And yet even this most body-based of genres manages to complicate the sex-gender system — especially on the side of the victim-hero, whose gender is clearly coded feminine (at least in the first phase of the story) but whose sex, it seems, is up for grabs" (157). The character's ambiguity gives her the power to defeat her rapists. As such, the rape victim moves entirely into the realm of the vixen and, more importantly, tends to stay there without repercussion.

The quintessential rape-revenge film is *I Spit on Your Grave* (1978). The film begins when a New York writer, Jennifer (Camille Keaton), decides to rent a summer home on a lake to write her novel. Viewers know things will go badly for her when she encounters a sneering, lecherous mechanic, Johnny (Eron Tabor), at the local gas station. While he pumps her gas, his two friends, Stanley (Anthony Nichols) and Andy (Gunter Kleeman), hold a knife-throwing contest. She tells Johnny that she is staying alone at one of the lake houses. Things go well for Jennifer at first, but while she is sunbathing on the lake in her canoe, Stanley and Andy come by in a motorboat, grab the canoe's rope, and pull her to a wooded area. Joined by Matthew (Richard Pace), a fourth friend, the four men proceed to rape her: twice in the woods and twice back at her home. Jennifer survives the trauma — Matthew is sent back to kill her but cannot — and decides to take her revenge. She seduces and kills both Matthew and Johnny: Matthew is strangled as she hangs him from a tree and Johnny bleeds to death after she cuts off his penis. After their two friends mysteriously disappear, Stanley and Andy come after Jennifer in the motorboat. She stabs Andy in the back with his ax and slices Stanley up with the boat's motor.

At first glance, it may seem as if Jennifer is entirely a vixen with no remaining feminine vestiges. Two of the most powerful scenes in the film do show Jennifer in complete control of the gaze, the motorboat, and Andy's weapon, all masculine-coded elements. As she comes after Andy, she has one hand on the boat's motor and the other holds the ax high above her head. The viewer watches as she comes right at the camera but then the viewer watches as Andy is killed. Although the viewer is placed in the role of victim for a brief moment, in the end it is Jennifer who controls the gaze, thus giving her complete control of the scene. The other scene shows Jennifer leaving the final murder scene. The camera follows her as she speeds down the lake in the motorboat. She has taken control of the very tool used to choreograph her rape. The canoe is useless — the vehicle of her femininity — and the motorboat has become a tool for her masculinization. Like the Final Girl, Jennifer has commandeered the murder weapons — literally castrating with her phallic tools (a knife and an ax) — and the gaze.

However, despite her masculinization at the film's end, Jennifer is still ensconced in her femininity; she, like other horror women before her, cannot break free from her specified gender role. The biggest demonstration of this adherence to gender stereotypes is her rape. She is the epitome of a victim while the men repeatedly hold her down and rape her. She has to be utterly degraded before she can recognize her strength. This certainly is not a new idea. Mina goes through a similar experience in Stoker's *Dracula*. It is only after Dracula forces Mina to drink his blood, thus making her a vampire, that she becomes a true monster hunter. Like Jennifer, Mina finds strength in her "rape" and is able to move on to monster hunting. In addition, Jennifer does something unique before her revenge: she enters a church, kneels and crosses herself, and asks forgiveness. In doing so, she aligns herself to both Marya and Irena as a sympathetic monster. She does not want to do what she is planning but sees no other course of action. Because the viewers are aligned with Jennifer throughout the film, the forgiveness is necessary for their continued sympathy. As Clover comments, "The female victim-hero is the one with a backstory and the one whose experience structures the action from beginning to end. Every narrative and cinematic device is deployed to draw us into her perceptions — her pain and humiliation at the rape, her revenge calculations, her grim satisfaction when she annihilates her assailant" (152). Since the viewer has been aligned with Jennifer from the very beginning, he will accept her strength and her revenge so long as she is not an evil person at heart.

In both the traditional slasher and the rape-revenge film, the Final Girl character must negotiate both the feminine and masculine spheres set by society. There is no doubt that these women do horrific things to their attackers. When they commandeer the phallic weapons and turn them on the film's monsters, they themselves become the monster. These women move from victim to vixen. Yet, even at their most monstrous these characters still elicit a sense of sympathy from the viewers. Like the early Hollywood vixens, they cannot help what they have become and regret their monstrous actions. What does this say about feminine power? Is there even a feminine power or is the term an oxymoron? If regret and guilt—two stereotypical feminine attributes—accompany these women as they are monsters, does that make them weaker than their male counterparts? These are difficult questions to answer. When it comes to early horror films and slasher films, there may not even be an answer. Because there were no strong female monster hunters at this time, these films had to create them. As such, the filmmakers had to carve out a new type of female role. In some ways—as with the movement between genders for the Final Girl—they succeeded in moving their female characters forward. In other ways—with Marya's and Irena's deaths, for example—they simply bought into the old ways of doing things. But whatever criticism these texts receive, they do, importantly, pave the way for female monster hunters. These texts, with their complicated victims and vixens dichotomy, become the inspiration for the new type of character who regendered the genre.

Regendering

The contemporary female monster hunter must be able to blend the power of the vixen with the humanity of the victim. Likewise, she must embrace both the Final Girl's rational fear (the fear of death which compels her to fight) with the power of the fearless victim from the rape-revenge film. This is certainly no easy task and it was not one for writers and filmmakers before the 1990s. Society just could not accept a truly feminized hero before then. This new character was not even a possibility until the advent of a new mindset toward women; that advent came with the third wave of feminism. The creation of Mina Harker came at the time of the New Woman, or first wave of feminism. The slasher film arose in the 1970s, the time of the second wave of feminism. Because these films reached their apex of popularity in the 1980s, they also experienced the repercussions of the second wave's backlash. The 1980s were a difficult decade for women; they were criticized for being outspoken and chided for their feminist ideologies. Those women wanting to have both careers and families were the target of much of this backlash, according to Susan Faludi, author of *Backlash: The Undeclared War Against American Women*. In talking about films from that decade, Faludi argues, "In so many of these movies, it is as if Hollywood has taken the feminist films and run the reels backward. The women now flee the office and hammer at the homestead door. Their new quest is to return to traditional marriage, not challenge its construction; they want to escape the workplace, not remake it" (126). In many ways, Laurie is permitted to live because she is the "good" girl. She is smart, she is resourceful, but she is neither sexually active (an ideal characteristic for a future wife and mother) nor particularly rebellious. She embodies the ideal woman who remains pure and passive, at least to some extent. It is her connection with the idealized wife and mother of the era that makes her palatable to an audience experiencing the beginning of a backlash against feminism.

Luckily, the backlash of the 1980s led to the third wave of feminism. According to Irene Karras, third wave feminists are those who were born after 1960 and who "came of age in the eighties and nineties" (par. 2). Her short definition of third wave feminism states, "[T]he second wave focused on changing women's social role; and the third wave's challenge is to ensure the rest of the world changes to keep up with women's changed roles" (par. 6). In other words, the third wave's challenge seems to be to avoid another backlash. It is up to the next generation, those women and men in their thirties and forties, to make sure that the media, the politicians, and the public do not slide back into the belief that women are happier at home. It is this desire to avoid another backlash that I believe gave birth to the contemporary female monster hunter as we know her today. Women's roles are changing in society and they need to change in horror as well. As long as she remains within the realm of either vixen or victim, the female horror character is easily classified. However, when female characters dare to move beyond these traditional gender stereotypes, they find themselves in a tricky position. Are they to be read as feminine, masculine, or as something new? Because of their refusal to play by traditional gender roles, female monster hunters are fraught with ambiguity, thus demonstrating that gender roles are never rigid.

One of the reasons why female monster hunters are so difficult to categorize is because, like their male counterparts, these women refuse to be held to an either/or dichotomy. Just as the male monster hunter is neither and yet both a monster and a hero, the female monster hunter is neither and yet both feminine and masculine. Reading these characters as an amalgamation of both is not unusual if we understand that gender is an act. According to feminist theorist Judith Butler,

> If one "is" a woman, that is surely not all one is; the term fails to be exhaustive, not because a pregendered "person" transcends the specific paraphernalia of its gender, but because gender is not always constituted coherently or consistently in different historical contexts, and because gender intersects with racial, class, ethnic, sexual, and regional modalities of discursively constituted identities [3].

Later in this chapter, Butler reiterates her argument that gender is nebulous: "[W]hat the person 'is,' and, indeed, what gender 'is,' is always relative to the constructed relations in which it is determined" (10). Butler understands that traditionally rigid labels such as feminine and masculine do not effectively reflect a person's gender. The context must be considered and, even then, it must be understood that gender is always already in flux.

Carol Clover also recognizes that gender is not rigid. However, she does believe that gender dictates action in the slasher film. As such, she sees a certain rigidity to the gender labels:

> The fact that female monsters and female heroes, when they do appear, are masculine in dress and behavior [...] and that male victims are shown in feminine postures at the moment of their extremity, would seem to suggest that gender inheres in the function itself—that there is something about the victim function that wants manifestation in a female, and something about the monster and hero functions that wants expression in a male [12–13].

Clover is not arguing here that heroes must be male and victims must be female. Instead, she insists that in the slasher film, masculinity is associated with the hero and femininity is associated with the victim. This argument contends that when the Final Girl becomes the monster's killer, she drops all pretense of femininity and becomes masculine in nature. Yet, why does the Final Girl have to be a specifically-gendered character? When male victims are shown in feminine postures, this does not necessarily mean that they have become entirely feminine in their gender. Likewise, when the Final Girl assumes a masculinized persona to kill the monster, she is not entirely masculine. Instead, these two characters are both at the same time. Whether an asexual tomboy or not, the Final Girl is always going to be a female character. If she takes on masculine attributes to survive, this does not necessarily mean that she is no longer feminine.

Even Clover seems to recognize the problems with the gendered hierarchy she proposes. Later in the same chapter she admits, "If *Psycho*, like other classic horror films, solves the femininity problem by obliterating the female and replacing her with representatives of the masculine order [...], the modern slasher solves it by regendering the woman" (59). The key here is that the Final Girl is regendered, thus making her more palatable to the slasher's target audience: the teenage boy. But why does this regendering need to take place? Because society has upheld this male-hero/female-victim dichotomy for so long, it is difficult for the male viewer of the slasher film to believe that the beautiful damsel in distress could save herself from the big, scary monster. To get around this perceptional dilemma, slasher filmmakers have created a character who is "a physical female and a characterological androgyne" (Clover 63). The Final Girl is acceptable because she is not entirely feminine or masculine. This kind of regendering may have seemed unimaginable to early horror audiences, yet glimpses of it have always been present. The tainted blood which infects Mina, the steely determination taken on by Nina, the sympathy for both Marya and Irena, the motherly qualities of Laurie, and the forgiveness asked by Jennifer demonstrate that these monstrous women—these vixens—still maintain feminine qualities even when they hold power. The regendering Clover discusses has its roots even as far back as the sexual repression of the Victorians.

This ability to be both genders at the same time is exactly the analytical direction Judith Halberstam travels in her discussion of the Final Girl. Halberstam also sees the character as regendered: "[I]mproperly or inadequately gendered bodies represent the limits of the human and they present a monstrous arrangement of skin, flesh, social mores, pleasures, dangers, and wounds" (141). Like her fellow posthumanists, Halberstam refuses to see the Final Girl as a binary: instead of an either/or gendered character, she is a new creation, one which will not succumb to traditional and societal boundaries between human and monster. In saying that the Final Girl is a "monstrous arrangement," Halberstam is not necessarily insisting that she is physically ugly. Rather, Halberstam argues that she is a new being, neither masculine nor feminine but, rather, "a gender that splatters, rips at the seams, and then is sutured together again as something much messier than male or female" (143). While Halberstam's regendering is specific to the Final Girl, the theoretical direction she takes can be applied to the female monster hunter as she is both monstrous and heroic, while at the same time distinctly feminine in appearance.

Lieutenant Ellen Ripley: The First Contemporary Female Monster Hunter

No female character better demonstrates Halberstam's regendering than Ellen Ripley (Sigourney Weaver) from the *Alien* franchise. These films span almost twenty years: *Alien* (1979), *Aliens* (1986), *Alien³* (1992), and *Alien: Resurrection* (1997). The franchise takes Ripley from a product of the second wave of feminism, through the backlash of the 1980s, and up to the regendering of the 1990s to become the first true female monster hunter.

In *Alien*, a salvage crew is awoken from hypersleep by a distress call. Three members of the crew go down to the planet LB426 to investigate. Once there, they find an alien life form. When Kane (John Hurt) is attacked by one of the creatures, the crew returns to their ship. Ripley, the commanding officer on the ship, refuses to let the three in because they need to remain in quarantine. She knows this difficult decision could lead to Kane's death but insists on following protocol despite being told otherwise by Captain Dallas (Tom Skerritt), who is with the landing party. Unfortunately, the science officer, Ash (Ian Holm), lets the three on to the ship. Within these few opening sequences, Ripley's decision is overridden by two different men. Although she is clearly correct in her decision—proof of which comes when an alien springs from Kane's stomach, grows up, and begins to kill off the crew—she is merely a woman and, despite her rank as lieutenant, can be easily pushed aside. For the remainder of the film, Ripley is the Final Girl. She alone manages to keep her wits about her long enough to save herself. Throughout the action she even demonstrates a little of the necessary maternal instinct when she risks her own life to go back and save Jonesy, the ship's cat. *Alien* does not necessarily do anything different for the Final Girl or the female monster hunter. Its importance, however, is in the creation of Ripley's character. Her strength, intellect, and maternity are all set up in this film so that the other films can see her grow.

In *Aliens*, Ripley's character really comes into her own. Found in hypersleep in her escape ship fifty years later, Ripley is blamed for the *Nostromo*'s destruction. (Ripley blew up her ship to kill the alien on board.) She takes the fall and picks up her existence on Earth. The company she worked for refuses to believe her story until people at the newly-created mining outpost on LB426 start disappearing. A man from the company, Burke (Paul Reiser), comes to her and asks for her help. The company is sending out a team of soldiers to look for survivors. This moment is where Ripley becomes a true monster hunter. She can refuse Burke's offer and remain on Earth with Jonesy; no one would fault her for her fear. However, as the only survivor of an alien encounter, Ripley has the knowledge needed to help the combat unit survive and she knows it. Rather than remain in safety, Ripley chooses to go to LB426 and lend her expertise.

This time around Ripley is not the only female monster hunter. One of the soldiers is a woman: Vasquez (Jenette Goldstein). While Ripley maintains her femininity — as will be seen — Vasquez is utterly masculinized. Immediately upon waking from hypersleep, Vasquez proceeds to do several pull-ups and clearly puts a great deal of stock in her muscles. In addition, she is not at all feminine in her appearance. Those muscles with her fatigues, short, spiked hairdo, and bandana all lend an air of masculinity to her. As if her appearance were not enough, Director James Cameron has her using the group's biggest weapon: a gun which stands in as an oversized phallic object. The most gung-ho of all the soldiers, Vasquez cannot wait to fight the aliens. In many ways, Vasquez represents the extreme to which the female monster hunter can go, utterly shedding one gender role for another. She is there to temper Ripley's own masculinity so that Ripley becomes more palatable for the male audience.[3]

At the beginning of the mission, the combat unit dismisses Ripley and her experience. However, once they encounter the complex alien hive under the surface of the mining town they begin to respect her suggestions. After the unit's sergeant is killed and their lieutenant proves useless, Ripley easily moves into the role of leader and proves her ability as monster hunter. As Thomas Doherty claims in his article on the franchise, "In *Aliens*, Ripley's aggressive self-sufficiency and ruthless logic is even more pronounced, more of a contrast to the men around her who freak out or freeze in the face of danger. [...] Quick-witted and courageous, she makes the tough decisions, initiates dramatic rescues, and assumes natural leadership over the macho squad" (194–195). Like Van Helsing in Stoker's novel, Ripley leads the young men and woman into a fierce battle with the monsters. She demonstrates Mina's "man's brain" in the way she maneuvers herself and her team in an attempt to escape the planet and save as many lives as possible in the process. She quickly learns the team's guns and soon manages to put two guns together into an even more efficient weapon. All of these elements demonstrate that Ripley is a true monster hunter.

Yet this film was released in a time of backlash against feminism. The tempering I spoke of earlier in terms of Ripley's gendering comes not entirely in her looks — although she is clearly made to look more feminine than Vasquez — but in her maternal instincts. There is one survivor of the mining colony: a young girl named Newt (Carrie Henn). Ripley discovers her and becomes her surrogate mother. For the remainder of the film, the girl rarely leaves Ripley's side. When Newt is taken by an alien, Ripley risks her life to save the child. According to Doherty, "Ripley is no Amazon. Tempering Ripley's masculine strength and assertiveness is her maternal devotion to the girl Newt [...] In comforting and protecting Newt, Ripley assumes a less threatening, more familiar female role" (195). Just as Laurie takes on the role of surrogate sacrificial mother, so too does Ripley in *Aliens*. To be a palatable monster hunter, then, a woman must never forgo her maternal side. This idea is begun in *Alien* with Ripley saving Jonesy and carried into full-blown theme in *Aliens*. In addition, Ripley has a love interest in the sequel: Corporal Hicks (Michael Biehn). During the backlash, women could not stray far from the ideal gender role put on them by patriarchy. Vasquez does and she fails to survive the film. Ripley, however, forms her own nuclear family unit with Newt and Hicks and becomes an acceptable female monster hunter. Although she actively pursues the alien — with Hicks taking orders from her — and saves what is left of the original military group, she comes out of the battle a pseudo wife and mother. As Doherty argues, "Investing the tough cookie with maternal longings created a kind of gender equipoise, balancing the harsh male proclivity for violence with a softer, feminine nurturing side. [...] Newt gives Ripley a culturally permissible way for a woman to fight and kill, not for her own satisfaction or career advancement but for her children" (195).

Alien[3] begins to move Ripley out of the backlash and into the regendering called for by Halberstam, yet the film also has its problems. Once again opening during hypersleep, Ripley, Hicks, and Newt's ship crashlands on Fury 161, a planet being used as a penal colony. Unfortunately, it turns out that there was an alien on the ship and its acidic blood leaks through and damages the ship. Ripley is the only survivor of the crash and finds herself in a refining plant full of men who are murderers, rapists, and thieves. As can be expected, the alien stowaway survives as well and starts killing the inmates.

The first thing that happens when Ripley awakens is a defeminizing process. Because of lice, she must shave her head. Her bald head serves two purposes. First, it makes her less appealing to the men who have not seen a woman in quite some time. Second, it allows her to blend in with those men. In addition, Ripley is given the same baggy, bland clothing as the men.

Carol Clover claims that the Final Girl is androgynous while I argue that she is still, and always will be, feminine. With *Alien*[3]'s Ripley, viewers have a character who is not feminine in her appearance. There is nothing about her appearance that would identify her as a woman. In addition, she eventually takes a leadership role over the inmates and tells them what to do to kill the alien. When she leads the men, she again has few, if any, feminine traits. But unlike Vasquez, who is a hyper-masculinized woman, Ripley just is. She is neither feminine nor masculine in the film.

This is not to say that some of Ripley's actions are not feminized. Her remorse over Newt's death reminds the viewer of Ripley's status as surrogate mother. Her sexuality is never in question either. Ripley seduces Dr. Clemens (Charles Dance)—the first time in three films that she has sex. A group of men also attempt to rape her, thus reminding viewers that even though she looks like the inmates, she is not one of them. In this way, it is difficult to determine what Ripley is in this film. She is certainly the regendered hero Halberstam refers to but she is also a sexualized being; she is both victim and vixen. In this regard, Doherty maintains, "*Alien³* can't decide whether it wants to eroticize or de-sex her, to celebrate her for being assertive or chastise her for being uppity" (196). I would argue that Ripley's gender is confusing because the filmmaker is trying to etch out a new gendering for her, one that goes beyond traditional notions of female and male. Why can't Ripley look like the inmates without sacrificing her sexuality? Does she show weakness when the inmates try to rape her? Perhaps viewers and critics have such a difficult time with Ripley because she is the first of her kind: a monster hunter who has managed to transcend gender boundaries.

While there may be questions as to Ripley's outward gender and actions, there are never questions about her maternal instinct. About halfway into the film Ripley discovers there is an alien in her, a mother. Rather than being in her chest cavity, as is normal, this alien is growing in Ripley's womb. Ripley may have been a surrogate mother to Newt in *Aliens*, but now she is a biological mother to an alien. Yet instead of wanting to protect her baby, Ripley refuses to unleash it on the world; her priority is to save humankind. The Company learns that Ripley has an alien inside her. As she backs away from Bishop (Lance Henriksen), the man they send after her, he promises her they will save her so she can have a normal life and maybe even have children. This offer does not sway Ripley. Instead of going with the company, she falls back into a vat of molten iron clutching the alien to her womb. Doherty sees this final action as problematic: "Her alert intelligence and active initiative cannot be contained by marriage, the conventional wrap-up for female-centered narratives, yet neither can she be unleashed to roam free in an uncharted feminist galaxy" (198). I would disagree. Ripley is not being punished here. Instead, she is doing what all monster hunters do: she is sacrificing herself to save the world. As will be seen, the female monster hunter is often willing to ignore her own personal happiness if it means that all of humanity can be saved, even if only for a short time. By embracing her nurturing instincts—seeing all of humankind as her children—Ripley is not punished for her gender transgressions; instead, she is embracing all gender traits that make her who she is: an intelligent, sexual, mother who is neither masculine nor feminine and yet is both.

If Ripley sacrifices herself in *Alien³*, how is it that she returns in *Alien: Resurrection*? Ripley has been cloned in an attempt to harvest the alien in her womb. After seven attempts, scientists finally succeed. They pull out the alien mother in a caesarian-section and then allow her to lay eggs. The eggs then spawn aliens which are allowed to infect a group of kidnapped miners. Of course, the scientists believe they can control the adult aliens and are quickly proven wrong. It is up to Ripley and a crew of space pirates—the same ones who kidnapped the miners—to destroy the aliens on the ship bound for Earth.

In this film, Ripley moves forward in her evolution. In addition to maintaining her gender transcendence, Ripley also achieves a level of posthuman traits. While she gives the alien a few human qualities, the alien gives her a few of its qualities. For one, Ripley possesses great speed and strength. Both of these characteristics make her masculine. Her embrace of both feminine and masculine traits appears in the scene where the pirates first meet Ripley. She is shooting hoops and one of the pirates—Johner (Ron Perlman)—comes on to her. He is clearly trying to show his sexual dominance by standing right up next to her in a pose of sexual intimidation. At first Ripley appears to return his sexual advances but soon outmaneuvers him and embarrasses him in front of the crew. Although she seems to demurely accept his sexual advances, it turns out that Ripley is as much the aggressor here as Johner, if not more. In addition to her speed and strength, Ripley's blood is acidic. The acidic blood demonstrates her connection to the aliens. Also, it demonstrates her move away from humanity; she is not like the humans on the ship. This difference is one which should not be forgotten for it also gives her a certain sympathy with the aliens which makes her, at first, a very reluctant monster hunter. In *Alien: Resurrection*, the very traits that make Ripley such a strong monster hunter—her ability to be both masculine and feminine—are combined with a stronger connection to the monster than even Linda Williams can imagine.

In the end, Ripley's ambivalence towards the human race is changed by another posthuman character: Call (Winona Ryder), a second-generation cyborg made by first-generation cyborgs. Cyborgs are not new creations to Ripley. Ash in *Alien* is one, as is Bishop (Lance Henriksen) in *Aliens*. In *Alien: Resurrection*, Call proves to be the most humane of the characters despite being a robot. She joins the pirate crew to gain access to the science ship so she can kill the aliens. She cannot imagine what will happen if the aliens escape. Whereas Ripley turns her maternal instincts, at first, on her alien offspring, Call uses her maternal instincts to try and save the world. Meanwhile, the pirate crew (all human) want nothing more than to get their money and save their own hides while the scientists (also all human) foolishly believe they can control the aliens and are completely ineffectual when the aliens escape. How interesting that the two posthuman characters end up being the most humane. At the film's beginning one scientist calls Ripley "a predator." By the end she is once again a monster hunter.[4]

The female monster hunter is a unique being who differs from her male counterparts and, in some respects, goes farther towards saving the world than they do. First, because women have always been monstrous, they do not feel a need to balance their record like the male monster hunter. As the Other in a patriarchal culture, women are often already somewhat in the abyss. When they become slightly monstrous — as Ripley does in *Alien: Resurrection* — they do not apologize. Ripley acknowledges that she is "the monster's mother" without regret and then moves on. The vixen of early horror texts has made the contemporary female monster hunter unapologetic of her stance beyond the borders of humanity. Second, these women recognize that all of humanity are their children. As such, self-sacrifice is always an option of last resort. They certainly do not wish to die, but the ideal of the sacrificial mother is never far removed from the female monster hunter's mind. Because they are willing to kill themselves, they never consider killing others for the greater good. No female monster hunter would make Ozymandias' sacrifice. Finally, the female monster hunter can do what the ubermensch cannot: she can overthrow patriarchal culture by refusing to give in to her idealized gender traits and roles. Instead, these female characters take the best of both masculine and feminine and use those attributes to their advantage. When these women refuse to live by patriarchal rules, they become empowered to chip away at the culture which made the rules. Ultimately, the female monster hunter will seek to make the world a better place by overthrowing her cultural bonds and giving all those considered Other a new opportunity at life.

The Contemporary Female Monster Hunters

Luckily, writers of fiction, television, and film caught on to Ripley's popularity. After her ability to be regendered proved a success, a few more female monster hunters popped up in popular culture. Anita Blake is the hero of Laurell K. Hamilton's book series about the undead. First appearing in 1993's *Guilty Pleasures*, Anita is an animator who can raise the dead. In a world of zombies, ghouls, and vampires, Anita is in a unique position. Her affinity with the dead—all dead, as she says—helps her determine whether a being is human or vampire. Because of her gift, she can avoid the mind games vampires like to play with the living. She is not easily controlled by their hypnotic gaze, so Anita becomes a vampire hunter. When the St. Louis courts issue a death warrant for a murderous vampire, Anita gets the call. The vampire community calls her the Executioner and with good reason. To date there have been fifteen Anita Blake books. For the sake of brevity, and to illustrate my argument that Anita is a monster hunter, I am only going to discuss the first two books: *Guilty Pleasures* and *The Laughing Corpse* (1994).

The first element of any female monster hunter is her appearance. Because she remains visually female, the character must weather criticism such as Cristina Lucia Stasia's of Lara Croft (Angelina Jolie) in the *Lara Croft* films: "The new female action hero [...] is neither masulinised nor muscularised. Rather she is hyperfeminised [...]. Clearly, this new female action hero is as titillating as she is threatening" (177), thus implying that a tough woman cannot also be sexy and beautiful. Yet, in a world of regendering this stereotype no longer holds true. Although readers must create their own image of Anita, Hamilton does provide some description like this one from *Guilty Pleasures*:

> I was wearing black jeans, knee-high boots, and a crimson blouse. My hair was made to order for the outfit, black curling just over the shoulders of the red blouse. The solid, nearly black-brown of my eyes matches the hair. Only the skin stands out, too pale, Germanic against the Latin darkness. A very ex-boyfriend once described me as a little china doll [11].

Anita should never be taken as a china doll. Despite her 5'3" frame, Anita is strong, intelligent, and quick. Even without her supernatural abilities she would be an admirable foe to anyone, male or female.

Anita does not apologize for her beauty and feminine qualities. She recognizes them as aspects of who she is, just like her animator ability is a part of her identity. Within her vampiric and patriarchal culture, Anita has managed to carve out a powerful niche for herself as a vampire killer, animator, and vampire expert. Traditionally these would be considered masculine attributes. Even St. Louis's vampire master, Jean-Claude, is a bit wary of Anita. When he attempts to make Anita his human servant (most humans are easily controlled by vampires and can be made into mindless servants), Jean-Claude learns that he cannot control this powerful woman. Because of her affinity with death, Anita can only be guided so far. Her strong will allows her to refuse Jean-Claude's commands. Her will, another traditionally male attribute, adds to her transgendered status. At the end of *The Laughing Corpse*, Anita is forced into raising a very old body. Instead of just raising that one, Anita raises every body in the cemetery, something only a very powerful necromancer can do. Having sent the bodies back to their graves, Anita sees Jean-Claude in the shadows and, after a brief exchange, asks him if he is afraid of her; his answer is only a shrug of his shoulders. Anita thinks, "He was afraid of me. It almost made some of this shit worthwhile" (291). No china doll could have done what Anita does in that cemetery. She proves to the most powerful male in St. Louis that she is even more powerful than he.

In Anita the victim and vixen come together to create the Executioner. Anita does not apologize for her nickname any more than she does for her femininity. Nor does she apologize for the role she must play to maintain that nickname, a role that requires her to be monstrous to "normal" St. Louis society. In addition, many people in Anita's world see animators as "bad" and, like most things people do not understand, are afraid of them. Because she is both an assassin and an animator, her society views Anita as living beyond the boundaries of civilization. Yet, Anita has her own self-imposed boundaries to live within. In her mind, it is one thing to raise the dead to resolve old business in a timely manner, which is what an animator does, but it is another thing entirely to rule over them and force them to do her bidding, like a necromancer — a line she refuses to cross until she is literally forced to do so in the cemetery or face death. Becoming a powerful necromancer is, for Anita, the same thing as falling into Nietzsche's abyss. After being forced into the role of necromancer, Anita knows there is something monstrous in her and acknowledges it. At the end of the exchange with Jean-Claude quoted above, Anita carries her friend, Wanda, out of the cemetery because Wanda will not allow Jean-Claude to touch her. Anita comments that Wanda's decision is "[a] choice of monsters" (291). But Anita also does not apologize to Wanda, even if she does not like the way Wanda treats her: "She jerked back at my touch. I guess I couldn't blame her, but it bothered me anyway" (290). When Wanda asks, "What are you?," Anita responds, "Today for the first time I didn't know how to answer that question. Human didn't seem to cover it. 'I'm an animator,' I said finally" (290). Anita understands that her monstrosity is simply who she is; she must either accept it and go on with her monster-hunting career or give in to Jean-Claude and all that is evil in St. Louis.

Anita's literary life has spanned over fourteen years and is still going strong. Hamilton's latest Anita Blake book, *The Harlequin*, was published in 2007 and she has another due out in 2008: *Blood Noir*. Anita certainly exhibits the many qualities that make up a female monster hunter: she is feminine in appearance, masculine in strength and power, refuses to care about the abyss, and wants to overthrow elements of her patriarchal culture. Although she may not be the fleshed-out monster hunter that exists in the Buffyverse, she is an important addition to any discussion of the female monster hunter.

The idea for *Buffy the Vampire Slayer* evolved out of Joss Whedon's interest in the slasher genre. In an interview with Beth Laski, Whedon explains that Buffy's origins came after years of watching slasher films in which "beautiful, vivacious blondes got themselves killed. I realized I wanted to see a movie in which the beautiful girl was the hero—that she was confronted and trounced [the monster]" (16). Buffy Summers is the outcome of that wish. Buffy is the Chosen One, the slayer. In every generation, there is a slayer who battles demons and vampires in order to make the world better, and when one slayer dies, another takes her place. This young girl—various episodes imply that slayers are almost always teenagers and rarely live through, or even to, their twenties—is supernaturally strong, heals quickly, and is quite agile. However, despite the superhero strength and abilities, the slayer is also very mortal and very much prone to the trauma of coming of age.

One of the biggest criticisms of Buffy is, oddly enough, her femininity. The costume designers on the show often dressed Buffy in the latest styles; this means she is often seen wearing miniskirts and low-cut or belly-baring (sometimes both) shirts. Going back to the Stasia quote I included earlier, it would seem that Buffy is to be titillating rather than feared. If we return even earlier in this chapter to Mila Bongco's comment that female comic book heroes do not seem to strike as much fear into the heart of a male villain, we might be led to believe that Buffy's wardrobe contradicts her power. However, we need to keep in mind that Joss Whedon knows and understands the female monster hunter. He clearly knows the character's history with the Final Girl, a character who often dresses in a conservative, and at times even dowdy, way. If Whedon truly wants Buffy to be the opposite of the traditional Final Girl, or at least move beyond the Final Girl, he would want her to not only act differently but also dress differently. Buffy's clothing, then, becomes not a way to attract male viewers but a sign of her refusal to mold herself to traditional genre and gender rules.

In addition to looking like a traditional vixen, Buffy also maintains the traditional vixen's sympathy: she did not choose to be a slayer. In fact, her birthright may make her more akin to the Final Girl than a true monster hunter because she never made the choice to be a slayer. In the show's opening episode, she expresses displeasure in her heritage when her new Watcher, Giles (Anthony Stewart Head), tells her about Sunnydale's vampires: "It's my first day [at a new school]. I was afraid that I was going to be behind in all my classes, that I wouldn't make any friends, that I would have last month's hair. I didn't think there'd be vampires on campus, and I don't care" ("Welcome to the Hellmouth"). The truth is Buffy does care. This complex commingling of desires—normalcy and slayer duties—is a constant source of anguish for Buffy. She wants desperately to wear miniskirts and become prom queen, but she realizes that her place is as a great monster hunter. When this woman fights, she is extremely powerful, but her personal battle is between her desire for what she considers a "normal" life and her duty. Eventually Buffy does, once and for all, make the choice to be a monster hunter. In the Season One finale, Buffy dies, albeit only for a moment. This death triggers the next slayer, Kendra (Bianca Lawson), who arrives in Sunnydale the following season. Once Kendra, and then Faith (Eliza Dushku)—who appears when Kendra dies—appear, Buffy has the chance to give up her slaying duties and have her ideal life. Her friends discuss it and her mother eventually encourages her to consider it. Yet, Buffy cannot. She is called to be a monster hunter and instead she searches for a way to be both slayer and young adult.

Whedon does not end his crusade for the female monster hunter with Buffy; he also gives the viewers Willow (Alyson Hannigan), Buffy's best friend and fellow Scoobie. At the show's beginning, she is a mousy girl with no superpowers but a vast intellect. Next to Giles, Willow becomes the "go-to girl" for knowledge and research. However, in Season Two, Willow picks up her own supernatural skill: witchcraft. The brainy, quiet girl of Season One slowly becomes a powerful monster hunter in her own right. She takes to magic so well that during Season Six she actually gets addicted to it. As we will see, when her girlfriend is accidentally killed, Willow uses her witchcraft for revenge, thus becoming the season's Big Bad and nastiest villain. In the first season, Willow is very much the traditional Final Girl; she could be Laurie's daughter. Over time, her self-esteem and power grow until she is a very powerful monster hunter. Her fall into the abyss in Season Six aligns her to some degree with the male monster hunter's plight for redemption, but she maintains her roots as both victim and vixen and turns her downward spiral not into a time for embarrassment but into one in which she learns something powerful about herself.

Finally, Faith completes Whedon's trio of powerful female monster hunters in his Buffyverse. She is the last to join Buffy and the one who, at first, may seem most monstrous. Faith is no ordinary slayer. She is a tough girl more prone to black leather than Buffy's favored miniskirts. Faith tries to fit in, but she cannot. Harboring jealousy towards Buffy and her perfect life, Faith turns traitor and works for Season Three's Big Bad. At the end of the season, the two slayers fight it out and Faith ends up in a coma. After waking, Faith wreaks havoc in Sunnydale for awhile and then leaves for L.A. where she meets up with Angel (David Boreanaz). It is Angel who convinces Faith to put her villainous past behind her and try to salvage her future. Because Angel sees in Faith a kindred spirit, and vice versa, he is the one who can help her overcome her personal demons. Like Call does for Ripley, Angel helps Faith regain her humanity.

Of the three characters, Buffy is the least monstrous and leads the most humane life. That said, she comes close to slipping into the abyss during the show's third season when Faith first comes to town. In many ways, Faith can be viewed as Buffy's darker side. Dressed in black leather, Faith is the eternal bad girl. After spending so much of her time as the good girl, Buffy uses Faith's arrival as an excuse to let loose. Soon, Buffy is dressing more like Faith and blowing off her friends to patrol with her fellow slayer. One night, Faith tells Buffy her motto: "Want. Take. Have" ("Bad Girls"). Faith then proceeds to steal weapons from a store, closely followed by Buffy. When the two are arrested by the police, they promptly escape from the patrol car. Then, when they are caught up in slaying, Faith stakes a human by mistake. Buffy yells for Faith to stop, but is too late. This scene is a parting of ways for the two slayers. While Faith continues her downward slide for a time, Buffy, turning back to her friends, sees her role as a champion for humanity. When she allows herself to abuse her powers, she immediately recognizes that the abyss is near and pulls back. Whedon is very clear in showing that it is Faith who kills the man, not Buffy. Although she feels guilty about the death for awhile, Buffy is reminded by Giles that it is not her fault. In many ways, this point in Buffy's life is akin to Browning's Mina telling Van Helsing that she, like Lucy, is monstrous. Van Helsing is sympathetic to Mina much as Giles is sympathetic to Buffy. Buffy has never been dangerously rebellious, like Faith, so her slight slip into the abyss is easily forgiven. Buffy and the Scoobies move on and she becomes a stronger monster hunter for it.

Faith, however, takes a bit longer to return from her abyss. Although she clearly regrets killing the man from the scene discussed above, she does not have a monster-hunting community to which she can turn. As a result, she instead turns to Sunnydale's mayor, the man's boss, and he uses her like a hired thug. After trying to kill Angel, falling in and out of a coma, and torturing Wesley (Alexis Denisof), Faith finally accepts Angel's help. In so doing, she once again aligns herself with a monster-hunting community. More than that, however, she also gives herself over to her society's humanizing apparatus: the law. Faith willingly goes to jail as part of her return to humanity. Yet, there is no sense that she sees prison as a place for rehabilitation. Faith does not need to be rehabilitated; rather, she feels the need to reconnect with her human side. Angel and prison do for Faith what Dr. Garth and Oliver can never do for Marya and Irena: they help Faith embrace both her victim and vixen sides. Unlike Angel's and Spike's (James Marsters) prison, their souls, Faith's prison is bricks and mortar, bars and cells, and her time there allows her to listen to her soul once again. Although she may not necessarily repent in prison, she at least recognizes that her powers should not be used for selfish purposes. After breaking out of prison to help Angel in L.A., Faith finally returns to Sunnydale to help Buffy and the Scoobies with the First Evil. When she arrives, Spike asks her why she did not break out of prison before this. Faith responds, "I stopped me. I got dangerous for awhile" ("Dirty Girls"). Although she may give herself over to society's humanizing apparatus, she is not controlled by it. She makes the choice to go to jail to think and she makes the choice to leave when the time is right. The patriarchal control of the law has no control over her. Granted, when Faith returns to Sunnydale she is not necessarily greeted with open arms; however, she is accepted back and acknowledged as a powerful ally. Other than Spike's question, she is not asked about her slip into the abyss, nor does she spend too much time worrying about her past actions. She has moved on from them, and understands that she is first and foremost a slayer. A monstrous past is only one small part of who she is.

Although Faith does commit murder, her slip into the abyss is nowhere near as all-encompassing as Willow's as she goes through the most dramatic change of the Buffyverse's three female monster hunters. When her girlfriend, Tara (Amber Benson), is shot and killed, Willow experiences deep pain and sorrow. As a result of her emotional distress, her magical abilities fly through the roof. After Tara's murder, Willow proceeds to the magic shop where she literally absorbs the magic from the black magic books.[5] When she needs a power boost, Willow goes to a local black magician and kills him, thus absorbing his power as well. All of the supernatural beings in Sunnydale can feel her wrath. With all this dark power, and her own anger, Willow physically takes on the traditional appearance of a villain: her eyes, hair, and clothing turn black. Buffy and Xander (Nicholas Brendon) try to stop her, but Willow is too powerful. Although they may agree that Warren (Adam Busch) — the man who shot Tara — deserves to die, they worry about Willow's humanity if she succeeds. Buffy explains, "We can't control the universe. If we were supposed to, then the magic wouldn't change Willow the way it does. [...] There are limits to what we can do. There should be. Willow doesn't want to believe that and now she's messing with forces that want to hurt her, all of us" ("Villains"). Her friends cannot save Warren from Willow, but they do try to save her from herself. After killing Warren, Willow tries to kill his two friends. Buffy and the remaining Scoobies do everything they can to keep Willow from the two innocents.

It is love that eventually saves Willow. Living in England now, Giles learns of Willow's power and comes running to Sunnydale. When he arrives, he brings with him a powerful coven's magic. The two engage in a magical showdown, but Willow finally gets the best of him and absorbs the coven's power. This is exactly what Giles hopes will happen. Suddenly, Willow can feel everyone on Earth and their suffering. Wanting to end that suffering, Willow attempts to destroy the world. Xander manages to save her by going to the cliff where Willow is trying to raise a pagan temple and telling her that he loves her: both the Willow from kindergarten and the scary, veiny Willow she is now. His love stops her and she collapses, sobbing, into his arms. As if to prove her return from the abyss, Willow's eyes, hair, and clothing turn back to their original colors. Although it is Xander who actually stops Willow, it is Giles's power that helps save her. As he explains, "The magic she took from me tapped into the spark of humanity she had left, helped her to feel again, gave Xander the opportunity to reach her" ("Grave"). Even though Willow commits murder and tries to destroy the world, she never truly loses her humanity. It is that glimmer of goodness which ultimately saves her from the abyss.

Willow spends the time between Seasons Six and Seven in England, training with the coven and learning to control her magic. For Willow, this is a period very much akin to Faith's brief stint in prison in that it allows her a time of self-reflection. Although she is very hesitant to return to Sunnydale, she finally does. Despite the fiasco at her return,[6] she is welcomed back. There is absolutely no mention of redemption. The times when she does refer to her brush with inhumanity, it is to poke fun at her transgression or as an example of why she now needs to keep her magic in check. Like Faith, she becomes more aware of her monstrous ability, but manages to keep it under control and uses it to her advantage. Willow is the most like Angel in that he, too, attempts to destroy the world, but she never feels the need to balance her record sheet. One could argue that this is because

Angel and Spike spend more time in the abyss, but I would argue that it is the female monster hunter's connection with and sympathy for the monster which allows her to accept her slip and move on.

Individually, these three women experience their own demons, power, and humanity. They attempt to merge their feminine and masculine attributes into a powerful combination. In her book *Action Chicks: New Images of Tough Women in Popular Culture*, Sherrie Inness comments that action women "can be rooted in stereotyped female roles but can simultaneously challenge such images" (6). Buffy, Faith, and Willow certainly challenge the traditional female roles, both in the horror genre and in their society as a whole. They dress provocatively, wield their power without remorse, and refuse to make amends for their wrongdoing. These women may adhere to society's humanizing apparatuses when necessary, but Whedon is always quick to remind the viewers that the women *choose* to adhere. Being more powerful than any mere human, each of these women could go entirely into the abyss and dominate the world. But they never do. Even when Willow attempts to destroy the world it is out of a misplaced empathy; she does not want others to suffer as she does. It is her grief and her desire to end grief for all people that dictates her actions. Frances Early argues, "[A]lthough Buffy is male-identified, she and her friends also partake of traditionally perceived female-gendered ways of thinking and behaving" (18). For these women, their "female-gendered ways of thinking and behaving" strengthen them and make them better monster hunters. When they embrace their empathy for the world — a feeling akin to the maternal nurturing instinct — these women become powerful forces ready to save their world not only from the short-term monsters but also from patriarchal control.

Throughout *Buffy the Vampire Slayer*, Buffy not only fights demons, but also fights the Watcher's Council. From the very first slayer, there has always been a Watcher's Council, a group that originated with the shadow men who created the first slayer, and continued throughout history to be primarily made up of men.[7] There is no doubt that Whedon intends the Council to represent patriarchy. The Council controls the slayer by monitoring her every move. In addition, they supply her with information only when they deem it necessary. These men are using the slayer for their own ends, although they justify this manipulation by claiming they are fighting a war against evil.

The first time Buffy refuses the Council occurs in "Graduation Day, Part 1" from Season Three. Faith has shot Angel with a poisoned arrow; only a slayer's blood will save him. When the Council refuses to help her, Buffy tells Wesley—her watcher after Giles's dismissal—that she is finished taking the Council's orders:

> **Buffy:** I don't think I'm going to be taking any more orders. Not from you, not from them.
> **Wesley:** You can't turn your back on the Council.
> **Buffy:** They're in England. I don't think they can tell which way my back is facing.

Wesley cannot believe that Buffy has the audacity to contradict him, an action he decries as mutiny; doing so means that she contradicts the Council's power. However, it is Buffy who holds the power here. Wesley can do nothing to stop her, nor can the Council. The only thing they can do in retaliation and to regain some level of control is to blame the whole thing on Wesley and fire him. Although this is only a first blow, Buffy continues her fight with the Council and, in Season Five, succeeds in completely destroying their patriarchal control.

The Council may believe they are fighting a war, but it is the slayer who is their general; without her, they have nothing, as is proven in the fifth season episode, "Checkpoint." Buffy is trying to fight a very powerful evil during the fifth season: the god Glory. No one in Sunnydale knows how to stop her. Quintin Travers (Harris Yulin), the head of the Council, appears in Sunnydale with a group of watchers, claiming to have information on Glory. He tells Buffy that they will give her the information only if she proves she is worthy enough by succeeding in a series of tests. Eventually, Buffy realizes that she is truly the one in control and tells Quintin, "You guys didn't come all the way from England to determine whether or not I was good enough to be let back in. You came to beg me to let you back in. To give your jobs, your lives, some semblance of meaning." No longer will the Watcher's Council be in charge of Buffy's life. This is the last time the Council tries to assert its power in Sunnydale. They can never wield the patriarchal domination they once did.

However, such episodes only demonstrate Buffy slaying her personal humanizing apparatus. In the final season of the show, in the finale in fact, Buffy and Willow manage to create a world that overthrows every last trace of the Council's power and saves an entire world of slayers. The evil to be destroyed in Season Seven is the First, an evil so ancient that it will take amazing strength to destroy it. The season begins with the First's minions killing potential slayers and their watchers. Eventually, the minions even blow up the entire Council, thus leaving the slayers without their patriarchal institution. Slowly, the potential slayers make their way to Sunnydale and to Buffy. Unfortunately, these slayers are not imbued with Buffy and

Faith's supernatural powers. In fact, these potentials are nothing more than frightened teenagers, running for their lives. For much of the final season, the Scoobies and the potentials are hunted. Here they are much more akin to the Final Girl than female monster hunters as they sit in Buffy's house, just waiting for the bad guys to arrive. But then, Buffy learns something remarkable: powerful women came before the shadow men. This realization gives her strength and helps her to stop doubting her choices and decisions as leader.

The First is trying to keep Buffy from a weapon, a scythe. When she finally finds it, Buffy feels as if the weapon is hers. There is power in the scythe, supernatural power. In "End of Days," Buffy learns that the scythe was made by women called Guardians. She meets the last of the Guardians, who tells her that the weapon was forged in secret and kept hidden from the shadow men who became watchers. And the women watched the watchers. This weapon was made specifically for the slayer to kill the First. The woman tells Buffy that the scythe and the Guardians are the last surprise. For Buffy, this surprise is a powerful one. It demonstrates that the Council does not know everything; they never held all the answers. In addition, it proves that the patriarchal order did not come first; long ago, and all along, women were and have been more powerful. She takes this knowledge back to the Scoobies and uses it not only to destroy the First, but also to deliver the final blow against the patriarchal hold of the Watcher's Council.

In order to succeed, Buffy will need the help of another powerful woman: Willow, who ends up being the most powerful character in the season finale; without her, the First could never be destroyed. Willow uses the power of the Guardians contained within the scythe to give every potential slayer power. Before going into the battle against the First, Buffy tells the gathered potential slayers:

> In every generation one slayer is born because a bunch of men who died thousands of years ago made up that rule. They were powerful men. This woman [Willow] is more powerful than all of them combined. So I say we change the rule. I say my power should be our power. Tomorrow, Willow will use the essence of this scythe to change our destiny. From now on, every girl in the world who might be a slayer, will be a slayer. Every girl who could have the power, will have the power. Can stand up, will stand up. Slayers, every one of us. Make your choice. Are you ready to be strong? ["Chosen"].

When Willow's spell succeeds, her girlfriend Kennedy (Iyari Limon) calls her a goddess, perhaps the most powerful feminine moniker of all. Although it is Buffy who delivers the final blow to the First, it is Willow who really turns the tide in the battle. These two women take the last vestiges of the patriarchal Watcher's Council and destroy them. Together, Buffy and Willow make all potential slayers equal slayers. Buffy's power becomes every potential slayer's power.

Buffy the Vampire Slayer's finale demonstrates the goal of third wave feminism on a large scale. The monster, patriarchy, is defeated by very strong women who are now all equals. As Irene Karras comments,

> Buffy would be the stereotypical last girl except that her friends are always left standing as well, and she saves not only herself at the end of each show, but all of humanity. [...] This marks a real shift in the genre that is distinctly third wave in its expression of the struggle against an inherited world of evil and the cooperation of women and men in addressing it [par. 13].

By embracing both their femininity and their masculinity, the female monster hunters of the Buffyverse are able to disrupt and disturb the patriarchal order of their world. These women do not just question the patriarchal order; along with their fellow third wave feminists, they shake its very foundation. Buffy, Faith, and Willow do exactly what Mina, Marya, Irena, and the Final Girl cannot: they break through the seams of patriarchy and construct a new identity for themselves which embraces both their masculine and feminine power. In doing so, these women become more powerful than their male counterparts. The Watcher's Council is right to want Buffy back with them, Faith deserves the respect of her fellow slayers, and Willow deserves to be called a goddess. These female monster hunters are ushering in a new millennium full of potential for all women of horror.

Thanks to characters like Anita and the Buffyverse women, there has even been a slight shift in the "tried and true" Final Girl. Although the Final Girl remains the same throughout most of the 1990s and into the new millennium, there is one slasher trilogy which begins to move the Final Girl from her traditional realm and into the realm of the contemporary female monster hunter: Wes Craven's *Scream* (1996), *Scream 2* (1997), and *Scream 3* (2000). These three films are all metanarratives of the very subgenre Craven helped launch into the mainstream in the 1980s, and they take a tongue-in-cheek look at the slasher phenomenon. However, *Scream*'s Final Girl is more akin to Buffy and Anita than Craven's own Nancy (Heather Langenkamp) from *A Nightmare on Elm Street*.

In the first two films, Sidney Prescott (Neve Campbell) is very much a traditional Final Girl; it is with *Scream 3* that Sidney becomes more of an active figure. The film begins in Hollywood on the set of *Stab 3*, the third film-within-a-film based on the murders surrounding Sidney. Someone is killing real-life Woodsboro people as well as members of the film's cast. Sidney, however, is safely away from all this, living in complete solitude in the mountains where she is protected by two alarm systems and a dog. While Sidney stays at home, Dewey (David Arquette) and Gale Weathers (Courtney Cox)—survivors of both previous *Scream* films-assist Detective Kincaid (Patrick Dempsey) in the murder investigation. Unfortunately, Sidney cannot remain removed from the events: she is soon contacted by the murderer and thus propelled once again into the action.

This time, however, Sidney does not wait for the killer to come to her. Realizing that she can help the police in their investigation, Sidney goes to Dewey and Detective Kincaid and offers to help catch the killer. While the typical Final Girl awaits her fate and fights only when provoked—just as Sidney has done in the previous two films—*Scream 3* shows a new, stronger Sidney; she chooses to fight on her own terms. Using his own tricks against him, Sidney is able to destroy the *Scream 3* killer. In the last of the *Scream* films, Sidney at least chooses to fight the monster, rather than waiting for the monster to come to her, thus making her more of a monster hunter than any of her Final Girl predecessors.

Sacrificial Heroines No More

Women in the horror genre are making strides towards overcoming the either/or dichotomy of victim and vixen. Yet, these strides are not without their consequences. In *Tough Girls*, Sherrie Inness claims, "[T]ough women are forced to walk a tightrope because they are impinging on male spheres of power. They must be perceived as neither too tough nor too weak and achieve what is an impossible balance" (20). Critics still have trouble with Buffy's and Faith's sexuality. They also occasionally chide Whedon for making Willow into a vamp with her tight outfits. Sometimes there is no pleasing audiences and critics. But these female monster hunters go further towards breaking gender stereotypes than any other women to date because they at least attempt a pairing of masculine and feminine qualities. Furthermore, these women do not even acknowledge they are being feminine in one moment and masculine in another. They move between gender roles seamlessly because they have a very important job to do: save the world.

In her article "The Cruelest Season: Female Heroes Snapped into Sacrificial Heroines," Sara Crosby argues that even the strongest female warriors are forced to sacrifice their lives in an attempt to make themselves less masculinized and more feminized, thus reversing the Final Girl's role. When discussing Buffy as sacrificial heroine, she targets Season Five's season finale when Buffy must kill herself to save both her sister and the world.

Crosby argues that before the female heroes sacrifice themselves, they must acknowledge three fundamental truths:

> First, like Eve, they bear a burden of guilt. [...] Tough female heroes feel guilt *because of* their heroism. [...] Second, the patriarchal community averts a collision with republican individualism by making women want to alienate their power. [...] They want to give it up and be "just normal girls," to let the men do the heroics. [...] Third, the only stable or pragmatic possible community is the patriarchal community [155].

At the end of Season Five, these three points may have applied to Buffy. But, looking back on the entire seven seasons, we can see that these points apply neither to Buffy nor to the other significant female monster hunters.

While Buffy, Willow, Faith, and Anita may not always appreciate their powers, they never feel guilty about them. They come from a history in which women are considered abject and other. Therefore, these women do not let guilt overpower them when they slip into the abyss. Yes, they recognize they have done wrong, but they do not dwell on this. Instead, they return to monster hunting with a passion. Their identity is interlaced with their power, and they realize that their power has consequences, but these consequences do not stop them from fighting. Buffy and Faith are always slayers just as Anita has always been able to raise the dead. If those powers get out of hand—if the female monster hunter becomes dangerous for awhile—so be it. That is a side effect of being powerful which the female monster hunter accepts.

Crosby believes that tough women want to give up their power and let the men be the heroes. To an extent, this may be true since even Buffy, in the first episode, would rather live a normal life and forget her slaying past. Unfortunately, she cannot because there will be no other slayer to take her place until she dies. After she dies and Kendra takes her place, Buffy could easily retire from slaying but chooses not to. In the end Buffy is the hero, not any of the men in her life. She is also aided by Willow and Faith who will not let their power be dominated by men. Likewise, the *Alien* franchise's Ripley always ends up controlling the men around her. Whether it is a commando unit, a group of felons, or a pirate crew, Ripley chooses to step up and be the hero. There is no indication that she would rather let these men lead her. None of the female monster hunters alienate their power for long and never do they give that power willingly to any men. If they did, they would not be monster hunters.

Finally, Crosby contends that the only possible community is a patriarchal community. Had she seen the final season of *Buffy the Vampire Slayer* before writing her article, Crosby would have known that patriarchy means little in the Buffyverse. Over and over again, Buffy and her friends manage to usurp patriarchy's power and assert their own feminist-driven control. These women do not let men control them. If that were the case, Faith would never have left prison, part of the patriarchal institution of law. Nor would Willow have been able to utilize the inherent female power of the scythe to topple the magic of the shadow men. No, these female monster hunters create their own female-centered world in which patriarchy is not a fundamental truth.

The contemporary female monster hunter is the culmination of almost a century's worth of potential—but never realized—female monster hunters. She is a little bit of the horror vixen, a little Mina Harker, a little Final Girl, and a little action chick all rolled into one. The female monster hunter understands her place in the world and that place is not on the sidelines, nor is it sitting at home waiting for the monster to attack. Ripley, Anita, Buffy, Willow, and Faith all demonstrate that we have entered a new period in both feminism and horror, one in which the woman will not stay home, safe from battle. In this era, women embrace who they are. The female monster hunter is both feminine and masculine and that combination is key to her survival and her success. She is able to transcend gender roles and boundaries and, in doing so, is capable of looking at the big picture. Without embracing all sides of herself, she could never question (and in some cases, even defeat) patriarchy. The female monster hunter is clearly a product of her time and her descendents will hopefully continue her battle and continue to save the world in years to come.

Chapter 5

MONSTER HUNTERS FOR THE NEW MILLENNIUM

"Hyde is love; love is a psychopath."

— *Jekyll*

Although he has long been a part of fantasy literature, the monster hunter has really only come into his own in the last few decades. Up until the 1990s, monster hunters were relegated to the sidelines to make way for the sexy monster and the beautiful victim. Thanks to a major shift in American thinking — brought on by Vietnam and Watergate — the monster hunter is slowly taking center stage. Because the world is a scary place full of unpredictable monsters, the public is drawn to unpredictable monster hunters. No time seems more unpredictable than the beginning of the twenty-first century. In less than a decade, the world has experienced shocking terrorism and unrest in the Middle East, ongoing genocide in Africa, and horrific natural disasters in Asia and the United States. According to Paul Wells, "The history of the horror film is essentially a history of anxiety in the twentieth century" (3). If this quote is true, and many horror critics would certainly agree with it, then it should come as no surprise that the monster hunter has been out in full force since the millennium's beginning. More importantly, since popular culture consumers are living in a time of such uncertainty and unrest, it should come as no surprise that the monster hunter is spilling over into several new genres.

The sci-fi/action films *Pitch Black* (2000) and *The Chronicles of Riddick* (2004) are one such franchise to focus on the contemporary monster hunter. The science-fiction aspects of the films do place them firmly in the realm of fantasy literature, but the focus on action within that setting places the films in a genre which has rarely seen a true monstrous monster hunter.[1]

In *Pitch Black* a ship crash-lands on an apparently deserted planet. All of the crew die but Carolyn Fry (Radha Mitchell). Fry and the surviving passengers set out to find water and a way to fix the ship. One of the survivors is a murderer named Richard Riddick (Vin Diesel). He is being transported by the bounty hunter Johns (Cole Hauser). Riddick is clearly the most powerful and dangerous man on the ship, which is probably why stowaway Jack (Rhiana Griffith) begins to idolize him. At first the survivors are curious about the deserted geology station they find, but then the planet's three suns are eclipsed and the dark-loving monstrous creatures of the planet come out to play. One by one the survivors are killed until only Riddick, Fry, Jack, and Imam (Keith David) are left. Riddick manages to save only Jack and Imam. In *The Chronicles of Riddick* the action picks up six years after *Pitch Black*. Riddick returns to Helion Prime—where he safely deposited Imam and Jack—to learn that an evil race of humans called Necromongers are about to land. Once they do, the people of Helion Prime are forced to convert or be killed. Riddick, however, cares only about saving Jack—who now goes by Kyra (Alexa Davalos)—who has been sent to the prison Crematoria. Riddick gets her out of prison only to have her taken by the Necromongers. When he goes to Helion Prime to confront the Necromongers' Lord Marshal (Colm Feore), he fulfills the ancient prophecy that only he can kill the man.

From *Pitch Black*'s beginning, Riddick is posited as an animal. Even Riddick himself considers his life as less than human. The opening lines are his: "They say most of your brain shuts down in cryosleep. All but the primitive side, the animal side. No wonder I'm still awake." Added to his connection with the primitive is an excellent sense of smell and hearing. Both of these heightened senses come about because of Riddick's eyes: he has silver eyes which allow him to see infrared images. Riddick sees more like an animal would see than a human. These animalistic sensibilities are reinforced in *Chronicles* when Riddick smells Lady Vaako (Thandie Newton) and says, "It's been a long time since I smelled beautiful." As if to further Riddick's comparison to an animal, David Twohy, *Chronicles*' director, includes a scene where monstrous hounds are released in Crematoria. While the inmates go running, Riddick stares one hound down. Another inmate watches as the hound lets Riddick pet it. Riddick tells the inmate, "It's an animal thing." All of these occurrences should lend an air of inhumanity to Riddick. Riddick thinks of himself as an animal and expects others to as well. However, these moments also serve to demonstrate that Riddick is not the monster he believes himself to be. Yes, it is clear that Riddick has some animal tendencies. However, in his case actions speak louder than his personality. While Riddick may claim to be an animal, he is never once inhumane. That said, viewers are to realize that Riddick does exist within the abyss. We do not know where Riddick was before the films — or even what he did — but this lack of knowledge is not important. What is important is the fact that, at the beginning, Riddick is thought to be the film's bad guy.

One of the main plot elements of both *Pitch Black* and *Chronicles* is the idea that Riddick may be a monster but there are worse monsters out there in the universe. In *Pitch Black*, the worse monsters are obviously the denizens of the planet who eat all humans. When Riddick is confronted by Fry, he comments, "All you people are so scared of me. Most days, I'd take that as a compliment. But it ain't me you gotta worry about now." Riddick is once again putting himself up as the bad guy but here he has a point: the creatures are certainly more dangerous than he is. By this point in the film Riddick could have easily killed all the crash survivors; he certainly does not need them to escape the planet. But Riddick has not killed anyone yet. A true psychopath without any feelings or emotions — or conscience — would have jumped at the chance to wreak havoc. Yet Riddick holds back; he controls whatever animal instincts he may have, thus making him appear less monstrous than he believes. While the creatures are clearly the film's true monsters, Riddick is also compared to his captor, Johns. David Twohy makes sure that viewers see Johns as no better, if not worse, than Riddick. Johns, a drug addict, steals drugs from the ship after the wreck. When a crewman is dying in agony, Johns refuses to give up his supply to make the crewman comfortable. Later, Johns tells Fry that he is going back on his deal with Riddick. Rather than setting Riddick free after they escape, Johns wants to kill him. Fry comments, "He hasn't harmed any of us. As far as I can tell, he hasn't even lied to us. Let's just stick to the deal." In addition, Johns suggests to Riddick that they use Jack as bait for the monsters since she is only a young girl. Surprisingly, Riddick refuses. (An odd choice for someone who claims to be an animal.) Who is the monstrous one here? Riddick may be a killer, but he is apparently an honest killer. To both Fry and the viewers, that fact is supposed to make a difference in their judgment of the two men. As the creatures eat Johns, no one mourns his death. Johns is clearly meant to be the bad human in this film. Even though Riddick threatens inhumane actions — as we will see later — he never follows through with them. Johns, on the other hand, is serious in his nasty proposals.

When Riddick is compared to more monstrous beings, his status as monster hunter is cemented. The previous monster hunters may save their societies from danger, but Riddick does them one better: he not only saves his immediate society from the monsters but he also manages to get them off the deserted planet. *Chronicles* further eliminates Riddick's monstrous status and elevates him to an even more blatant savior role. At the film's beginning, viewers are told of the Necromongers in a voice-over by Aereon (Judi Dench). After giving a brief background of this monstrous race, Aereon claims, "If we are to survive, a new balance must be found. In normal times, evil would be fought by good. But in times like these, well, it should be fought by another kind of evil." The image cuts from a ship-eye's view of a planet to Riddick running from mercenaries. It is clear that director Twohy wants viewers to recognize that Riddick is a monster. That said, once again the implication of Riddick's inhumanity is overshadowed by his actions. When he learns that Imam has issued the current bounty, Riddick is angry. When Riddick reaches Helion Prime, Imam tells him that the bounty was simply a way to get him there to fight the Necromongers. Riddick — always the loner — wants nothing to do with helping Helion Prime. His resolve melts just slightly when Imam's daughter Ziza (Alexis Llewellyn) asks, "Are you going to stop the new monsters now?" Animal or not, evil or not, Riddick once again recognizes that he is not the worst thing roaming through the galaxy. For him, total annihilation of the human race is unthinkable. It is not a stretch of the imagination to think that Riddick may like humanity in the same way a pre-soul Spike does: it is a fun place that lets him get away with most anything. Despite his outward refusal, Riddick most likely does care about Helion Prime, Imam, and the rest of the galaxy. When Kyra comments, "Shit. I hate not being the bad guys," she is echoing what Riddick might be thinking throughout both films.

This explanation is not to say that Riddick altruistically helps the crash survivors in *Pitch Black* and the inhabitants of Helion Prime in *Chronicles*. On the contrary, Riddick is an extremely selfish person and, like many contemporary male monster hunters at first, would never simply save the world for truly unselfish reasons. Riddick is like his contemporaries in that he needs a bit of motivation to move him from the abyss into the so-called light. In *Pitch Black*, Riddick agrees to help because he wants off the planet. He does not care about anyone, at first. It is the stowaway, Jack, who helps crack Riddick's veneer. Jack's absolute idolization of Riddick makes an impression on the man. When Jack is in danger, Riddick makes a point to go back and save her. There is no outward reason why Riddick connects with Jack, but he does. And this connection helps him make a major decision about his escape. When Riddick finally reaches the ship, he begins to prep it for take-off. Fry gets there and tells him she will not leave without Imam and Jack, who are hiding in a cave. Riddick tries to get her on the ship but she asks, "Come on Riddick. There's gotta be some part of you that wants to rejoin the human race." Riddick responds, "Truthfully, I wouldn't know how." When Fry tells Riddick she would die for Imam and Jack, Riddick responds, "How interesting," and goes back for them. At this moment Riddick has made the first steps towards joining the human race. We do not know how much Riddick's connection to Jack influences his decision in this moment, but given his attachment to her in *Chronicles* it must have some effect. While Riddick does not show any such connection to Imam, it is clear he likes Jack and, given this bit of dialogue, may be willing to die for her.

When Riddick returns to the ship with Imam and Jack, his move to humanity is made slightly stronger. He is helping Fry get on the ship when one of the creatures kills her. As she is pulled into the sky, Riddick yells, "Not for me!" It was Fry's willingness to die for Imam and Jack—two helpless humans—that gets Riddick to save them. However, in his mind it is not acceptable for her to die for him. He never sees himself as part of the human race. This lack of self-awareness is precisely what makes him a new member of humanity. His refusal to accept Fry's selfless action shows that Riddick has some type of conscience, or soul. Johns would have no trouble sacrificing Imam and Jack and he would not regret Fry's death. Riddick, on the other hand, does have a clear sense of right and wrong instilled in him from somewhere. Even though he may not give in to his society's humanizing ideals, he can recognize irony when it occurs. He cannot abide that Fry has died for what he considers to be an animal. In this moment Riddick is no longer an animal at all.

This glimmer of caring develops into a full-blown love in *Chronicles*. Once again it is Jack who connects Riddick to humanity. For six years Riddick has kept the mercenaries away from Helion Prime to protect Jack, for he knows the men would use her as bait to get to him. Once he gets to Crematoria and the two are face-to-face, Riddick learns that he should have stayed for Kyra instead of running. Kyra tells Riddick that she tried to find him. In her search, she joined a group of mercenaries who—by the sounds of it—were not very nice to the teenager. Although he is angry, Riddick is more upset at the knowledge that he is responsible for Kyra's downfall into the abyss. She is now a murderer, just like him. Once again, it is Riddick's grasp of the situation's irony that makes him humane. In this brief exchange, the viewer can also see that Riddick actually loves Kyra, but this love is not a sexual love. Instead, Riddick has adopted Jack as a little sister much like V adopts Evey in Moore's graphic novel. From the ending of *Pitch Black* to the end of *Chronicles*, Riddick is motivated not to simply escape the planet and stop the Necromongers but to save Kyra. She is his connection to humanity whether he recognizes it or not. In the end, it is her loyalty to him that saves Riddick. The Lord Marshal has turned Kyra into a Necromonger. This breaks Riddick's heart because he believes she has left him. He is no longer the ferocious warrior once Kyra turns; his heart is no longer in the struggle. However, during Riddick's battle with the Lord Marshal Kyra attacks the Lord Marshal and he flings her back into a spike. As Kyra dies, she tells Riddick that she was always with him. This realization that Kyra is no Necromonger gives Riddick the strength and motivation to kill the Lord Marshal.

Riddick is certainly not a "good" man in the traditional sense of the word. He is an animal who has done — we are told but not shown — horrific things. Yet, somehow this monster does manage a slight return to humanity. Through Kyra's love he moves out of the abyss and into humanity, even though he claims to not know how or, more importantly, to not care. Whether he actively realizes it or not, by saving Imam and Jack Riddick enters into a community and begins the road to humankind. Thanks to this connection, he also saves the entire galaxy, at least for the immediate future. Yet, while the other monster hunters in this study continue the battle, it is difficult to know what will happen with Riddick. The Necromonger rule is, "You keep what you kill." The final scene of *Chronicles* shows Riddick on the Lord Marshal's throne with Kyra dead at his feet. With his connection to humanity severed, it is difficult to say what will happen to Riddick. He now rules the Necromongers, which could make him more dangerous than ever. However, the viewer is left with a sense that Riddick may do some good on that throne. After all, it is Ziza's question that helps prompt some of his actions. When she asks if he is going to stop the new monsters he hesitates for a moment as if considering the child's question after refusing her father. After he returns to Helion Prime to fight the Lord Marshal, Imam's necklace is left on his front door for Ziza to find, another tender moment between the monster hunter and the child. Perhaps Riddick has moved farther into humanity than even he is willing to admit to.

Another character who hangs out on the fringes of humanity and is reluctantly drawn into an epic battle is John Constantine. John was first created by Alan Moore who used him in a Swamp Thing storyline. A very ambiguous human being with knowledge of the supernatural, John soon found himself in his own series, *Hellblazer*, initially written by Jamie Delano and drawn by John Ridgway. In 2005, a film adaptation appeared starring Keanu Reeves in the title role. Unlike most of Moore's creations, John Constantine managed to retain his moral ambiguity — although it was toned down a bit — and still appealed to mass audiences. According to the Internet Movie Database, *Constantine* had grossed $75 million in the United States within three months of opening and the film ended up making over $230 million worldwide. A little action and a little horror/fantasy, this film clearly appealed to a wide audience. The basic plot can be boiled down to a story about John himself. John Constantine is a man with a mission: he is trying to buy his way into Heaven. John was born with the ability to see demons and angels, something few others can do. As a teenager, John wants nothing more than to stop the visions, so he commits suicide. The doctors manage to bring him back to life, but not before John experiences the fire and brimstone of Hell, thus showing him that the visions are real. But now John has a big problem: according to the Catholic faith, suicides do not get into Heaven. Twenty years later, John knows exactly what awaits him after death, and he believes that if he completes enough exorcisms—sends enough demons back to Hell—he will be able to balance his books and go to Heaven.

However, John is running out of time: early in the film, he learns that he is dying of lung cancer. After meeting with his doctor, John goes to see Angel Gabriel (Tilda Swinton) to try and buy more time on Earth:

Gabriel: You're still trying to buy your way into Heaven?
John: What about the minions I've sent back? That alone should guarantee my entry.
Gabriel: How many times have I told you, that's not the way this works.
John: Haven't I served him enough? What does he want from me?
Gabriel: Only the usual: self-sacrifice, belief.

At this point, John does not realize what Gabriel is saying. He is still convinced that he can achieve redemption through selfish means. In many ways, John's actions as an exorcist are comparable to Angel's and Rorschach's actions as vigilantes. As long as these men are stuck obsessing over their own personal battles, they cannot move beyond this selfishness to embrace the full implications of monster hunting, which in many ways involves self-sacrifice.

To come to terms with his role as monster hunter, John must take the path of his contemporaries. First, John needs to move from his self-imposed alienation into a community. John keeps his fellow fighters at arm's length. In addition, there are times when it seems like he is using those friends for personal gain. For example, he allows Chas (Shia LaBeouf) to drive him around but does not connect with him in any other ways. Likewise, he uses Beeman (Max Baher) to track down religious artifacts and cough suppressant but never is overly friendly. It is almost as if John needs to keep these men at arm's length to protect both himself and them. It is difficult to understand the motive behind John's alienation. In the comic book, John's friends always end up dead so he tries not to connect with anyone. Then, to make matters worse, the ghosts of his friends—as well as other people he has gotten killed—follow him around. With such an unusual circle of groupies, it comes as no surprise that John wants to remain alone. However, there is no indication that this is occurring with the film's John. Instead, his refusal to connect with anyone makes him seem aloof and uncaring.

While it can be said that John does have a few distant friends, it is not until he connects with Angela (Rachel Weisz) that he moves towards his ultimate goal of redemption. It is Angela's desire to save the soul of her sister after her sister commits suicide. Like John, Angela's sister can no longer handle her visions. In Chapter 2, I argued that the humanity of a community is vital to a monster's transformation to monster hunter. When John allows himself to connect with Angela, he begins to share her quest, thus giving him an end goal that does not involve his own soul. In addition, John is infatuated with Angela. While there is no indication that the two are in love, there are hints that their relationship is more than just friendly, as when John flirts with Angela before helping her regain her visionary ability. Once his community is in place, it will help save John's soul and, ultimately, his life. With the help of Beeman, John learns that Satan's son is trying to be reborn so he can rule the Earth. If he succeeds, humanity will experience a Hell greater than anyone can imagine. The forces from Hell kill Father Hennessey (Pruit Taylor Vince) and Beeman to keep them from helping John. After their deaths, John is spurred on to help Angela and to save the world. He even finally allows Chas to assist him and mourns when his apprentice is killed. The fact that Satan's son wants to use Angela's body as a host even furthers John's mission. In John's case, his community does not do much to help him regain his humanity. Instead, the slow destruction of his community spurs him on to selfless monster hunting. This is a slight switch from what we have seen in other monster-hunting narratives, but could be a signifier of a new direction in the subgenre. To some extent, Imam's, Fry's, and Kyra's deaths truly propel Riddick on to moral judgment so maybe the death of community members is the new motivation for contemporary male monster hunters. This change would not be out of place given the aggression Americans have had towards countries like Afghanistan, Iraq, and Iran in the wake of the 9/11 terrorist attacks. Provocation by destroying a community rather than the desire to be a part of a community may very well become the new monster-hunting motivation.

John's connection to his community and his desire to save both Angela and the world from Satan's son leads to his moment of self-sacrifice and his epiphany. As Gabriel is about to kill Angela, thus releasing Satan's son, John does the one thing he believes will save her: he commits suicide, again. Lucifer (Peter Stormare) arrives to claim John's soul and John tells him about his son. When he learns the truth, Lucifer sends his son straight back to Hell and then goes for John. But first, he asks John what he wants as a reward. Instead of asking for his own life, John asks that Angela's twin sister be allowed to enter Heaven. Because Lucifer has control over those souls in Hell, he releases Angela's sister. This is John's self-sacrifice: he is willing to spend eternity in Hell to save another soul. John's reward is his redemption and he rises towards Heaven. However, at the last moment, Lucifer reaches into John's chest, removes all of the tar and thus the cancer, and tells John, "You will live. You will have the chance to prove that your soul truly belongs in Hell." Lucifer does not actually believe that John has learned anything and thinks he has merely given John more time to return to his previous selfishness. This slip back into the abyss is always a risk for contemporary monster hunters. Their personal monstrosities do not just disappear when they decide to take up the monster-hunting call. Their personal demons are constantly trying to rear their ugly heads. As a result, these characters not only battle the world's monsters but also their own. Will John eventually go to Heaven? The truth is that it does not matter. Just like in other monster-hunting narratives of the new millennium, nothing is guaranteed. What is important is that John has made the world a little safer for the time being.

Thanks to a couple of memorable characters, the twenty-first century has seen a continuation of monstrous monster hunters on the big screen. Because these films were made for and marketed to the masses, they bring a favorite horror type to a new audience. On television, a similar shift is occurring. Few outside the realm of horror or vampire aficionados were drawn to shows like *Forever Knight* and *Buffy the Vampire Slayer*. Such specialized shows in the occult are still a hard sell today despite *Buffy*'s critical success, and they certainly were not embraced before the 1990s on any wide consumer range. While vampires still may be few and far between on television, the monster hunter is growing ever more popular. Due to their naturally violent nature, these shows are found on cable networks, which give them smaller audiences, but their very appearance is a win for monster hunters everywhere.

The first show to put the contemporary monster hunter to the test was HBO's *Deadwood* (2004–2006). Set in Deadwood, South Dakota, in the late 1870s, the series follows the mining town through gold rushes and a move to statehood. The main character, Seth Bullock (Timothy Olyphant), is also the main monster hunter and he certainly embodies ambiguity. The opening scenes of the first episode show Bullock getting ready to leave Montana, where he is Marshall, for Deadwood. He has in the jail a horse thief. When a lynch mob comes for the man, Bullock decides to hang him from "under the banner of law" ("Deadwood"). Before he does that, though, he asks the man for last words and demands someone in the lynch mob deliver those words to the man's sister. When the man's neck remains unbroken, Bullock reaches up and pulls on his legs. Right from the show's beginning, Bullock is a contradiction. On one hand, he respects the law and upholds that law; on the other hand, he is a hard man willing to do whatever it takes to accomplish a job. This character clearly sympathizes with people but is also a man with a very high sense of responsibility. But helping a man to die as quickly and as painlessly as possible does not make Bullock a monster, the hallmark of the contemporary monster hunter.

What makes Bullock a monster is his mean temper. When angry he may beat someone almost to death. In Deadwood, Bullock meets Bill Hickok (Keith Carradine). After Bill is murdered by Jack McCall (Garret Dillahunt), Bullock goes to where Jack is being held and proceeds to strangle him for no reason other than anger and vengeance—certainly not something the law would condone. Although he tries to play by the rules, Bullock's extreme anger management issues often cause him to slip into the abyss. Bill's friend Charlie (Dayton Callie) tells Bullock, "You got some of Bill's qualities but then you got something he's missing. Get along with people, turn a dollar, look out for yourself. He don't know how to do that" ("Deep Water"). It is difficult to determine the qualities Bullock and Hickok have in common. Given what viewers are shown in the first few episodes, the qualities could be respect and a sense of justice. However, those qualities could just as easily be a sense of righteousness and a need to avenge either oneself or others. Either way, the implication is that Bullock has a conscience and an honest concern for others. He may act out in his anger, but then he feels great regret for his actions. Of the twenty-first-century monster hunters, Bullock is the quickest to feel remorse and clearly yearns to be free of his own personal monsters. After nearly killing Jack, Bullock then decides to see him safely to his trial in the Territory. Monstrous though he may be, Bullock honestly tries to avoid the abyss. One of the elements that helps him avoid the abyss is his connection to the law. When Deadwood needs a sheriff, Bullock at first refuses. In the Season One finale, a visiting general tells Bullock, "[I]n a camp where the sheriff can be bought for bacon grease, a man, a former Marshall who understands the danger of his own temperament, might consider serving his fellows" ("Sold Under Sin"). Bullock chooses to put his demons to work for the greater good and starts protecting the community.

When it comes to Deadwood's monsters, Bullock is really the least of the town's worries. Upon arriving in Deadwood, Bullock must contend with Al Swearengen (Ian McShane) who runs the mining community with an iron fist. The saloon owner is a force to be reckoned with. If he wants someone killed—and he often does—no one even tries to oppose him. As godfather of Deadwood, Al believes himself above the law and above Bullock. In Season Two's final episodes an even greater threat arrives: George Hearst (Gerald McRaney). Hearst uses even dirtier tactics than Swearengen to get what he wants. While Swearengen may never balk at murder, in his mind the murders are necessary to protect himself and Deadwood. Hearst, on the other hand, is motivated purely by greed.

Because both Bullock and Swearengen actually care about Deadwood, they team up to rid the town of Hearst. One would assume that this pairing is like the other monster-hunting team of Angel and Spike. Yet, it is very different. While it is true that Bullock and Swearengen are monstrous monster hunters trying to defeat Deadwood's bigger evil, they are the first of their kind to actually fail. In the last episode of the show, Hearst finally gets the gold mine he wants and leaves the town. In addition, he has succeeded in buying enough votes to ensure Bullock's defeat as sheriff in the upcoming election. Although Deadwood itself still stands, Hearst has rendered its most formidable monster hunter impotent. It is unclear what will happen to Swearengen — presumably his life will be business as usual — but viewers are left watching Bullock's back as he walks home to a life that no longer includes the law.

This loss is surprising given the contemporary monster hunter's usual short-term success. While there is never a guarantee that the monster hunter's world will remain safe for long, he is always shown as successful. Bullock's defeat here may be indicative of a new trend in monster-hunting narratives, one more in line with the current state of affairs in the Middle East. Although *Deadwood*'s creator and writers could not change history by killing off George Hearst — the show always featured some level of historical accuracy — they did not need to highlight Bullock's defeat so brilliantly. The show's finale implies that no matter how much right may be on a monster hunter's side, he is not infallible. Sometimes the monster will be bigger, smarter, nastier, and better. This message is certainly a difficult one for viewers to take, but does mirror the seemingly no-win situation in the Middle East. Just as the slasher's chaotic monster seemed to continually triumph in the years following the turbulent 1970s, perhaps the twenty-first-century monsters will start defeating their monstrously heroic foes.

This morbid view of the future may not sit will with more optimistic viewers and fans of monster-hunting narratives but seems a potential outcome for a genre that has sometimes mirrored historical trends. *Deadwood* is the first to allow such an outcome and is presently the only with such a dramatic conclusion. Only time will tell if more monster hunters will see their defeat at the hands of more villainous monsters. One of the nice things television has always offered the monster hunter is a chance to evolve. Over the course of several seasons a monster hunter can reinvent himself, as was seen with the long-running *Buffy* and *Angel*. Another show that is currently experimenting with reinvention is Showtime's *Dexter* (2006-) which is giving its viewers the most unusually inhumane monster hunter yet: Dexter Morgan (Michael C. Hall).

Dexter is a blood-splatter expert for the Miami Police Department. He should be an expert, because in his spare time he moonlights as a serial killer. Yet, Dexter has standards for his victims. He only murders people who deserve it; people who are themselves monstrous (i.e. pedophiles, rapists). Through flashbacks, viewers are introduced to Dexter's deceased adopted father, Harry (James Remar). When Harry — a Miami cop — realizes that Dexter is "different" (Dexter has been killing animals), Harry teaches Dexter to control his impulses. When those impulses become too much to handle, as Harry knows they will, Harry teaches Dexter how to kill without getting caught. More importantly, it is Harry who instills in Dexter what the serial killer calls the Code of Harry. In "Popping Cherry," Harry tells Dexter, "When you take a man's life you're not just killing him. You're snuffing out all the things he'll ever become. [...] Killing would serve a purpose otherwise it's just plain murder." Dexter lives by the Code of Harry and manages to escape detection.

One of the interesting elements of *Dexter* is that Dexter lives entirely in the abyss; more importantly, he knows he lives in the abyss. Dexter believes he has absolutely no soul. In the first episode, Dexter makes two revealing comments. The first is, "My name is Dexter, Dexter Morgan. I don't know what made me the way I am but whatever it was left a hollow place inside" ("Dexter"). As the season progresses, viewers learn that when Dexter was a small child he witnessed his mother's brutal murder, along with the murders of several others. After two days, Dexter is found by Harry sitting in blood. Although he was only three when the horrific murders occurred, the experience has clearly caused Dexter to become a murderer. It is Dexter's "hollow place" that makes him believe he is inhuman. More importantly, Dexter's "hollow place" keeps him from truly connecting with humanity. Like Riddick, Dexter does not know how to make this connection. Again it is Harry who helps his son cope, knowing that being a loner can be a warning sign for criminal behavior. Throughout the first season viewers see flashbacks showing Harry telling Dexter to smile at family outings and to ask a girl to a dance, things Dexter has no desire to do and no understanding of. The other contemporary monster hunters like Nick Knight and Angel can hide themselves from the world to deal with their inhumanity. They are vampires and really do not have to be "human" at all by conforming to society's standards. Dexter, on the other hand, must live in the world despite his lack of humanity. Dexter's dilemma of living in the abyss but having to pretend to live within humanity's borders is one of the great traits Dexter gives to the twenty-first-century monster-hunting narrative. As the series progresses, viewers really experience Dexter's quandary along with him, making them more aware of the monster hunter's plight.

Even without wanting to be human, Dexter has a clear mission as a monster hunter. As Dexter goes about the murder of a pedophile in the very first episode, he tells the man, "Soon you'll be packed into a few neatly wrapped Hefties and my own small corner of the world will be a neater, happier place. A better place" ("Dexter"). This murder is the first glimpse viewers have of Dexter and it is an important one. Within the first moments of the first episode viewers understand that Dexter, although a murderer, is not entirely a bad guy. Like Riddick, Dexter is a different kind of evil from Miami's "true" evil. Because he is himself a monster, he knows how to track down and catch others of his kind. And because he works outside the parameters of society's humanizing apparatuses, he is more effective than the police — the humane and traditional monster hunters around him. In the episode "Let's Give the Boy a Hand," the Ice Truck Killer leaves Dexter a victim ready for the taking. However, Dexter lives by the Code of Harry and calls the police. Later Dexter says, "My new friend thought I wouldn't be able to resist the kill he left for me. But I did. I'm not the monster he wants me to be. So I'm neither man nor beast. I'm something new entirely. My own set of rules." It is Dexter's own set of rules that makes him so effective; unfortunately, it is this set of rules that also forces him to live outside humanity. In the Season One finale Dexter envisions what life would be like if people knew about his secret. Because he only kills monsters, Dexter envisions a ticker-tape parade (of sorts) with everyone applauding him. Sadly, he acknowledges the truth that all monstrous monster hunters must face: the majority of society, encased within their humanizing apparatuses, would never accept him and would see him only as a monster.

Despite his own recognition of living outside the bounds of humanity, there are moments when Dexter does dangle a toe into the world around him, and it is the love of his community members that brings him closer to humanity. The second revelation Dexter gives in "Dexter" is, "I don't have feelings about anything but if I could have feelings at all I'd have them for Deb." Deb (Jennifer Carpenter) is Harry's biological daughter. Like her father, Deb is a cop with the Miami Police Department. Deb clearly loves Dexter and sees him as an amazing big brother; obviously she has no idea that he is a serial killer. Since Harry is dead, Deb is Dexter's only family. And while Dexter may believe he has no true feelings for Deb, Dexter will find, just like Riddick, that his actions speak louder than words. Throughout the show's first season, the Miami Police Department is trying to track down a serial killer called the Ice Truck Killer. So is Dexter. This killer knows Dexter's secret and Dexter is intrigued. The killer turns out to be Rudy (Christian Camargo), Deb's boyfriend. More importantly, Rudy is Dexter's biological brother and his murderous ways are also a result of being held in a bloody cargo container for two days. In "Born Free," the Season One finale, Dexter—with Rudy's help—remembers his childhood. He is now torn between Rudy and Deb, whom Rudy has bound and prepared for murder. Dexter is torn between a brother who accepts him as he is and a sister he must hide from. In the end, the Code of Harry prevails and Dexter kills Rudy, claiming it is for Deb's safety. Whether he acknowledges it or not, Dexter does feel something for Deb. He could have easily let her go, but he does not. In "Popping Cherry" Dexter claims, "But there was something Harry didn't teach me, something he didn't know, couldn't possibly know. The willful taking of life represents the ultimate disconnect from humanity. It leaves you outside, forever looking in, searching for company to keep." His actions in "Born Free" show that Dexter is much closer to his community—and, by extension, humanity—than even he realizes. Dexter could join Rudy and fall entirely into the abyss but chooses not to.

The other person who helps Dexter connect to humanity is his girlfriend, Rita (Julie Benz). Deb introduces the two and Dexter pursues his usual mock relationship with Rita. At first, Dexter likes this victim of domestic violence and abuse because he says that she is broken, just like him. As the relationship progresses, Rita heals and wants to have sex with Dexter. At this point, Dexter is wary because all his other relationships have failed when he cannot connect with a woman during sex; he believes it is the moment they get a glimpse that he is not "normal." During this episode Dexter masquerades as a therapy patient to catch a murderous psychiatrist. His sessions help him have a breakthrough and he and Rita's relationship actually strengthens after sex, at least from Rita's point of view. Truthfully, it is difficult to say how much of Dexter's relationship with Rita is just an act and how much is real. There are no moments with Rita where Dexter must choose to be a monster or human, at least not to the extent he does with Deb. But Dexter's sexual breakthrough definitely implies that Rita affects him in a way no other woman ever has. When he is with her and her children, he is a different person.

Because *Dexter* is an ongoing show at the time of this writing, it will be interesting to see how his character develops. Of all the contemporary monster hunters, he is the most self-reflective and the most self-aware. He lives by a clear monster-hunting creed and tries to use his own inhumanity to make his world safer. Despite his self-proclaimed nothingness, he still has glimmers of humanity. In "Return to Sender"—the episode where he almost gets caught—he has his very first nightmare and claims, "When I sleep, all of me sleeps. Nothing ever goes bump in Dexter's night. I've never felt a moment of remorse, doubt, regret. What's happening to me?" It is possible that what is happening is a move towards his culture's definition of human. In the final moments of this same episode Dexter says, "I realize now my days are numbered, so I better make the most of them." Immediately following this revelation he grabs Rita's son to play. Some people argue that if one plays a part long enough, that person will actually become the person he is playing. It is possible this phenomenon is happening to Dexter. Serial killer he may be, but Dexter has a clear purpose in life: he is a monster hunter. Perhaps along the way he will also become human.

Among male monster hunters there have been some interesting developments, both in film and on television. Given the financial and critical successes of these texts, it is clear that mainstream audiences are beginning to embrace a monstrous monster hunter, which then allows the characters to move from fantasy literature into other genres with wider appeal. Parallel to a burgeoning appeal of monster-hunting narratives is an emergence of monster-hunter characteristics in other types of narratives. Two of the most interesting examples of these characteristics are the BBC television series *Jekyll* (2007) and J. K. Rowling's *Harry Potter*.

Although only six episodes in length, *Jekyll* epitomizes what it takes to make a contemporary monster hunter: love. The series follows Dr. Tom Jackman (James Nesbitt) on his quest to contain and control his alter-ego, Hyde (also played by Nesbitt). Jackman is the direct descendent not of Dr. Jekyll but of Mr. Hyde. Through flashbacks, viewers watch as Hyde slowly emerges. Unfortunately, Jackman's secret is not a secret at all. His whole life he has been watched and nurtured by the Institute, an organization that wants to control him. They use his wife Claire (Gina Bellman) as bait and think they manage to force Hyde to take control over Tom. However, the two entities work together to save Claire and their sons and, they believe, bring down the Institute.

The first important element at work in *Jekyll* that reflects the monster-hunting trend is love. At first, Tom sees himself as a different person from Hyde. Because Hyde cannot tell what Tom is thinking, nor does he have access to Tom's memories, Tom believes he is protecting his wife and sons. He never tells Hyde about his family. Yet, when Hyde learns of their existence, he does not hurt Claire and the boys. Tom believes that since Hyde is nothing more than a monster, he cannot understand love. In the final episode, Tom's mother (Linda Marlowe) contradicts this belief when she tells Claire, "Hyde is love; love is a psychopath" ("Episode 1.6"). The truth is that love is, and has always been, the key to Hyde's existence. In a flashback to Dr. Jekyll's study, Hyde learns that Jekyll (also played by Nesbitt) is transformed because of his fierce love for his maid, Alice (also played by Bellman), not a potion. Hyde is there when Jekyll comments, "Oh Alice. You're the only thing that keeps me here. Without you I'm just ... him" ("Episode 1.5"). In fact, in an earlier episode it is Claire who keeps Hyde from killing. When she finally learns Tom's secret and meets Hyde, she confronts him calling Hyde her husband and demanding that he realize it. Claire's love here tempers Hyde and moves him in a new direction. When Benjamin (Paterson Joseph), the man heading up Hyde's capture, tells Hyde that Jackman's family is Tom's weakness, Hyde responds, "Are you threatening *my* family [emphasis mine]?" ("Episode 1.3"). This is the first time Hyde makes any reference to the fact that he and Tom are one and the same. Until this point they consider themselves two different people. As he leaves Claire in the company of the men from the Institute, after killing Benjamin, Hyde says, "Gentlemen, if any harm should come to Mrs. Jackman, I will kill all of you one by one. And I shall take my time" ("Episode 1.3"). The brief moment of thinking of himself as Tom is over. But the viewer is left with the idea that Claire has made an impression on Hyde and that that impression could lead to something more.

Love being one of the main ingredients in the movement of monster to monster hunter, it is easy to understand Hyde's personification of love. Love is the main reason why monsters come out of the abyss. But love is a strong emotion. Tom's mother, before revealing the fact that Hyde is love, asks Claire the first time she realized she could kill another person. Claire responds that it is the day she had her twins. In that moment she loved someone so much she would do anything to protect him, thus demonstrating how Hyde can be so strong and ferocious. Although Hyde's killings may seem random, his killings do take on a purpose thanks to love, even if he does not know it. In one flashback viewers learn that Hyde first appears after Tom and Claire have a run-in with a street punk who sexually assaults Claire. Tom does nothing, but when Hyde appears he claims to want to hurt the punk without knowing why. Likewise, when Hyde first goes to meet Claire and the boys, claiming to be Uncle Billy, he only plays the night away. Although he does not consciously realize it, Tom's love for his family drives Hyde. Unfortunately — or fortunately when dealing with the Institute — this drive is taken to a brutal extreme by Hyde; he can do what Tom cannot. When Hyde tries to help Claire and the boys escape from the Institute, he tells her, "I'm so strong I walk through this funny little world of yours and I don't notice it. It bores me. But you, you Mrs. Jackman, you make me weak. I notice you" ("Episode 1.5"). But Hyde is not weakened by love. Ask any mother who has picked up a car or sprinted a long distance to save her child what love can do and she will tell you it gives strength, not depletes it. Like the other monster hunters, Hyde's strength comes from his love.

To truly become as strong as possible, Hyde and Tom must do what all monster hunters—especially the doppelganger type — must do: embrace both sides. Although the Institute truly believes they have suppressed Tom, Hyde digs deep into his psyche and finds his Other. When the two of them finally meet face-to-face they shake hands in agreement over their mission: save Claire and the boys. At this point Tom and Hyde are truly one, something that rarely happens in the Jekyll/Hyde narratives. When they reach this point, they learn that they can equally exist in one psyche yet keep the other from harm. (Tom realizes the cut Hyde receives does not appear on his hand.) As one person, they are stronger and faster than anyone else. More importantly, when sharing a psyche Hyde also has a conscience. In the final episode, Hyde sacrifices himself knowing that Tom will survive, as will Claire and the boys. In Chapter 2 I suggested an alternate reading of the end of Stevenson's novel where Hyde becomes a monster hunter by killing himself. It appears that *Jekyll*'s creator took a similar view of the ending. When Hyde kills himself so that Tom and his (both Hyde's and Tom's) family can live, he achieves the label of monster hunter.

While *Jekyll* is not a monster-hunting narrative per se, the elements of the contemporary male monster hunter clearly permeate the show. As of my writing there is no word whether the show will see a second season or not, but the final episode certainly opens the door. In the season's final scene, Tom goes to see his mother, who had abandoned him as a baby.

There he learns that it was she who passed on Hyde's genetic legacy and hints that Tom's Hyde may not actually be dead. In the final moments she turns into a Hyde of her own, the woman who runs the Institute. Is Tom's Hyde really gone? More importantly, is the Institute? Viewers are left with the possibility that he can come back. Given his strength and superhuman abilities, it is not a stretch to claim that Hyde may also possess regenerative abilities. If so, the two may find themselves with a second season in which they face even bigger monsters.

There is one more character who deserves mention in this section before I turn to the fate of the female monster hunter: Severus Snape. It took J. K. Rowling ten years to finish the Harry Potter series. For those dozen or so people who have not read or heard of the series, Severus Snape, the Potions Master, is Harry's main nemesis at Hogwarts School of Witchcraft and Wizardry. He continually gives Harry a hard time in class and enjoys deflating the boy's ego. Snape also works as a spy for Hogwart's Headmaster, Albus Dumbledore. Having once been a follower of the evil Lord Voldemort, Snape now works as a double agent. Throughout the entire run, readers were left wondering just why Professor Dumbledore trusted the Potions Master when no one else did. Over and over — in every book in fact — Snape does something to deter Harry, whether it is let Peter Pettigrew escape in *The Prisoner of Azkaban* (1999) or refuse to continue Harry's occlumency lessons in *The Order of the Phoenix* (2003). In fact, it even appears that Snape kills Dumbledore at the end of *The Half-Blood Prince* (2005). For readers, all of Rowling's hints pointed to the fact that this Dark Arts-lover never truly joined the good side and always worked as a spy for Lord Voldemort. So it was with bated breath that fans waited to see Snape's fate in *The Deathly Hallows* (2007).

In the end, readers learned that Dumbledore always knew what he was doing. Whether the revelation about Snape surprised fans or not, it did provide him a place among monstrous monster hunters. In one of the last chapters of *Deathly Hallows*, Voldemort kills Snape. Harry witnesses this murder and stands over Snape as he dies. Before he does, Snape gives Harry a memory, which Harry then views in the Pensieve. Through this memory Harry learns that Snape loved his mother, Lily. While Snape does, indeed, become a Death Eater — one of Voldemort's loyal followers — his love eventually brings him back to Dumbledore. It is Snape's ill-gotten information that causes Voldemort to kill Lily and James Potter. Snape's extreme guilt and regret at inadvertently killing his life-long love makes him loyal to Albus Dumbledore. This loyalty is strongest during the final moments of Snape's memory:

> From the tip of his [Snape's] wand burst the silver doe: She landed on the office floor, bounded once across the office, and soared out of the window. Dumbledore watched her fly away, and as her silvery glow faded he turned back to Snape, and his eyes were full of tears.
> "After all this time?"
> "Always," said Snape [687].

Severus Snape's petronus is the same is Lily's, thus demonstrating his unwavering love for her even after years have passed. For, in the wizarding world, a petronus takes on the form of the symbol of the person closest to you. Lily's own petronus was a doe so it makes sense that Snape's is as well.

Harry also learns that Dumbledore entrusted Snape with two extraordinarily difficult tasks. The first is to kill Dumbledore. After being cursed, Dumbledore knows he is going to die. To keep his wand from Harry, Dumbledore asks Snape to kill him so that the wand will be rendered useless. Snape protests, but Dumbledore makes him promise. This glimpse of the past explains why Snape becomes a murderer in *Half-Blood Prince*. Second, Dumbledore tells Snape that he must tell Harry that the only way to defeat Voldemort is to die. Snape balks at this, saying, "I thought ... all these years ... that we were protecting him for her. For Lily. [...] You have kept him alive so that he can die at the right moment?" (686–687). But, just as he does kill Dumbledore, Snape also gives Harry the news. This one chapter assures Snape's place as a hero in the wizarding world, not a villain. In the end, Harry recognizes that Snape's double life was a difficult one and names one of his sons Albus Severus: "Albus Severus [...] you were named for two headmasters of Hogwarts. One of them was a Slytherin [Snape] and he was probably the bravest man I ever knew" (758). Severus Snape may have seemed to be Harry's enemy, but in reality he was always Harry's begrudging protector, and he did it all out of love for Lily.

The male monster hunter is alive and well in all realms of popular culture, mainstream and non-mainstream alike. The character continues to grow and evolve thanks to love and an ever-emerging conscience. He is bringing in money at the box office and awards for the small screen.[2] However, mainstream artists and audiences of the new millennium do not appear to have the same interest in the female monster hunter. In the first decade of the twenty-first century only one true female monster hunter has emerged: Selene (Kate Beckinsale) from *Underworld* (2003) and *Underworld: Evolution* (2006).

Underworld follows the adventures of vampire Selene (Kate Beckinsale), a Death Dealer, or assassin. She is the adopted daughter of her coven's elder, Viktor (Bill Nighy). As a Death Dealer, it is her job to hunt and kill werewolves as the vampires and werewolves have been locked in battle for centuries. Selene must also deal with the advances of her coven's temporary leader, Kraven (Shane Brolly).[3] Selene is not attracted to Kraven, and his advances reflect a desire for power, not love; because of her connection with Viktor, having Selene as his mate would ensure Kraven's leadership role. While hunting two werewolves, Selene tries to save a mortal, Michael (Scott Speedman), from them. Unfortunately, he is bitten anyway. In the film, memories can be passed on when one supernatural being bites another. From his bite, Michael inherits the memories of Lucian (Michael Sheen), his sire, and learns that, at one time, the werewolves were bred as slaves for the vampires. When Lucian fell in love with and impregnated Viktor's daughter, Viktor had her killed, which prompts Lucian to escape and declare war on the vampires. Since then, he has been trying to create a hybrid creature, one both vampire and werewolf. Lucian succeeds when Selene bites Michael — which the werewolf tells Selene to do in order to save Michael from death — thus causing werewolf and vampire blood to commingle.[4] The film ends with Viktor trying to destroy Michael. Now that she knows the truth about the war, Selene fights and kills Viktor after deciding that he is the true monster.

Selene is like the women discussed in Chapter 4, as she continues to blur the line between victim and vixen. In fact, she goes even further over that line than her predecessors because she is rarely a victim in either the first or second film. The only truly feminine attribute Selene possesses in *Underworld* is her clothing and even that borders more on masculine than feminine.

Her leather outfit may be considered sexy in the fact that it molds to her shape but it is certainly not scanty: it covers her entire body, and she often wears a long black duster as well. The other female vampires in the coven wear elaborate period dresses, which makes Selene's choice to wear something more masculine out of the ordinary for her culture, just as Buffy's choice to wear skimpy clothing while she patrols for demons is out of the ordinary for slayers. Yet, for both characters, this choice not only sets them apart from the crowd, it also allows them to embrace both their feminine and masculine attributes — they can still fight in those outfits. In addition, Kate Beckinsale's own beauty is downplayed in such a way that while she may be considered sexy as a vampire, she is not immediately associated with traditional feminine beauty. In other words, she does not have Buffy's long, blond locks that immediately stereotype her as a bombshell. There is something slightly androgynous in Selene's look which helps to move her beyond the traditional, obviously erotic, feminine stereotype of the victim.

Not only does Selene's appearance allow her to move beyond traditional gender coding of the horror film, but her strength and power do as well. Throughout the film, Selene is the primary vampire fighter; her strength is never in question. In the final battle scene, however, the viewer realizes just how powerful she is. This battle begins with Michael and Viktor, and, for awhile, it looks as if Michael will be able to defeat the vampire elder. Then, the tables turn and Viktor appears to have the upper-hand. Selene enters the fight when a trio of vampires bursts in and starts shooting at Michael. After she takes care of the vampires, Selene turns on Viktor, who throws her across the room. Viktor and Michael continue to fight until Selene picks up a sword and takes a swing at Viktor. Michael is released from Viktor's chokehold and Viktor turns his attention to Selene. Just as he begins to advance, Selene raises her sword in front of her face so that the viewer can see the blood drip down it; Selene has taken off half of Viktor's head, thus killing him. Although this summary does not do the battle's special effects justice, it does show that Selene ultimately has the power. While Michael and Viktor appear to be equally matched, it is Selene who triumphs over the elder. This is yet another way in which *Underworld* continues to uproot traditional gender roles. By being physically powerful, Selene continues what the other female monster hunters began.

By transcending traditional gender roles, the female monster hunters are able to disrupt their patriarchal cultures. Selene is no different. The power in *Underworld* is almost entirely male-dominated. Two of the three elders are male — the female elder, Amelia (Zita Gorog), is murdered almost as soon as she appears — and other than Selene, the Death Dealers are all men. The only other significant female vampire is Erika (Sophia Myles), and her greatest aspiration is to be Kraven's significant other. There are no female werewolves at all. As if the patriarchal structure were not clear enough, Viktor elaborates on Selene's supposed weakness. When Selene asks the elder why he trusts Kraven over her, he responds, "Because he is not the one who has been tainted by an animal," a comment alluding to Selene's love for Michael. But, as has been shown throughout this study, love can make a monster hunter even more powerful. In fact, it is Selene's love for Michael that causes her to enter the aforementioned battle and kill Viktor. When Selene kills the elder, she brings about the possibility of a new supernatural order. Having been proven a traitor, Kraven runs away.[5] At the moment, there is no active vampire elder because Marcus, the only one left, has yet to be awakened from his hibernation. In crossing the lines of battle, Selene has offered a new option to her fellow supernatural creatures: vampires and werewolves can rethink their alliances, thus creating an opening for an entirely new social order. As her voiceover at the film's end states, "Two vampire elders have been slain, one by my own hand. Soon, Marcus will take the throne and a tide of anger and retribution will spill out into the night. Differences will be set aside, allegiances will be made. And soon, I will become the hunted." Like her fellow female monster hunters, Selene has created a world of possibilities for women and werewolves, both of whom have long resided outside their culture's patriarchal power structure. Of course, like most contemporary monster-hunting narratives, *Underworld*'s ending is not entirely optimistic. When Marcus awakens he will prove to be even more powerful than Viktor and much more ruthless. Even though she has defeated one patriarchal structure, there is no guarantee that another one will not take its place.

In the sequel, *Underworld: Evolution*, Selene continues to seek freedom for both herself and Michael. She and Michael are running from Marcus (Tony Curran), who has awoken. While much of the film is focused on special-effects-driven battles, there are two significant occurrences that deserve attention. The first is not so much about the monster hunter as it is a change in the role of women — a role which I saw as problematic in the first film. As I mentioned earlier, in *Underworld* the female vampire elder — Amelia — is given little to do before her murder. However, she proves to be a powerful warrior in the sequel. *Underworld: Evolution* begins with a flashback to the eleventh century. The three vampire elders are trying to capture William (Brian Steele), the first and most powerful werewolf, who is also Marcus's twin brother. Amelia is instrumental in this battle, more active as a fighter than either of the other two elders. Although she is not a monster hunter, the fact that she has been given a powerful role in the sequel demonstrates that female characters in horror are, on the whole, becoming more aggressive.

The other occurrence that bears discussion here is Selene's transformation at the end of the film. Because Marcus is the first vampire, he is stronger than any other supernatural creature. Selene meets Marcus's father, Corvinus (Derek Jacobi), who is neither a vampire nor a werewolf, but has the gift of longevity. After Marcus stabs him with a sword, a dying Corvinus explains to Selene that she is not strong enough to defeat Marcus and tells Selene to drink his blood. Corvinus's own type of immortality combines with Selene's vampire blood to make her strong enough to fight the remaining vampire elder. After killing Marcus, Selene stands in the sunlight without burning; she is a new breed of vampire. Again, in killing the remaining vampire elder, Selene has succeeded in breaking through the patriarchal structures surrounding her. However, as with the ending of the first film, Selene and Michael's fate is left open. Her final voiceover states, "An unknown chapter lies ahead. The lines that have divided the clans have now been blurred. Chaos and in-fighting are inevitable. All that is certain is that darkness is still ahead. But for now, for the first time, I look into the light with new hope." *Underworld: Evolution* may leave viewers with another strong female monster hunter, but it also leaves them with just as many questions as the first film.

Unfortunately, other than Selene there has not been another significant monstrous female monster hunter in the new millennium's popular culture. However, it is difficult to pinpoint a reason why. Women are making their way into male-dominated roles in other genres. For example, Sarah Conner (Linda Hamilton), the fierce warrior in the action films *Terminator* (1984) and *Terminator 2: Judgment Day* (1991), is slated to appear in a television series, *Terminator: The Sarah Conner Chronicles*, in Spring 2008. Also on television, Sydney Bristow (Jennifer Garner) battled bad guys as a CIA agent in *Alias* (2001–2006) and the Bionic Woman (Michelle Ryan) returned to television in Fall 2007. Yet, these women are not monstrous like Ripley, Buffy, Anita, and Selene. They are strong warrior women—there will be no argument on that account from me—but they do not have a monstrous side that assists them with their battles. In this respect, they are not monstrous monster hunters. For some reason, film and television creators just do not want to create an army of monstrous female monster hunters. Perhaps society as a whole still needs the victim/vixen dichotomy. Perhaps society just cannot accept a monstrous woman. Whatever the reason, female monster hunters—although they have come a long way—still have a long way to go to become as popular as their male contemporaries. That said, the rape-revenge subgenre seems to be coming back into vogue. In 2007 such movies as *The Brave One* with Jodi Foster and *Descent* with Rosario Dawson featured a "wronged" woman out for justice against the men, or man, who wronged her. Again, it is difficult to guess as to why these women appear, but women like Faith and Willow do not. Although a few women manage to transcend gender boundaries, perhaps the American society at large is not yet ready for a new set of gender rules.

What audiences are apparently ready for is love. Love clearly makes the characters stronger, male or female. More importantly, it is often the villain's ignorance of the power of love that makes him fail in the monster-hunting narratives of the twenty-first century. This is certainly clear in *Dexter* when Rudy believes biological ties will overcome the love Harry and Deb give to Dexter. Likewise, the Lord Marshal underestimates Kyra's love for Riddick in *The Chronicles of Riddick*. But no text better demonstrates the importance of love than *Harry Potter and the Deathly Hallows*. Throughout the series Dumbledore continually reminds Harry how love is its own type of powerful magic; after all, it is Lily's love for Harry that saves the infant from Voldemort's killing curse. In *Deathly Hallows*, Harry confronts Voldemort with the power of love and explains to the Dark Lord how Snape continually bested the powerful wizard. When Harry faces Voldemort in the novel's final battle, Voldemort laughs at Harry's belief in love: "'Is it love again?' said Voldemort, his snake's face jeering. 'Dumbledore's favorite solution, *love*, which he claimed conquered death, though love did not stop him falling from the tower and breaking like an old waxwork? *Love*, which did not prevent me stamping out your Mudblood mother like a cockroach, Potter...'" (739). But Harry does know the power of love and tells Voldemort, "'Severus Snape wasn't yours,' said Harry. 'Snape was Dumbledore's, Dumbledore's from the moment you started hunting down my mother. And you never realized it, because of the thing you can't understand'" (740). At this moment Voldemort realizes that Snape tricked him. This realization does not actually lead to Voldemort's death — Harry's spell combined with Dumbledore's Elder Wand does that — but it does drill into the reader that love is a mighty powerful emotion.

Yet, love does not necessarily bring hope in the twenty-first-century, monster-hunting narrative. While the key to the monster hunter's strength may revolve around love, love does not guarantee victory. Kyra lies dead at Riddick's feet at the end of *Chronicles*. John Constantine has lost Chas and Beeman. Bullock loses his job, his reason for being, in his attempt to save the woman he truly loves. Dexter must kill the one man who truly understands him. These are not happy endings. To understand the complications of love in the monster-hunter narratives we must remember that love is a psychopath; it can do great and powerful things but the flip side is that it can bring great and powerful suffering. Just because a monster has love does not mean he is going to conquer evil once and for all. Even in *Jekyll* and *Underworld: Evolution*, where the monster hunters seem to succeed, there is no guarantee that life will be easy or that another evil — perhaps even a greater one than before — will not emerge. What these twenty-first-century texts do show is that with love comes motivation and that motivation can propel any monster, no matter how inhuman, out of the abyss and towards humanity.

Conclusion

"We love and need the concept of monstrosity because it is a reaffirmation of the order we all crave as human beings"
— *Danse Macabre*

Horror of the 1950s came on a wave of invasion narratives. Because World War II brought with it the deaths of millions of people by the atomic bomb and the extermination camp, Americans did not want to face the immediate possibility of more mass death, a fear which hung over them at the start of the Cold War. According to David Skal, "Most Americans found it easier not to face invasion/annihilation anxieties directly; they found indirect expression in McCarthyism, UFO hysteria, and, perhaps most pointedly, in the popular medium of lurid and sensational comic books that had been growing steadily in circulation since the end of World War II" (230). The popular films of the 1950s predominantly feature either aliens attacking the United States—like *Earth vs the Flying Saucers* (1956)—or animals growing to enormous size and attacking the United States—like *Them!* (1954) and *It Came from Beneath the Sea* (1955). These films attempt to mirror the invasions of Communism and technology in such a way that the American people did not have to relive the gruesome deaths and atrocities of war.

But no matter what the invader, it was the military's job to defend the nation, frustrate the invasion, and keep Americans safe and secure. According to Paul Wells, "Republican president and World War Two military hero General Eisenhower presided over a government which ultimately sought to appease liberals and conservatives at a time when the Korean war, McCarthyism, and the emergent Civil Rights movement threatened to destabilise political and cultural life" (61). It was a period of anxiety in that Americans realized dangerous entities were gathering force both beyond the borders of the United States and within them, but it was also a time of hope that a strong government, a strong military, and a strong leader would eventually keep these external forces at bay, thus maintaining the American way of life. By having the military succeed, horror reflected the belief that our leaders just might be able to protect us, come what may.

Unfortunately, much happened during the second half of the twentieth century to displace the unwavering American belief in our military power and stable home life. Vietnam was a shock as the American military's reputation was brought to its knees. Not only did we fail to win the war, but our soldiers proved to be less than heroic. News of destroyed villages, rapes, and murders reached America, causing the pride of the 1950s to be replaced with shame and shock because America was not the unstoppable world power its citizens thought it was. Our military members were not heroes; in some cases, they were nothing but monsters. In addition, on the domestic front Americans were dealing with such issues as the legalization of abortion and no-fault divorce. It must have seemed as if the fabric of the United States was being ripped at the seams; the brute-force power of both the male-dominated military and the patriarchal household was crumbling. Movie audiences of this era no longer hoped that their leaders and military would keep the monsters at bay. By the 1970s, as Jonathan Lake Crane comments, "It is difficult to imagine any contemporary audience entertaining the utterly perverse idea, the idea that drives almost all atomic films, that the world can be rescued from the brink by ordinary folks with good hearts" (135). It is during this time that monster hunters like Van Helsing almost completely disappear from the genre and the monster almost gains full reign over everyone and everything.

As a reaction to the significant domestic changes of the 1970s, films of the 1980s became nostalgic, yearning for a more traditional way of life, a 1950s way of life to be exact. In his book *Flatlining on the Field of Dreams*, Alan Nadel discusses the Reagan Era as a time when America wanted to partake of a collective amnesia to return the country to that time of peace and security before the Vietnam War. He criticizes the Reagan Era films as offering forgiveness and forgetfulness too easily: "What these films are attempting to forget through amnesia, nostalgia, [and] retreat from the present [...] is the 1960s in general and Vietnam in particular" (67). The horror film was no exception. In his 1981 essay on *The Shining*, Fredric Jameson argues, "This is the situation in which the new wave of occult films [...] may rather be seen as expressing the nostalgia for a system in which Good and Evil are absolute black-and-white categories: they do not express a new Cold War psychology as much as they express the longing and the regret for a Cold

War period in which things were still simple" (124). Jameson criticizes horror films—slashers to be specific—for trying to do what other films of the 1980s did: present the world in an easy "us-versus-them," or "good-versus-evil," black-and-white manner. Unfortunately, the troubles of the time were not so easily glossed over. By the 1960s humanity and inhumanity were no longer perceived by everyone as two separate beings. When both good and evil are present in the same character, the "us-versus-them" mentality no longer works.

The chaos of the 1970s slasher monster and the backlash over the "us-versus-them" nostalgia fused into a new being: the contemporary monster hunter. The character who once took part in chaotic villainy is driven by love, a community, and a conscience to become the new Van Helsing. A group of ordinary folks with good hearts could no longer best the villain, but another villainous being could. However, this new type of monster hunter is without the guarantee of the old. At the end of Stoker's novel, Mina and her boys can rest easy knowing their job is done. No contemporary monster hunter has this luxury. In fact, not all contemporary monster hunters—like Seth Bullock—even fully succeed in their quest.

If there is no closure to any of these monster-hunting texts, why are they maintaining their popularity? I believe that the main reason these texts are popular is that they ultimately present a new way of looking at contemporary culture. Invasion narratives are coming back, but this time it is a different type of invasion, one which cannot be so easily stopped as those in the 1950s. The invaders this time are what Andrew Tudor calls the "lurkers." In Chapter 1, I focused on Tudor's observation about horror texts of the 1980s: "Van Helsing is in his grave, the old remedies do not work and the lurker has crossed the threshold for good" (184). Tudor is referring specifically to the slasher villains as "lurkers," but could the term also include other monsters and even women? If so, why should we be so wary of lurkers crossing the threshold? Perhaps because of its strong female monster hunters and conflicted male monster hunters, horror is proving that absolute power held only by men is, and has always been, fleeting at best. Because the films of the 1980s were so steeped in nostalgia, this power shift was difficult to recognize. The 1980s were a last-ditch attempt to recapture the lost gender coding of the 1950s. Today, being masculine does not guarantee dominance, nor does being feminine force one to be submissive. As if to illustrate this gender shift, *Constantine* presents an androgynous Angel Gabriel. Tilda Swinton is neither masculine nor feminine in this film, yet the other angels and demons all have specific gender coding. By portraying the most famous, and perhaps most powerful, of angels as androgynous,

Constantine forces its viewers to rethink traditional gender roles. And the trend continues.

I used the following quote in Chapter 5 but it bears repeating here: "The history of the horror film is essentially the history of anxiety in the twentieth century" (Wells 3). I have touched on some of those anxieties throughout this study — anxiety like sexuality, Communism, and feminism, just to name a few. But as we enter the twenty-first century, what are our anxieties? Having begun the century with the terrorist attacks of 9/11, terrorism seems to be high on the anxiety list. But there is also the ever-present fear of technology begun in 1818 with Mary Shelley's *Frankenstein*. Not only do we now have cloning, and with it the fear that our doctors and scientists are coming too close to playing God, but there is also the fear of technology on a smaller scale: the internet. Chatrooms can contain child molesters and murderers, while online purchases can lead to identity theft and financial ruin. In addition, we are destroying our environment, and plagues like HIV and the more recent community-based MRSA outbreaks seem to have no cure in sight. And these are just the tip of the anxiety iceberg. We are but a few years into the new millennium and life has certainly not gotten easier, nor have we cut back on the number of anxieties we face; they have just changed. A look at the box office records for the first three months of 2006 illustrates the fact that anxiety is still every bit as lucrative as it has always been: *When a Stranger Calls* (2006) — the remake of the classic babysitting urban legend — *Underworld: Evolution*, and *Hostel* (2005) all topped the weekend box office charts with *Final Destination 3* (2006) premiering at number two and *The Hills Have Eyes* (2006) — another remake — premiering at number three. Horror is still reflecting our anxieties, and the genre does not appear to be in any sort of financial or popular decline.

But, for the first time in horror history, some of the lurkers are actually becoming heroes. Does this mean we should no longer fear our monsters? Should we welcome all lurkers with open arms? Certainly not. The slasher film is still going strong; of the five films I mentioned above, only *Underworld: Evolution* is not a slasher. In Chapter 1, I quoted Stephen King's *Danse Macabre*: "We love and need the concept of monstrosity because it is a reaffirmation of the order we all crave as human beings" (39). If all monsters became heroes, the audience members would lose this reaffirmation of order. The monster is present in society to allow that society's members to experience the repressed within a contained environment. This becomes an outlet for repressions that need to be released from time to time. The majority of monsters are remaining well within the abyss of inhumanity, still representing the repressed, and still reflecting our anxieties just as they always have. This is not a bad thing, nor do I see it changing any time in the near future.

This brings us to one final question: are the monsters who become monster hunters representing hope or fear? Perhaps, in the end, it is a little of both. The very fact that the monster can make its way out of the abyss to humanity may, at first glance, demonstrate that the new millennium brings with it possibility and some level of optimism akin to the 1950s belief that a strong leader and a strong military can protect the American people. Yet, if we look closer, we see that by refusing these characters any semblance of closure, contemporary horror texts remind readers and viewers that nothing is guaranteed and we are no closer to truly exorcising our monsters now than we were in the 1950s. Paul Wells comments, "[T]he 1950s alien can be construed as future-oriented, unknown, and modern; often accidentally, but necessarily, invited into the agencies of American progress. This horror, although unwelcome, was inevitable, and would have profound consequences" (62). Just as the alien invasions of the 1950s brought with them the unknowable, so too do the monster hunters of the twenty-first century. It is possible that these characters will help save the world, but it is equally possible that they will, in the end, slip back into the abyss just as Lucifer believes will happen to John Constantine.

Because it represents the unpleasant side of culture, horror will never end. Although some aspects of the genre never change, like an uneasiness around new technology, others are constantly in flux, like sexuality and gender coding. It is not unusual that the popularity of the monster hunter ebbs and flows. At one time, horror audiences have wanted this character to provide them with closure and a feeling of security. At other times, the monster hunter is considered useless or not even present in the text. Now the monster hunter is reemerging as something new, yet still rooted in a tradition stretching back to Bram Stoker. What this new character will ultimately achieve has yet to be determined. One thing is for sure, however: The iron nerve, temper of the ice-brook, indomitable resolution, self-command and toleration exalted from virtues to blessings, and kindliest and truest heart that beats have not disappeared entirely from the genre.

Chapter Notes

Chapter 1

1. I am lumping all viewers together here; however, different critics have different views on how gender affects spectatorship. Gender spectatorship is the topic of Rhona J. Berenstein's *Attack of the Leading Ladies: Gender, Sexuality, and Spectatorship in Classic Horror Cinema* (1995), in which she claims that watching horror films allows men and women to play a specific gender role that may be different from normal gender expectations. The seminal text, "When the Woman Looks," by Linda Williams, claims that in classic horror cinema female spectators found in the monster a kind of kindred spirit as both were displaced creatures within patriarchy. Peter Hutchings' article, "Masculinity and the Horror Film" (1993)— discusses the idea that male horror viewers react through a type of masochism. Isabel Cristina Pinedo's *Recreational Terror: Women and the Pleasures of Horror Film Viewing* (1997) further examines the role of women as horror spectators.

2. Tod Browning is, after all, the director who made *Freaks* the year after *Dracula*. Although he presents his assortment of sideshow freaks as the true "humans" in this film, it caused such an uproar that his career was over.

3. Appropriately enough, the name "Scoobies" is taken from the cartoon series *Scooby Doo* as the Buffyverse Scoobies consider themselves to be like the cartoon detectives. In addition, this name demonstrates Whedon's continual use of pop culture references in his television series.

4. For a brief discussion of Van Helsing as a Christ figure, see Anne McWhir's essay, "Pollution and Redemption in *Dracula*."

Chapter 2

1. Paul Wells sees films such as *The Incredible Shrinking Man* (1957) and *Attack of the Fifty Foot Woman* (1958) as threatening the physical power of masculinity by reducing men in the former and presenting the possibility of larger-than-life women in the latter. Both of these films damage the traditional male power structure by offering other options to that power.

2. For this study I am focusing solely on Season One of the television show. While characters came and went throughout the seasons, the episodes' basic format remained the same. There was no significant character development like on *Buffy the Vampire Slayer* and *Angel*.

3. Although Joss Whedon has not mentioned *Forever Knight* as an inspiration, the similarities between Nick, Angel, and Spike are prominent. It would be surprising if Whedon had never seen the television movie or series.

4. The *Blade* comic book series was created in 1973 by Marv Wolfman and Gene Colan for Marvel Comics.

5 There have only been two people who have ever been able to give Angel his soul. The first is a gypsy woman and the second is Willow. Both are witches who have mastered the necessary magic spell. In addition, there have been two characters capable of removing Angel's soul through magic. Both of these men have done so (or pretended to do so) using a magical incantation.

6. To learn of a demonic plan to block out the sun, the members of Angel Investigations— Angel's detective agency — have Angel's soul removed so that they can confer with Angelus, who knows the demon in question. To keep it safe and within reach, the sorcerer who performs

the spell places Angel's soul within a special glass jar. This jar must then be broken and Angel's soul released before it can be placed back into him.

7. Lacroix returns in future seasons and continues to tempt Nick.

8. After having sex with Buffy, Angel loses his soul and reverts back to his pre-soul evil vampire personality, Angelus. Angelus then goes to Spike and Drusilla and takes charge of their plans to kill the slayer. Having been injured trying to save Drusilla, Spike is in a wheelchair and is incapable of leaving the lair. Angelus spends a great deal of time out with Drusilla, thus causing Spike to be jealous. Truthfully, one of Spike's reasons for siding with Buffy is his desire to win back Drusilla's affections, not just to keep Earth out of Hell.

9. There is a time in *Blade II* when Blade must drink blood to regain his strength. In this scene, though, the blood is already in a vat and so the scene seems less ominous and less like a slip into the abyss.

10. A moment of true happiness—sex with Buffy—causes Angel to lose his soul and become the evil Angelus. Because being around Buffy is a temptation, Angel feels that leaving Sunnydale is the best idea for both of them.

11. It is never made absolutely clear what Angel's destiny actually is. His friends, Cordelia and Wesley, believe that his destiny is to help as many of the hopeless in L.A. as he can. Wolfram & Hart (the evil law firm bent on destroying Angel or getting him on their side) believes that Angel's destiny is to play a major role in the battle between good and evil.

12. In yet another attempt at getting Angel to do their bidding, Wolfram & Hart offer Angel Investigations their L.A. branch. The crew accepts, thinking that working from inside the belly of the beast will help them to better fight evil. Instead, they find themselves bogged down in paperwork and unable to accomplish anything substantial—which is, the viewer presumes, exactly what Wolfram & Hart hoped would happen.

Chapter 3

1. This is an action frighteningly parallel to America's own post-9/11 experience.

2. Fans of the movie, which will be discussed shortly, will notice the significant script change. In the film, the destruction of Big Ben and Parliament is the climactic final moment of the story.

3. Mina could be the monster given the many allusions to her vampiric nature, but readers never witness her acting like a vampire.

4. Moore does, however, remind readers that Hyde is still a monster. Before going to his death, Hyde asks to both kiss Mina and touch her breast, which she allows.

5. There is a two-page series of panels in the graphic novel from which the inspiration for the girl is taken. The reader watches as she spray-paints a "V" on the side of a brick wall. However, the small aside is not nearly as pivotal in the graphic novel as the girl's storyline is in the film.

6. The tree here refers to the end of *The Count of Monte Cristo*, V's favorite film. He and Evey watch it together and it becomes a parallel story to their own. At the end of the film, the hero and heroine are alone in their tree, enjoying their happily ever after.

7. It should be noted that Sean Connery was an Executive Producer on the film. This could, possibly, account for the significant change to Allan Quatermain's persona.

8. The addition of Tom Sawyer completely negates the purpose of Moore's League, which is to bring together characters that would have been alive in England at the same time. When creating the League, Moore made the publication dates of the tales the time when they were actually occurring (unless otherwise noted in the stories). In this way, it would be possible for the five characters to meet up. *Tom Sawyer*, however, was published in 1876. If he is a boy at this time, he would be well into his thirties by the time *League* takes place. Having a twenty-something actor play the character seriously damages Moore's intention.

Chapter 4

1. I want to clarify here that I do mean Mina of the novel, not of the film adaptations; in the novel, Mina has some level of agency and monster-hunting abilities while in many of the adaptations she is nothing more than a victim.

2. In *Cat People*'s 1944 sequel, *The Curse of the Cat People*, Irena returns as a guardian angel to Oliver and Alice's daughter, Amy. By becoming an angel, the viewer knows that Irena's sins have been forgiven and she has been redeemed.

3. The opposite of this pairing occurs in *Alien*. There is a second woman on the crew: Lambert (Veronica Cartwright). To make Ripley more masculine, Lambert serves to be Clover's abject fear personified; she spends most of her on-screen time in panic mode and screams a great deal. In *Alien*, Lambert shows the viewers how feminine a character can be, thus making Ripley more respected and, as gender roles dictate, more masculine.

4. It should be noted that Joss Whedon wrote the script for *Alien: Resurrection*. It seems that when it comes to the creation and evolution of the contemporary male and female monster hunters, Whedon is the expert.

5. By placing her hands on the open books, Willow receives all of their knowledge through a type of osmosis. The viewer sees the spells literally moving from the page to Willow's flesh. When she is through, the books are blank.

6. On the plane home, Willow accidentally puts a spell on herself so that she cannot see Buffy and Xander, nor can they see her. This accident almost leads to her death as she is attacked by a demon who paralyzes her and begins to eat her skin. (This is ironic considering that evil Willow flayed Warren.) But, at the last minute, she is able to lift the spell and is saved by her friends.

7. The two significant Watchers have been male: Giles and Wesley. The only significant female Watcher was evil and died. When a large group of Watchers come to see Buffy in Season Five, the group only contains one woman. Due to these women's secondary roles and the mythology of the Watcher's origination, I am led to believe that the group is mostly male.

Chapter 5

1. It is true that some other sci-fi/action films get close like *Terminator 2: Judgment Day* and *Terminator 3: Rise of the Machines*. Both of these films feature an assassin robot (Arnold Schwarzenegger) reprogrammed to protect the hope of all humankind: John Connor. However, the robot never really copes with his villainous past so it does not affect his role as bodyguard.

2. *Deadwood* has been nominated for many Emmy awards, most notably in 2005 for Ian McShane as Outstanding Lead Actor in a Drama Series and in 2004 for Brad Dourif as Outstanding Supporting Actor in a Drama Series and Robin Weigert for Outstanding Supporting Actress in a Drama Series. It has won several technical Emmys. In 2005 Ian McShane won a Golden Globe for Best Performance by an Actor in a Television Series—Drama, and the show was nominated for Best Television Series—Drama. *Dexter* has also been nominated for, and won, several awards including Michael C. Hall's 2007 and 2008 Golden Gobe nominations for Best Performance by an Actor in a Television Series—Drama. Even *Jekyll* earned a 2008 Golden Globe nomination for James Nesbitt—Best Performance by an Actor in a Mini-Series or a Motion Picture Made for Television.

3. In the vampire community there are three elders: Viktor, Amelia, and Marcus. Only one is awake at a time, thus allowing them to "piggy-back" through history, as Viktor explains to Selene. When a coven's elder is sleeping, a temporary leader takes his place. At the film's beginning, Viktor is hibernating while Amelia is the active elder. The plot never really explains why Amelia is not in charge of Selene's coven; the assumption is that each elder has his own coven.

4. It is interesting to note that Lucian's name is very similar to "Lucifer." However, Lucian acts as more savior than devil in that he is trying to save the werewolves from persecution at the vampires' hands. In some ways, *Underworld* could be read as symbolic of the fall from grace. *Underworld: Evolution* (2006), on the other hand, has some elements of New Testament redemption with Selene as savior for the supernatural realm.

5. Selene proves that Kraven was always in league with Lucian, and that his touted victory over the werewolf was nothing but a sham. He runs away rather than face the coven's wrath.

WORKS CITED

Abbott, Stacey. "Walking the Fine Line Between Angel and Angelus." *Slayage: The Online International Journal of Buffy Studies* 3.1 (August 2003). 31 Dec. 2004 <http://slayageonline.com/essays/slayage9/Abbott.htm>.

Alias. By J. J. Abrams. Perf. Jennifer Garner, Ron Rifkin. ABC. Sept. 2001–May 2006.

Alien. Dir. Ridley Scott. Perf. Sigourney Weaver, Tom Skerritt. Twentieth Century-Fox, 1979.

Alien[3]. Dir. David Fincher. Perf. Sigourney Weaver, Charles S. Dutton. Twentieth Century-Fox, 1992.

Alien: Resurrection. Dir. Jean-Pierre Jeunet. Perf. Sigourney Weaver, Winona Ryder. Twentieth Century-Fox, 1997.

Aliens. Dir. James Cameron. Perf. Sigourney Weaver, Michael Biehn, Lance Henriksen. Twentieth Century-Fox, 1986.

"Angel." *Buffy the Vampire Slayer*. WB. 14 April 1997.

Angel. By Joss Whedon. Perf. David Boreanaz, Charisma Carpenter. WB. Oct. 1999-May 2004.

Attack of the 50 Foot Woman. Dir. Nathan Juran. Perf. Allison Hayes, William Hudson. Woolner Brothers Pictures Inc., 1958.

Auerbach, Nina. *Our Vampires, Ourselves*. Chicago: University of Chicago Press, 1995.

"Bad Girls." *Buffy the Vampire Slayer*. WB. 9 Feb. 1999.

Badmington, Neil. *Alien Chic: Posthumanism and the Other Within*. London: Routledge, 2004.

_____. "Introduction." In *Posthumanism*, edited by Neil Badmington, 1–10. New York: Palgrave, 2000.

_____, ed. *Posthumanism*. New York: Palgrave, 2000.

Barbour, Dennis H. "Heroism and Redemption." *Journal of Film and Television* 27.3 (Fall 1999): 28–34.

Batman Begins. Dir. Christopher Nolan. Perf. Christian Bale, Michael Caine. Warner Bros. Pictures, 2005.

"Becoming: Part 1." *Buffy the Vampire Slayer*. WB. 12 May 1998.

"Becoming: Part 2." *Buffy the Vampire Slayer*. WB. 19 May 1998.

Berenstein, Rhona J. *Attack of the Leading Ladies: Gender, Sexuality, and Spectatorship in Classic Horror Cinema*. New York: Columbia University Press, 1996.

Bernard, Mark, and James Bucky Carter. "Alan Moore and the Graphic Novel: Confronting the Fourth Dimension." *ImageTexT: Interdisciplinary Comics Studies* 1.2 (Winter 2004). 6 Feb. 2007 <http://www.english.ufl.edu/imagetext/archives/v1_2/carter/>.

Bionic Woman. By David Eick. Perf. Michelle Ryan, Lucy Hale. NBC. 26 Sept. 2007-Present.

Blacula. Dir. William Crain. Perf. William Marshall, Vonetta McGee. American International Pictures, 1972.

Blade. Dir. Stephen Norrington. Perf. Wesley Snipes, Stephen Dorff, Kris Kristofferson. New Line Cinema, 1998.

Blade II. Dir. Guillermo del Toro. Perf. Wesley Snipes, Kris Kristofferson. New Line Cinema, 2002.

Blade: Trinity. David S. Goyer. Perf. Wesley Snipes, Jessica Biel. New Line Cinema, 2004.

Bongco, Mila. *Reading Comics: Language, Culture, and the Concept of the Superhero in Comic Books*. New York: Garland Publishing, Inc., 2000.

"Born Free." *Dexter*. Showtime. 17 Dec. 2006.

Boyette, Michele. "The Comic Anti-hero in *Buffy the Vampire Slayer*, or Silly Villain: Spike is for Kicks." *Slayage: The Online In-

ternational Journal of Buffy Studies 1.4 (December 2001). 31 Dec. 2004 <http://slayageonline.com/essays/slayage4/boyette.htm>.
Bram Stoker's Dracula. Dir. Francis Ford Coppola. Perf. Gary Oldman, Anthony Hopkins, Winona Ryder. Columbia Pictures, 1992.
The Brave One. Dir. Neil Jordan. Perf. Jodi Foster, Terrence Howard. Redemption Pictures, 2007.
Brennan, Matthew C. "Repression, Knowledge, and Saving Souls: The Role of the "New Woman" in Stoker's Dracula and Murnau's Nosferatu." Studies in the Humanities 19.1 (June 1992): 1–10.
Buffy the Vampire Slayer. By Joss Whedon. Perf. Sarah Michelle Gellar, Anthony Stewart Head, Alyson Hannigan. WB and UPN. March 1997–May 2003.
Buffy the Vampire Slayer. Dir. Fran Rubel Kuzui. Perf. Kristy Swanson, Donald Sutherland, and Rutger Hauer. Twentieth Century-Fox 1992.
Butler, Judith. Gender Trouble: Feminism and the Subversion of Identity. New York: Routledge, 1999.
Captain Kronos — Vampire Hunter. Dir. Brian Clemens. Perf. Horst Janson, John Carson. Hammer Studios, 1974.
Carter, Margaret L. "The Vampire as Alien in Contemporary Fiction." In Blood Read: The Vampire as Metaphor in Contemporary Culture, edited by Joan Gordon and Veronica Hollinger, 27–44. Philadelphia: University of Pennsylvania Press, 1997.
Cat People. Dir. Jacques Tourneur. Perf. Simone Simon, Tom Conway. RKO Radio Pictures Inc., 1942.
"Checkpoint." Buffy the Vampire Slayer. WB. 23 Jan. 2001.
"Chosen." Buffy the Vampire Slayer. UPN. 20 May 2003.
The Chronicles of Riddick. Dir. David Twohy. Perf. Vin Diesel, Judi Dench, Thandie Newton. Universal, 2004.
"City Of." Angel. WB. 5 Oct. 1999.
Clover, Carol J. Men, Women, and Chain Saws: Gender in the Modern Horror Film. Princeton: Princeton University Press, 1992.
Constantine. Dir. Francis Lawrence. Perf. Keanu Reeves, Rachel Weisz. Warner Bros., 2005.
Crane, Jonathan Lake. Terror and Everyday Life: Singular Moments in the History of the Horror Film. London: Sage Publications, 1994.
Crosby, Sara. "The Cruelest Season: Female Heroes Snapped into Sacrificial Heroines." In Action Chicks: New Images of Tough Women in Popular Culture, edited by Sherrie A. Inness,153–178. New York: Palgrave Macmillan, 2004.

"Crush." Buffy the Vampire Slayer. WB. 13 Feb. 2001.
The Curse of the Cat People. Dir. Gunther von Fritsch and Robert Wise. Perf. Kent Smith, Simone Simon, Jane Randolph. RKO Radio Pictures, 1944.
"Dark Knight." Forever Knight. USA Network. 5 May 1992.
Davenport-Hines, Richard. Gothic: Four Hundred Years of Excess, Horror, Evil and Ruin. New York: North Point Press, 1998.
Deacy, Christopher. "The Christian Concept of Redemption and Its Application through the Films of Martin Scorsese." Religious Studies and Theology 17 (June 1998): 46–70.
Deadwood. By David Milch. Perf. Timothy Olyphant, Ian McShane. HBO. March 2004–Aug. 2006.
"Deadwood." Deadwood. HBO. 21 March 2004.
"Deep Water." Deadwood. HBO. 28 March 2004.
DeKelb-Rittenhouse, Diane. "Sex and the Single Vampire: The Evolution of the Vampire Lothario and Its Representation in Buffy." In Fighting the Forces: What's at Stake in Buffy the Vampire Slayer, edited by Rhonda Wilcox and David Lavery,143–52. Lanham: Rowman & Littlefield, 2002.
Delano, Jamie, John Ridgway, and Alfredo Alcala. Hellblazer: Original Sins. New York: DC Comics, 1992.
The Departed. Dir. Martin Scorsese. Perf. Jack Nicholson, Leonardo DiCaprio. Warner Bros. Pictures, 2006.
Descent. Dir. Talia Lugacy. Perf. Rosario Dawson, Chad Faust. Descent, 2007.
Dexter. By Jeff Lindsay and James Manos, Jr. Perf. Michael C. Hall, Julie Benz, Jennifer Carpenter. Showtime. Oct. 2006-Present.
"Dexter." Dexter. Showtime. 1 Oct. 2006.
"Dirty Girls." Buffy the Vampire Slayer. UPN. 15 April 2003.
Doherty, Thomas. "Genre, Gender, and the Aliens Trilogy." In The Dread of Difference: Gender and the Horror Film, edited by Barry Keith Grant, 181–199. Austin: University of Texas Press, 1996.
"Doomed." Buffy the Vampire Slayer. WB. 18 Jan. 2000.
Dracula. Dir. John Badham. Perf. Frank Langella, Kate Nelligan, Laurence Olivier. Universal, 1979.
Dracula. Dir. Tod Browning. Perf. Bela Lugosi, Helen Chandler, David Manners. Universal, 1931.
Dracula's Daughter. Lambert Hillyer. Perf. Otto Kruger, Gloria Holden, Marguerite Churchill. Universal, 1936.
Early, Frances H. "Staking Her Claim: Buffy the Vampire Slayer as Transgressive Woman

Warrior." *Journal of Popular Culture* 35.3 (Winter 2001): 11–27.
Earth vs. the Flying Saucers. Dir. Fred F. Sears. Perf. Hugh Marlowe, Joan Taylor. Columbia Pictures, 1956.
Edmundson, Mark. *Nightmare on Main Street: Angels, Sadomasochism, and the Culture of Gothic*. Cambridge, MA: Harvard University Press, 1997.
"End of Days." *Buffy the Vampire Slayer*. UPN. 13 May 2003.
"Epiphany." *Angel*. WB. 27 Feb. 2001.
"Episode 1.3." *Jekyll*. BBC. 30 June 2007.
"Episode 1.5." *Jekyll*. BBC. 21 July 2007.
"Episode 1.6." *Jekyll*. BBC. 28 July 2007.
"False Witness." *Forever Knight*. USA Network. 4 Aug. 1992.
Faludi, Susan. *Backlash: The Undeclared War Against American Women*. New York: Crown Publishers, Inc., 1991.
"Father Figure." *Forever Knight*. USA Network. 13 Oct. 1992.
The Fearless Vampire Killers. Dir. Roman Polanski. Perf. Jack MacGowran, Roman Polanski, Sharon Tate. MGM, 1967.
"Feeding the Beast." *Forever Knight*. USA Network. 1 Dec. 1992.
Fenn, Richard K. "Soul-Loss Revisited." In *On Losing the Soul: Essays in the Social Psychology of Religion*, edited by Richard K. Fenn, et al., 231–244. Albany: State University of New York Press, 1995.
Fenn, Richard K., et al., eds. *On Losing the Soul: Essays in the Social Psychology of Religion*. Albany: State University of New York Press, 1995.
Final Destination 3. Dir. James Wong. Perf. Mary Elizabeth Winstead, Ryan Merriman. New Line Cinema, 2006.
"For I Have Sinned." *Forever Knight*. USA Network. 12 May 1992.
Forever Knight. By Barney Cohen and James D. Parriott. Perf. Geraint Wyn Davies, Catherine Disher. USA Network. May 1992–May 1996.
Fossey, Claire. "Never Hurt the Feelings of a Brutal Killer: Spike and the Underground Man." *Slayage: The Online International Journal of Buffy Studies* 2.4 (March 2003). 31 Dec. 2004 <http://slayageonline.com/essays/slayage8/Fossey.htm>.
Foucault, Michel. *Discipline and Punish: The Birth of the Prison*. New York: Vintage Books, 1995.
_____. "Technologies of the Self." In *Technologies of the Self: A Seminar With Michel Foucault*, edited by Luther H. Martin, Huck Gutman, and Patrick H. Hutton, 16–49. Amherst: University of Massachusetts Press, 1988.
Frankenstein. Dir. James Whale. Perf. Colin Clive, Boris Karloff, Mae Clarke. Universal, 1931.
Frazer, Sir James George. *The Golden Bough: A Study in Magic and Religion*. New York: The Macmillan Company, 1956.
Freaks. Dir. Tod Browning. Perf. Wallace Ford, Leila Hyams. MGM, 1932.
Freddy vs. Jason. Dir. Ronny Yu. Perf. Robert Englund, Ken Kirzinger. New Line Cinema, 2003.
Friday the 13th Part 2. Dir. Steve Miner. Perf. Amy Steel, John Furey. Georgetown Productions, Inc., 1981.
Fry, Carrol L. "'Unfit for Earth, Undoomed for Heaven': The Genesis of Coppola's Byronic Dracula." *Literature Film Quarterly* 30.4 (2002): 271–278.
Gibson, Pamela Church. "Queer Looks, Male Gazes, Taut Torsos and Designer Labels: Contemporary Cinema, Consumption and Masculinity." In *The Trouble with Men: Masculinities in European and Hollywood Cinema*, edited by Phil Powrie, Ann Davies, and Bruce Babington, 176–186. London: Wallflower Press, 2004.
Gillis, Stacy, Gillian Howie, and Rebecca Munford, eds. *Third Wave Feminism: A Critical Exploration*. New York: Palgrave Macmillan, 2004.
"The Girl Who Overcame Time." *Inuyasha*. Cartoon Network. 31 August 2002.
Gordon, Joan and Veronica Hollinger, eds. *Blood Read: The Vampire as Metaphor in Contemporary Culture*. Philadelphia: University of Pennsylvania Press, 1997.
"Graduation Day, Part 1." *Buffy the Vampire Slayer*. WB. 18 May 1999.
Grant, Barry Keith, ed. *The Dread of Difference: Gender and the Horror Film*. Austin: University of Texas Press, 1996.
_____. *Planks of Reason: Essays on the Horror Film*. Metuchen: Scarecrow Press, 1984.
"Grave." *Buffy the Vampire Slayer*. UPN. 21 May 2002.
Greene, Richard and Wayne Yuen. "Why We Can't Spike Spike?: Moral Themes in *Buffy the Vampire Slayer*." *Slayage: The Online International Journal of Buffy Studies* 1.2 (March 2001). 31 Dec. 2004 <http://slayageonline.com/essays/slayage2/greeneandyuen.htm>.
Groth, Gary and Robert Fiore. *The New Comics: Interviews from the Pages of "The Comics Journal."* New York: Berkley Books, 1988.
Halberstam, Judith. *Skin Shows: Gothic Horror and the Technology of Monsters*. Durham, North Carolina: Duke University Press, 1995.
Halloween. Dir. John Carpenter. Perf. Donald Pleasence, Jamie Lee Curtis. Anchor Bay Entertainment, 1978.

Hamilton, Laurell K. *Guilty Pleasures*. New York: Berkley Books, 1993.
___. *The Harlequin*. Berkley Hardcover, 2007.
___. *The Laughing Corpse*. 1994. New York: Jove Books, 2002.
Haraway, Donna J. "A Cyborg Manifesto: Science, Technology, and Socialist-Feminism in the Late Twentieth Century." In *Simians, Cyborgs, and Women: The Reinvention of Nature*, edited by Donna J. Haraway, 149–181. New York: Routledge, 1991.
___, ed. *Simians, Cyborgs, and Women: The Reinvention of Nature*. New York: Routledge, 1991.
Heldreth, Leonard G. and Mary Pharr, eds. *The Blood is the Life: Vampires in Literature*. Bowling Green, Ohio: Bowling Green State University Popular Press, 1999.
"Hell Bound." *Angel*. WB. 22 Oct. 2003.
The Hills Have Eyes. Dir. Alexandre Aja. Perf. Aaron Stanford, Kathleen Quinlan. Craven-Maddalena Films, 2006.
Hollinger, Karen. "The Monster as Woman: Two Generations of Cat People." In *The Dread of Difference: Gender and the Horror Film*, edited by Barry Keith Grant, 296–308. Austin: University of Texas Press, 1996.
Hollinger, Veronica. "Fantasies of Absence: The Postmodern Vampire." In *Blood Read: The Vampire as Metaphor in Contemporary Culture*, edited by Joan Gordon and Veronica Hollinger,199–212. Philadelphia: University of Pennsylvania Press, 1997.
Horror of Dracula. Dir. Terence Fisher. Perf. Peter Cushing, Christopher Lee. Hammer Studios, 1958.
Hostel. Dir. Eli Roth. Perf. Jay Hernandez, Derek Richardson. Hostel LLC, 2005.
"The House Always Wins." *Angel*. WB. 20 Oct. 2002.
Hughes, Jamie A. "'Who Watches the Watchmen?': Ideology and 'Real World' Superheroes." *Journal of Popular Culture*. 39.4 (2006): 546–557.
Hutchings, Peter. "Masculinity and the Horror Film." In *You Tarzan: Masculinity, Movies, and Men*, edited by. Pat Kirkham and Janet Thumim, 84–94. New York: St. Martin's Press, 1993.
I Spit On Your Grave. Dir. Meir Zarchi. Perf. Camille Keaton, Eron Tabor. Cinemagic Pictures, 1978.
The Incredible Shrinking Man. Dir. Jack Arnold. Perf. Grant Williams, Randy Stuart. Universal International Pictures, 1957.
Inness, Sherrie A, ed. *Action Chicks: New Images of Tough Women in Popular Culture*. New York: Palgrave Macmillan, 2004.
___. *Tough Girls: Women Warriors and Wonder Women in Popular Culture*. Philadelphia: University of Pennsylvania Press, 1999.
The Internet Movie Database. 2008. 21 Jan. 2008 <http://www.imdb.com>.
Inuyasha. By Michihiko Suwa and Hideyuki Tomioka. Perf. Kappei Yamaguchi and Satsuki Yukino. Cartoon Network. August 2002–June 2004.
It Came from Beneath the Sea. Dir. Robert Gordon. Perf. Kenneth Tobey, Faith Domergue. Columbia Pictures, 1955.
Jackson, Rosemary. *Fantasy: The Literature of Subversion*. London: Routledge, 1993.
Jameson, Fredric. "*The Shining*." *Social Text* 4 (Autumn 1981): 114–125.
Jekyll. By Steven Moffat. Perf. James Nesbitt, Gina Bellman. BBC. June 2007–July 2007.
Jensen, Jeff. "*Watchmen*: An Oral History." *Entertainment Weekly* 847 (28 Oct. 2005): 44–49.
"Just Rewards." *Angel*. WB. 8 Oct. 2003.
Kaplan, E. Ann. "The Case of the Missing Mother: Maternal Issues in Vidor's *Stella Dallas*." *Feminism and Film*. Edited by E. Ann Kaplan, 466–478. Oxford: Oxford University Press, 2000.
___, Ed. *Feminism and Film*. Oxford, Oxford University Press, 2000.
Karras, Irene. "The Third Wave's Final Girl: *Buffy the Vampire Slayer*." *thirdspace* 1/2 (March 2002). 3 Oct. 2005 <http://www.thirdspace.ca/journal/issue/view/2>.
King, Stephen. *Danse Macabre*. New York: Berkley, 1981.
Kirkham, Pat and Janet Thumim, eds. *You Tarzan: Masculinity, Movies and Men*. New York: St. Martin's Press, 1993.
Lara Croft Tomb Raider. Dir. Simon West. Perf. Angelina Jolie, Jon Voight. Paramount Pictures, 2001.
Lara Croft Tomb Raider: The Cradle of Life. Dir. Jan de Bont. Perf. Angelina Jolie, Gerard Butler. Paramount Pictures, 2003.
Laski, Beth. "Television Quest." *Buffy the Vampire Slayer Magazine* 1.1 (Fall 1998): 12–16.
The League of Extraordinary Gentlemen. Dir. Stephen Norrington. Perf. Sean Connery, Peta Wilson, Stuart Townsend. Twentieth-Century Fox, 2003.
"Let's Give the Boy a Hand." *Dexter*. Showtime. 22 Oct. 2006.
Lorrah, Jean. "Dracula Meets the New Woman." In *The Blood is the Life: Vampires in Literature*, edited by Leonard G. Heldreth and Mary Pharr, 31–42. Bowling Green: Bowling Green State University Popular Press, 1999.
Mad Max. Dir. George Miller. Perf. Mel Gibson, Joanne Samuel. Roadshow Entertainment, 1979.

Mad Max 2: The Road Warrior. Dir. George Miller. Perf. Mel Gibson, Bruce Spence. Kennedy Miller Productions, 1981.

Mad Max Beyond Thunderdome. Dir. George Miller and George Ogilvie. Perf. Mel Gibson, Tina Turner. Kennedy Miller Productions, 1985.

McWhir, Anne. "Pollution and Redemption in Dracula." Modern Language Studies 17.3 (Summer 1987): 31–40.

Miller, Frank, Klaus Janson, and Lynn Varley. Batman: The Dark Knight Returns. New York: DC Comics, 2002.

Moore, Alan and David Gibbons. Watchmen. New York: DC Comics, 1987.

Moore Alan, and David Lloyd. V for Vendetta. New York: DC Comics, 1989.

Moore, Alan and Kevin O'Neill. The League of Extraordinary Gentlemen: Volume 1. La Jolla, CA: America's Best Comics, 1999.

———. The League of Extraordinary Gentlemen: Volume II. La Jolla, CA: America's Best Comics, 2003.

Mulvey, Laura. Visual and Other Pleasures. Bloomington: Indiana University Press, 1989.

Nadel, Alan. Flatlining of the Field of Dreams: Cultural Narratives in the Films of President Reagan's America. New Brunswick, NJ: Rutgers University Press, 1997.

Nelson, Susan L. "Soul-Loss and Sin: A Dance of Alienation." In On Losing the Soul: Essays in the Social Psychology of Religion, edited by Richard K. Fenn et al., 97–116. Albany: State University of New York Press, 1995.

Newman, Kim. Anno Dracula. New York: Avon Books, 1992.

Nietzsche, Friedrich. Beyond Good and Evil in the Philosophy of Nietzsche. Trans. Helen Zimmern, Ed. Willard Huntington Wright. New York: The Modern Library, Inc., 1954.

A Nightmare on Elm Street. Dir. Wes Craven. Perf. Robert Englund, Heather Langenkamp. New Line Cinema, 1984.

Nosferatu. Dir. F. W. Murnau. Perf. Max Schreck. Prana Films, 1921.

"Not Fade Away." Angel. WB. 19 May 2004.

"Only the Lonely." Forever Knight. USA Network. 17 Nov. 1992.

"Orpheus." Angel. WB. 19 March 2003.

Pearson, Roberta E. and William Uricchio, Eds. The Many Lives of the Batman: Critical Approaches to a Superhero and his Media. New York: Routledge, 1991.

Penley, Constance, ed. Feminism and Film Theory. New York: Routledge, 1988.

———. "The Lady Doesn't Vanish: Feminism and Film Theory." In Feminism and Film Theory, edited by Constance Penley, 1–24. New York: Routledge, 1988.

"Phases." Buffy the Vampire Slayer. WB. 27 Jan. 1998.

Pinedo, Isabel Cristina. Recreational Terror: Women and the Pleasures of Horror Film Viewing. Albany: State University of New York Press, 1987.

Pitch Black. Dir. David Twohy. Perf. Vin Diesel, Radha Mitchell. Interscope Communications, 2000.

"Popping Cherry." Dexter. Showtime. 15 Oct. 2006.

Powrie, Phil, Ann Davies, and Bruce Babington, eds. The Trouble with Men: Masculinities in European and Hollywood Cinema. London: Wallflower Press, 2004.

Psycho. Dir. Alfred Hitchcock. Perf. Anthony Perkins, Vera Miles, Janet Leigh. Universal, 1960.

"Reprise." Angel. WB. 20 Feb. 2001.

"Return to Sender." Dexter. Showtime. 5 Nov. 2006.

"Reunion." Angel. WB. 19 Dec. 2000.

Rice, Anne. Interview with the Vampire. New York: Ballantine Books, 1976.

Robinson, Tasha. "Joss Whedon." A. V. Club 5 Sept. 2001. 28 Jan. 2006 <http://www.avclub.com/content/node/24238>.

Rowling, J. K. Harry Potter and the Deathly Hallows. New York: Arthur A. Levine Books, 2007.

———. Harry Potter and the Half-Blood Prince. New York: Arthur A. Levine Books, 2005.

———. Harry Potter and the Order of the Phoenix. New York: Arthur A. Levine Books, 2003.

———. Harry Potter and the Prisoner of Azkaban. New York: Arthur A. Levine Books, 1999.

"School Hard." Buffy the Vampire Slayer. WB. 29 Sept. 1997.

Schrag, Calvin O. The Self after Postmodernity. New Haven: Yale University Press, 1997.

Scream. Dir. Wes Craven. Perf. Neve Campbell, David Arquette. Dimension Films, 1996.

Scream 2. Dir. Wes Craven. Perf. Neve Campbell, David Arquette. Dimension Films, 1997.

Scream 3. Dir. Wes Craven. Perf. Neve Campbell, David Arquette. Dimension Films, 2000.

"Seeing Red." Buffy the Vampire Slayer. UPN. 7 May 2002.

Senf, Carol A. "Dracula: Stoker's Response to the New Woman." Victorian Studies 26.1 (Autumn 1982): 33–49.

Sharrett, Christopher. "Batman and the Twilight of the Idols: An Interview with Frank Miller." In The Many Lives of the Batman: Critical Approaches to a Superhero and His

Media, edited by Roberta E. Pearson and William Uricchio, 33–46. New York: Routledge, 1991.

Shatz, David. "Introduction." In *Tikkun Olam: Social Responsibility in Jewish Thought and Law*, edited by David Shatz, Chaim I. Waxman, and Nathan Diament, 1–16. Northvale, NJ: Jason Aronson, 1997.

Shatz, David, Chaim I. Waxman, and Nathan J. Diament, eds. *Tikkun Olam: Social Responsibility in Jewish Thought and Law*. Northvale, NJ: Jason Aronson, 1997.

Sheehan, James J. and Morton Sosna, eds. *The Boundaries of Humanity: Humans, Animals, Machines*. Berkeley: University of California Press, 1991.

Shelley, Mary. *Frankenstein*. 1818. Ed. Johanna M. Smith. Boston: Bedford/St. Martin's, 1992.

Skal, David J. *The Monster Book: A Cultural History of Horror*. New York: W. W. Norton, 2001.

"Smashed." *Buffy the Vampire Slayer*. UPN. 20 Nov. 2001.

"Sold Under Sin." *Deadwood*. HBO. 13 June 2004.

Stableford, Brian. *The Empire of Fear*. New York: Ballantine Books, 1988.

Stasia, Cristina Lucia. "'Wham! Bam! Thank you Ma'am!': The New Public/Private Female Action Hero." In *Third Wave Feminism: A Critical Exploration*, edited by Stacy Gillis, Gillian Howie, and Rebecca Munford, 175–184. New York: Palgrave Macmillan, 2004.

Stevenson, Robert Louis. *The Strange Case of Dr Jekyll and Mr Hyde and Weir of Hermiston*. 1886. Oxford: Oxford University Press, 1998.

Stoker, Bram. *Dracula*. 1897. Ed. John Paul Riquelme. Boston: Bedford/St. Martin's, 2002.

"Surprise." *Buffy the Vampire Slayer*. WB. 19 Jan. 1998.

Them! Dir. Gordon Douglas. Perf. James Whitmore, Edmund Gwenn. Warner Bros., 1954.

The Terminator. Dir. James Cameron. Perf. Arnold Schwarzenegger, Linda Hamilton. Hemdale Film, 1984.

Terminator 2: Judgment Day. Dir. James Cameron. Perf. Arnold Schwarzenegger, Linda Hamilton. Canal+, 1991.

Terminator 3: Rise of the Machines. Dir. Jonathan Mostow. Perf. Arnold Schwarzenegger, Nick Stahl. C-2 Pictures, 2003.

Terminator: The Sarah Connor Chronicles. By Josh Friedman. Perf. Summer Glau, Lena Headey, Thomas Dekkar. Fox. January 2008–Present.

Thompson, Kim. "Frank Miller." In *The New Comics: Interviews from the Pages of The Comics Journal*, edited by Gary Groth and Robert Fiore, 61–70. New York: Berkley Books, 1988.

"To Shanshu in L.A." *Angel*. WB. 23 May 2000.

Tudor, Andrew. *Monsters and Mad Scientists: A Cultural History of Horror Movies*. Oxford: Blackwell, 1989.

Underworld. Dir. Len Wiseman. Perf. Kate Beckinsale, Scott Speedman. Lakeshore Entertainment, 2003.

Underworld: Evolution. Dir. Len Wiseman. Perf. Kate Beckinsale, Scott Speedman. Lakeshore Entertainment, 2006.

Vampire Hunter D [Kyuketsuki Hunter D]. Dir. Toyoo Ashida and Carl Macek. Perf. Michael McConnohie, Steve Bulen. CBS Sony Group, Inc., 1985.

Van Helsing. Dir. Stephen Sommers. Perf. Hugh Jackman, Kate Beckinsale. Universal, 2004.

V for Vendetta. Dir. James McTeigue. Perf. Natalie Portman, Hugo Weaving. Silver Pictures, 2005.

"Villains." *Buffy the Vampire Slayer*. UPN. 14 May 2002.

"Welcome to the Hellmouth." *Buffy the Vampire Slayer*. WB. 3 March 1997.

Wells, Paul. *The Horror Genre: From Beelzebub to Blair Witch*. London: Wallflower Press, 2000.

When a Stranger Calls. Dir. Simon West. Perf. Camilla Belle, Tommy Flanagan. Screen Gems Inc., 2006.

Wilcox, Rhonda and David Lavery, eds. *Fighting the Forces: What's at Stake in Buffy the Vampire Slayer*. Lanham: Rowman & Littlefield, 2002.

Williams, Bernard. "Prologue: Making Sense of Humanity." In *The Boundaries of Humanity: Humans, Animals, Machines*, edited by James J. Sheehan and Morton Sosna, 13–23. Berkeley: University of California Press, 1991.

Williams, Henry A. *True Resurrection*. London: Mitchell Beazley, 1972.

Williams, Linda. "When the Woman Looks." In *The Dread of Difference: Gender and the Horror Film*, edited by Barry Keith Grant, 15–34. Austin: University of Texas Press, 1996.

Wolf-Meyer, Matthew. "The World Ozymandias Made: Utopias in the Superhero Comic, Subculture, and the Conservation of Difference." *Journal of Popular Culture* 36.3 (Winter 2003): 497–517.

Wood, Robin. "An Introduction to the American Horror Film." In *Planks of Reason: Essays on the Horror Film*, edited by Barry Keith Grant, 164–200. Metuchen: Scarecrow Press, 1984.

INDEX

Abbott, Stacey 55, 60
abyss 59, 60, 61, 65, 72, 77–78, 100, 127, 129, 131–135, 140, 144–147, 150–151, 153, 155, 157, 165, 169–170, 172
adaptation 92, 94–95, 100, 107–108, 147, 172
agency 101–103, 107–108, 113, 172
Alias 164
Alien 101, 122, 124, 126, 172
Alien: Resurrection 122, 126–127, 173
Alien³ 122, 124–126
alienation 52, 54, 57, 61, 140, 148–149
Aliens 122–125, 126
ambiguity 96–97, 99, 116, 119, 147, 151
anarchy 67, 85, 93
Angel 2, 5, 29, 30, 31, 44, 45, 47–48, 54, 59, 63, 153, 171–172; "City Of" 60; "Epiphany" 63, 87; "Hellbound" 64; "The House Always Wins" 48; "Just Rewards" 63; "Not Fade Away" 64; "Orpheus" 54; "Reprise" 63; "Reunion" 62; "To Shanshu in L.A." 61
Angel (David Boreanaz) 5, 29, 45, 46, 48–49, 52, 53, 54–55, 56, 57, 60–64, 65–66, 71, 73, 74, 78, 80, 81, 85, 87, 132–133, 134–135, 148, 152, 154, 171, 172
Angel Investigations 57, 61, 62, 64, 171
Angela (Rachel Weisz) 149–150
Angelus (David Boreanaz) 55–56, 57, 171, 172
anime 4, 33, 34
atonement 28, 44, 66
Auerbach, Nina 3, 12, 13, 17, 19, 21, 24, 37, 39

backlash 119, 122–123, 168
Badham, John 27, 39–40, 42
Badmington, Neil 22–23
Barbour, Dennis H. 52
Batman Begins 75
Batman/Bruce Wayne 70–75, 76, 77, 78, 84, 99

Batman: The Dark Knight Returns 3, 70, 72, 76
Bennett, Rita (Julie Benz) 155–156
Berenstein, Rhona J. 107, 171
Bernard, Mark 80
Bionic Woman 164
Blacula 27, 37–39, 42
Blacula (William Marshall) 38, 40, 42, 54
Blade 5, 21, 30, 31, 44, 46, 50, 59
Blade (Wesley Snipes) 5, 30, 31, 32, 46, 50–52, 53, 57–58, 59–60, 65–66, 71, 72, 74
Blade 2 30, 46, 172
Blade: Trinity 30, 46, 58
Blake, Anita 5, 101, 128–130, 138, 140, 141, 164
Bongco, Mila 68–69, 103, 105, 130
Boyette, Michele 56
Bram Stoker's Dracula 27, 37, 40
The Brave One 4, 33, 164
Brennan, Matthew 113
Browning, Tod 15, 17, 37, 107–109, 110, 132, 171
Buffy the Vampire Slayer (film) 45
Buffy the Vampire Slayer (television) 2, 5, 29, 44, 45–46, 49, 55, 63, 101, 130, 135, 138, 140, 150, 153, 171; "Angel" 47; "Bad Girls" 132; "Becoming, Part 1" 48, 54; "Becoming, Part 2" 55; "Checkpoint" 136; "Chosen" 137; "Crush" 55, 56; "Doomed" 61; "Dirty Girls" 133; "End of Days" 137; "Grave" 56, 134; "Graduation Day, Part 1" 135; "Phases" 29; "School Hard" 46; "Seeing Red" 29; "Smashed" 61; "Surprise" 55; "Villains" 134; "Welcome to the Hellmouth" 131
Buffyverse 29, 47, 48, 49, 50, 62, 72, 130, 132, 133, 138, 140, 171
Bullock, Seth (Timothy Olyphant) 151–152, 135, 168
Butler, Judith 120

Index

Call (Winona Ryder) 126–127, 132
Captain Kronos, Vampire Hunter 20–21
Carl (David Wenham) 21, 31
Carter, James Bucky 80
Carter, Margaret 23
Cat People 107, 110, 172
Chase, Cordelia 61, 62, 172
Chosen One 29, 45, 130
The Chronicles of Riddick 142–147, 164–165
Claudia (Rice) 25–26
Clover, Carol 114–117, 120–121, 124, 172
Cold War 5, 166, 167–168
community 46, 52–53, 57–61, 64, 65, 75, 132–133, 140, 147, 148–149, 152, 155, 168
conscience 29, 44, 47–52, 54, 56, 57, 62, 144, 146, 151, 158, 160, 168
Constantine 148, 168, 170
Constantine, John (Keanu Reeves) 147–150, 165–166
Coppola, Francis Ford 27, 40–42
Crain, William 27, 38, 42
Crane, Jonathan Lake 3, 23, 167
Craven, Wes 138
Crosby, Sara 139–140
The Curse of the Cat People 172

Danse Macabre 166, 169
Darla (Julie Benz) 54, 57, 62–63
Davenport-Hines, Richard 8
Deacy, Christopher 65
Deadwood 3, 4, 150, 152–153, 173; "Deadwood" 151; "Deep Water" 151; "Sold Under Sin" 151–152
DeKelb-Rittenhouse, Diane 47
demon(s) 29, 35, 46, 56, 65, 130, 132, 135, 148, 150, 152, 161, 168, 173
The Departed 33
Descent 4, 164
The Descent 2
Dexter 3, 4, 153, 156, 164, 173; "Born Free" 155; "Dexter" 153–155; "Let's Give the Boy a Hand" 154; "Popping Cherry" 153, 155; "Return to Sender" 156
Doherty, Thomas 123–125
doppelganger 17, 158
Dracula (Badham) 27, 37
Dracula (Browning) 13, 15, 17, 18, 19, 110, 171
Dracula (Stoker) 8, 37, 40, 43, 104, 107, 112, 117
Dracula, Count (Bela Lugosi) 15–17, 18, 24, 27, 108–109
Dracula, Count (Christopher Lee) 18–20, 24, 39
Dracula, Count (Frank Langella) 39–40, 42
Dracula, Count (Gary Oldman) 40–41, 42
Dracula, Count (Richard Roxburgh) 31–32
Dracula, Count (Stoker) 8, 9, 10, 12, 14, 40, 44, 59, 79, 105–106, 117
Dracula's Daughter 109–110, 111, 116

Drusilla (Juliet Landau) 54, 55, 56, 57, 62–63, 172
dualism 44, 74, 100

Early, Frances 135
Earth vs. The Flying Saucers 166
Edmundson, Mark 69–70
Evey (Moore) 82–83, 85–87, 93, 95, 146
Evey (Natalie Portman) 96–95, 96, 99, 172
Faith (Eliza Dushku) 29–30, 131–135, 137–138, 139–141, 164
Faludi, Susan 119
The Fearless Vampire Killers 20, 21, 39
femininity 38, 101, 103, 104–106, 111, 112–114, 116–118, 119–121, 123–127, 128–130, 135, 137–138, 139, 141, 161, 168, 172
Final Destination 3 169
Final Girl 5, 14, 101, 114–116, 117–118, 120–121, 122, 124, 130–131, 137, 138–139, 141
Finch, Edward (Moore) 85–87
Finch, Edward (Stephen Rea) 95–96
Fisher, Terence 18, 19, 20
Forever Knight 5, 28, 44, 50, 59, 150, 171; "Dark Knight" 53; "False Witness" 53; "Father Figure" 51; "Feeding the Beast" 59; "For I Have Sinned" 50
forgiveness 44, 117, 121
Fossey, Claire 56
Foucault, Michel 22, 49, 50
Frankenstein (Shelley) 2, 43, 169
Frankenstein (Whale) 92
Frankenstein's Monster (Boris Karloff) 92
Frankenstein's Monster (Shelley) 11–12, 27, 52
Frazer, James George 48
Freaks 171
Friday the Thirteenth, Part 2 23
Frost, Deacon (Stephen Dorff) 30, 58, 59–60
Fry, Caroline (Radha Mitchell) 143–146, 149
Fry, Carrol L. 34

Garth, Jeffrey (Otto Kruger) 109–110, 111, 133
the gaze 102, 115, 117
Gibson, Pamela Church 46
Giles, Rupert (Anthony Stewart Head) 45, 48, 55, 131, 132, 134, 136, 173
graphic novels 3, 5, 33, 67–69, 73, 74, 75, 79–80, 87, 89, 93, 94–96, 97, 98–100, 146
Gray, Dorian (Stuart Townsend) 97, 98–99
Greene, Richard 62
Griffen, Hawley 33, 88–89, 91, 96–97, 99
Guilty Pleasures 128
Gunn, Charles (J. August Richards) 48, 62

Halberstam, Judith 121, 122, 124–125
half-breed 30, 34, 35, 46, 58
Halloween 23, 114–116

Hamilton, Laurell K. 101, 128, 130
Hammer Studios 17, 18, 19, 20
Haraway, Donna J. 22–23
Harker, John (David Manners) 15–16, 107–110
Harker, Jonathan (John Van Eyssen) 18–19
Harker, Jonathan (Keanu Reeves) 40–41
Harker, Jonathan (Stoker) 9, 10–11, 12, 15, 19, 59, 106
Harker, Jonathan (Trevor Eve) 39
Harker, Mina (Peta Wilson) 97–99
Harker, Mina (Stoker) 5, 10–11, 12, 59, 79, 101, 103, 104–107, 108, 109, 112, 113, 114, 117, 118, 121, 123, 138, 141, 168, 172
Harris, Xander (Nicholas Brendon) 45, 61, 133–134, 173
Harry Potter and the Deathly Hallows 159, 165
Harry Potter and the Half-Blood Prince 159–160
Harry Potter and the Order of the Phoenix 159
Harry Potter and the Prisoner of Azkaban 159
Hellblazer 147
Hills, Jennifer (Camille Keaton) 116–118, 121
The Hills Have Eyes 169
Hillyer, Lambert 109
Hitchcock, Alfred 14
Hollinger, Karen 107
Hollinger, Veronica 12
Holmwood, Arthur (Cary Elwes) 41
Holmwood, Arthur (Michael Gough) 18–20
Holmwood, Arthur (Stoker) 11, 59
Holmwood, Lucy (Carol Marsh) 18–19
Holmwood, Mina (Melissa Stribling) 18–20
homogeneity 7, 10, 22, 38
horror archetypes 11–12, 37
Horror of Dracula 18
Hostel 169
Hughes, Jamie 76, 77–78
humanity 8, 10, 11, 13, 14, 17, 24–27, 28, 33, 34, 35, 36, 38, 39, 42, 44, 46, 47, 49–50, 51, 52, 54–61, 63–66, 77, 78–79, 80, 81, 84, 85, 88, 90–91, 92, 112, 118, 126–127, 132–135, 138, 145–147, 149, 154–156, 165, 168, 170
humanizing 15, 94–95
humanizing agent 9
humanizing apparatuses 8, 10, 12, 14, 22, 48–49, 67, 86, 102, 133, 135–136, 154
Hutchings, Peter 171
Hutter, Johnathon (Gustav von Wangenheim) 112–113
Hutter, Nina (Greta Schroeder) 112–114, 121
Hyde, Edward (James Nesbitt) 156–159
Hyde, Edward (Jason Flemyng) 97–98
Hyde, Edward (Moore) 33, 88–92, 96–98, 172
Hyde, Edward (Stevenson) 43–44, 91, 158

I Spit on Your Grave 116
inhuman/inhumane 7, 8, 22, 28, 34, 47, 49, 89–90, 107, 110, 144, 153, 165
inhumanity 23, 24–25, 89, 134, 143, 145, 154, 156, 168, 169
Inness, Sherrie 135, 139
Interview with the Vampire 24, 26, 27, 28, 55
Inuyasha 35; "The Girl Who Overcame Time" 35
It Came from Beneath the Sea 166

Jack (Rhiana Griffith) 143–147
Jackman, Claire (Gina Bellman) 157–158
Jackman, Tom (James Nesbitt) 156–159
Jackson, Rosemary 67
Jameson, Fredric 167–166
Jane Eyre 2
Janet (Maguerite Churchill) 110
Janette (Deborah Duchene) 28, 50–51, 53–54
Jekyll 142, 156–158, 173
Jekyll, Henry (Jason Flemyng) 98
Jekyll, Henry (Moore) 33, 88–90, 98
Jekyll, Henry (Stevenson) 42–44, 52
Jensen, Jeff 77, 78, 80
Jenson, Karen (N'Bushe Wright) 30, 51, 57, 60
Johns, William (Cole Hauser) 143–144, 146

Kaplan, E. Ann 115
Karras, Irene 119, 138
King, Stephen 10, 169
Knight, Nick (Geraint Wyn Davies) 5, 28, 44–45, 46, 50–54, 59, 60, 65–66, 71, 72, 74, 154, 171, 172
Krueger, Freddy (Robert Englund) 1, 59
Kyra (Alexa Davalos) 143, 145–147, 149, 164–165

Lacroix (Nigel Bennett) 28, 45, 51, 53–54, 172
Lambert, Natalie (Catherine Disher) 44, 53–5
Lara Croft 128
Laski, Beth 130
The Laughing Corpse 128, 129
The League of Extraordinary Gentlemen 33, 88–91, 96–97, 172
The League of Extraordinary Gentlemen (film) 92, 96, 99
The League of Extraordinary Gentlemen, Volume I (Moore) 3, 33, 88, 96, 172
The League of Extraordinary Gentlemen, Volume II (Moore) 88
Lestat (Rice) 24–26
Lorrah, Jean 104, 106
Louis (Rice) 24–27, 34, 55

Maclay, Tara (Amber Benson) 29, 133–134
Mad Max 52

Manhattan, Doctor 79–81
masculinity 38, 103, 104–106, 112–114, 116–118, 119–121, 123–127, 130, 135, 138, 139, 141, 161, 168, 172
McTeigue, James 93
McWhir, Ann 171
Miller, Frank 3, 5, 69, 70–75, 76, 77, 92
Moore, Alan 3, 5, 33, 34, 69, 75, 77–80, 81–83, 85, 88–92, 93–94, 96, 98–99, 146, 147, 172
Morgan, Deb (Jennifer Carpenter) 155–156, 164
Morgan, Dexter (Michael C. Hall) 153–156, 164–165
Morris, Quincey (Bill Campbell) 41
Morris, Quincey (Stoker) 10, 11, 59
Mulvey, Laura 102
Murnau, F. W. 112
Murray, Mina (Moore) 33, 34, 88, 90–91, 96, 172
Murray, Mina (Winona Ryder) 40–42
Myers, Michael (Tony Moran) 1, 23, 114–116

Nadel, Alan 167
Nelson, Susan 57
Nemo, Captain 33, 88–89, 96
Nemo, Captain (Naseeruddin Shah) 97–98
The New Woman 103–104, 106, 107, 113, 118
Newman, Kim 12
Nietzsche, Friedrich 59, 72, 77, 12
A Nightmare on Elm Street 116, 138
9/11 73, 149, 169, 172
Nite Owl/ Dreiberg, Dan (Moore) 76, 78
Norrington, Stephen 96
Nosferatu 112–113

O'Neill, Kevin 88–89
Orlak, Count (Max Schreck) 112–113
The Other 10, 12, 105, 127, 158
Ozymandias/Adrian Veidt 70, 76, 78–79, 80, 81–82, 83, 85, 86, 99, 127

patriarchy 38, 39, 101–103, 105, 107, 110, 112, 115, 124, 127, 128, 130, 133, 135–138, 140–141, 162–163, 167
penitence 44
Penley, Constance 102
Pinedo, Isabel Cristina 171
Pitch Black 3, 142–145
posthuman 29, 67, 71, 126–127
posthumanism 3, 22, 27, 28, 32, 44, 66, 71, 102, 121
postmodern 23, 52
Prescott, Sidney (Neve Campbell) 138–139
pseudo-soul 49, 55, 56, 61
Psycho 14, 120

Quatermain, Allan (Moore) 33, 88–90, 96–97

Quatermain, Allan (Sean Connery) 97, 98, 172

rape-revenge films 116, 118
redemption 28, 47, 50, 56, 61, 63–65, 131, 134, 148–150, 173
Reed, Irena Dubrovna (Simone Simon) 110–111, 113, 117–118, 121, 133, 138, 172
Reed, Oliver (Kent Smith) 110–111, 112–133
regender(ing) 118, 121–122, 124–125, 127
remorse 37, 44, 83, 135
repentance 29, 30
repression 10, 24, 102
revenge 11, 82, 84, 85, 116–118, 131
Rice, Anne 24, 25, 29, 34
Riddick, Richard (Vin Diesel) 143–147, 149, 154–155, 164–165
Ripley, Ellen (Sigourney Weaver) 4, 5, 122–127, 132, 140, 141, 164, 172
Robinson, James 96
Rorschach (Moore) 76–78, 79, 80, 81–83, 86, 99, 148
Rosenberg, Willow (Alyson Hannigan) 29, 45, 131, 133–138, 139–141, 164, 171, 173
Rowling, J.K. 156, 159

Sandor (Irving Pichel) 109–110, 111
Sawyer, Tom (Shane West) 97–98, 172
Schanke, Don (John Kapelos) 28, 53
Schrag, Calvin O. 53–54, 57, 58, 62
Scoobies 29, 45–46, 49, 55, 57, 61, 131–134, 137
Scream 138–139
Scream 2 138–139
Scream 3 138–139
Selene (Kate Beckinsale) 160–164, 173
Senf, Carol 106
Seward, Jack (Donald Pleasence) 39
Seward, Jack (Herbert Bunston) 15–16, 108
Seward, Jack (Richard E. Grant) 41
Seward, John (Stoker) 8, 11, 31, 59, 105
Seward, Lucy (Kate Nelligan) 39–40, 42
Seward, Mina (Helen Chandler) 15–16, 107–109, 110, 132
sexuality 10, 18, 19, 94–95, 97–98, 99, 107–110, 113, 121, 124, 126, 139, 169, 170
Shanshu Prophecy 37, 61, 63, 64
Sharrett, Christopher 70–72, 75
Shatz, David 64
Shelley, Mary 27, 37, 43, 92, 169
Silk Spectre/Laurie 76, 80
Skal, David 166
Skinner, Rodney (Tony Curran) 97
slasher films 14, 23, 37, 114, 116, 118, 120–121, 138, 168–169
slasher villains/monsters 14, 23, 59, 152, 168
slayer 29, 45, 54, 56, 130–132, 135–138, 140, 161, 172
Snape, Severus 4, 159–160, 165

The Shining (Kubrick) 2, 167
soul 29, 46, 47–52, 54, 56, 57, 61, 65, 133, 146, 149–150, 153, 172
Spike (James Marsters) 5, 29, 32, 45, 46, 49, 52, 53, 54, 55–57, 60, 61, 63–66, 71, 74, 78, 80, 85, 133, 135, 145, 152, 171, 172
Stableford, Brian 22
The Stand 2
Stasia, Cristina Lucia 128, 130
status quo 9, 10, 17, 20, 23, 28, 38, 40, 86
Stevenson, Robert Louis 33, 42–44, 88, 91, 158
Stoker, Bram 4, 5, 8, 9, 13, 14, 15, 17, 18, 19, 20, 30, 31, 32, 35, 37, 39, 43, 51, 58, 66, 68, 101, 103–104, 105–106, 107–108, 109, 112, 113, 114, 117, 123, 168, 170
The Strange Case of Dr Jekyll and Mr Hyde 42–43, 91
Strode, Laurie (Jamie Lee Curtis) 114–115, 119, 124, 131
Summers, Buffy (Sarah Michelle Gellar) 4, 5, 29, 30, 45, 47, 48, 49, 54–55, 56, 57, 60, 61, 130–138, 139–141, 161, 164, 172, 173
superhero 68–69, 70, 75–76, 80–81, 82, 92, 103, 130
Superman 92
super-villain 72–74, 84
Swearengen, Al (Ian McShane) 152
sympathy 27, 37, 38, 40, 42, 44, 74, 80, 84, 86, 93–94, 97, 99, 109–111, 116–118, 121, 126, 131–132, 135

The Terminator 164
Terminator: Judgment Day 164, 173
Terminator 3: Rise of the Machines 173
Terminator: The Sarah Connor Chronicles 4, 164
Them! 166
third wave feminism 118–119, 138
Thomas, Gordan (Thalmus Rasulala) 38–39, 42
Thompson, Kim 92
tikkun olam 64
Tourneur, Jacques 110–111
Tudor, Andrew 9, 14, 20, 73, 168
Twohy, David 143–145

Underground comix 68
Underworld 160–163, 173
Underworld: Evolution 160, 163–164, 169, 173
Universal Studios 18, 19, 31

V (Hugo Weaving) 93–95, 96, 99, 172
V (Moore) 81–87, 93, 95, 146
V for Vendetta (film) 92–93, 96, 99
V for Vendetta (Moore) 3, 67, 81, 83, 85, 86
Vampire Hunter D 34

vampire–turned-monster hunter 25, 26, 45, 46, 50, 59, 71
Van Helsing 2, 7, 21, 31
Van Helsing (Hugh Jackman) 31–32
Van Helsing (Peter Cushing) 17, 18–20
Van Helsing, Abraham (Anthony Hopkins) 41–42
Van Helsing, Abraham (Edward Van Sloan) 15–17, 18–19, 108–110, 132
Van Helsing, Abraham (Laurence Olivier) 39
Van Helsing, Abraham (Stoker) 4, 8, 9, 10, 12–13, 14, 26, 28, 30–31, 32, 35, 43, 58–59, 68, 79, 86, 87, 104–105, 106, 123, 167–168, 171
victim 101, 107–110, 112, 114–118, 119, 120–121, 125, 129, 131, 133, 142, 155, 161, 164, 172
Victorian England 9, 10, 11, 12, 20, 42–43, 68–69, 96–97, 104, 106, 121
Vietnam War 3, 5, 21, 23, 64, 142, 167
vigilantism 58, 61–63, 67, 71–72, 73–74, 76–78, 81, 84, 86, 99–100, 148
vixen 101–102, 107–112, 113, 114–118, 119, 121, 125, 127, 130–131, 141, 161, 164
Voorhees, Jason 1, 23, 59

Wachowski, Andy 93–94
Wachowski, Larry 93–94
watcher 30, 45, 131, 172
Watcher's Council 135–138
Watchmen 3, 70, 75–76, 78, 99
Watergate 5, 21, 23, 65, 142
Wells, Paul 3, 38, 142, 166, 169, 170
Westenra, Lucy (Sadie Frost) 41
Westenra, Lucy (Stoker) 107
Weston, Lucy (Frances Dade) 15, 108–109, 132
Whale, James 92
Whedon, Joss 29, 45, 47, 48, 49, 50, 80, 101, 130–132, 135, 139, 171, 173
When a Stranger Calls 169
Whistler, Abraham (Kris Kristofferson) 21, 30, 46, 51, 57, 58
Wilde, Oscar 99
Williams, Bernard 7
Williams, Henry A. 65
Williams, Linda 102–103, 105, 126, 171
Wolf-Myer, Matthew 81, 85
Wolfram & Hart 62, 63, 64, 172
Wood, Robin 10
Wyndam-Price, Wesley (Alexis Denisof) 30, 62, 133, 136, 172, 173

Yuen, Wayne 62

Zaleska, Marya (Gloria Holden) 109–110, 111, 113, 117–118, 121, 133, 138

www.ingramcontent.com/pod-product-compliance
Ingram Content Group UK Ltd.
Pitfield, Milton Keynes, MK11 3LW, UK
UKHW042014140426
5217IPUK00015B/1169